The Rules for
Growing
Rich

THE RULES FOR
GROWING
RICH

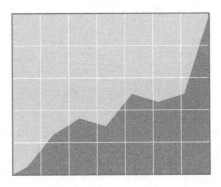

Making Money in the
New Information Economy

DAVID A. LEREAH

CROWN
BUSINESS
NEW YORK

Published by Crown Publishers, New York, New York. Member of the Crown Publishing Group.

Random House, Inc. New York, Toronto, London, Sydney, Auckland
www.randomhouse.com

Crown Business is a trademark of Random House, Inc.

Printed in the United States of America

Design by Publications Development Company of Texas

Library of Congress Cataloging-in-Publication Data

Lereah, David.
    The rules for growing rich : making money in the new information economy/ David Lereah.
      p. cm.
    1. Investments—United States. I. Title.
  HG4910.L456   2000
  332.63′2′0973—dc21   99-056474

ISBN 0-8129-3056-8

10 9 8 7 6 4 3 2 1

First Edition

To Wendy, Abbey, Jeff, and Jenna

PREFACE

Today's new information economy has the investment world by its not-so-gentle hands. On the one hand, the new information age has created an extraordinary backdrop for investors seeking to build wealth in a short period of time with equity investments. The 1990s technology boon created the longest economic expansion in U.S. history, pushing equity values to all-time highs. Multi-millionaires were made in a matter of months rather than years, as equity values soared on many technology related companies including initial public offerings.

However, the new information economy also presents great challenges for today's investor. Investors have almost instantaneous access to an abundance of investment data, once available only to professional investors. Understanding how to sort, interpret and evaluate this information is critical in developing successful investment strategies.

The new information age has also split America's economy in two—the traditional economy and the new information economy, creating confusion among investors. What creates value in the traditional economy not necessarily creates value in the new economy. There is a new set of laws and values emerging in the new economy that are heavily influencing consumer and business activities, promising to impact the value of investments for years to come.

Companies in the new information economy have become the new darlings of the investment community, associated with high price/earnings ratios and high growth rates in terms of market capitalization. As of this writing, these companies were dominating the National Association of Securities Dealers, NASDAQ Exchange, attracting investment funds away from the more traditional S&P 500 companies traded on the New York Stock Exchange.

Investors are in the best of times but also in the most fragile of times. Most investors appear overwhelmed by the reams of economic, financial and investment data that are displayed daily on the Internet. Some feel compelled to base their investment decisions on this information only to find that the connection between the information and investment values are nontrivial. Others are intimidated by the data and are missing exciting investment opportunities by avoiding the information altogether.

This book is for both types of investors, and particularly for those who want to use the Internet and take control of their investment life. The end zone for this book is to help investors make the connection among the Internet, the economy and investments. For some investors, this book will help them replace the traditional stockbroker with Internet investment sites. For others, the lessons and rules learned throughout these pages will lessen, but not eliminate, the need for stockbrokers. Remember, stockbrokers (or account executives) are specialists in the world of investments. Their fingers are supposed to be on the pulse of the markets. They also have access to financial rumors, technical analysis and share allotments to initial public offerings. It would be difficult and probably unwise for Internet-driven investors (remember we all have day jobs) to go it alone in the wonderful world of investing.

On a more personal level, I am indebted to a number of individuals who have contributed in some meaningful manner to the final pages of this book. I owe a special debt of gratitude to my Random House-Times Books editor, John Mahaney, who helped inspire, shape, and edit the entire manuscript. I would also like to pay special thanks to Dewey Daane and Lyle Gramley, both former Governors of the Federal Reserve Board, who let me know in no uncertain terms when I veered off course with content and direction. In no particular order I would also like to thank Rick Shomo for giving me a reality check in the equity markets; my wife Wendy for applying her accountant's eye to the tax-deferred material; Brian Carey and Veronica Warnock for their timely data gathering and analysis; Janet Hewitt for her organizational advice; Sandie Peguero for her continual administrative assistance throughout the entire writing process; and to everyone from the Publications Development Company who put a professional package around my words—thank you.

I would be remiss if I did not thank my agent, Alice Martell, who made this book a reality by introducing me to Random House, and Ilyce Glink, who early on gave me a swift kick in the rear when I was ready to throw in the towel. Of course, I alone am responsible for the contents of this book and for whatever misuse I might have made of the suggestions from others.

DAVID A. LEREAH

CONTENTS

PART THREE
THE NEW INFORMATION ECONOMY

PART ONE

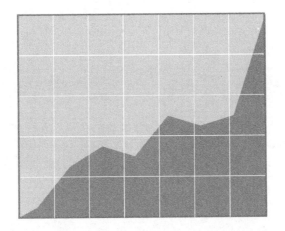

THE ROAD TO GROWING RICH

1

BECOMING A NEW
MILLENNIUM INVESTOR

The 1990s have become known as the "information decade," a time when personal computers went mainstream and the Internet became a way of life. Almost overnight, everyday households had direct access to a full array of financial investment information, ranging from timely U.S. Government economic releases to stock price movements on companies traded on the European and Asian exchanges. Savvy investors—those who learned how to collect and use this new information—grew rich throughout the decade. Not surprisingly, besides generating financial gains for a lot of people, the 1990s' economic boom created even larger wealth for those individuals who understood how to play the PC/Internet revolution.

Today's new information economy is a residual from a technological revolution that strikingly reminds us of the "industrial revolution" that shaped the world during the late 1800s. In fact, the reach of today's technological innovation may eventually dwarf the advances made during the industrial revolution, and the implications are enormous for the world of investments. As technological changes have produced a transformation of communications and commerce from the physical world to the virtual (electronic) world, they have generated unprecedented investment opportunities for equities and bonds as well as real estate, international, and retirement investments.

As we enter the twenty-first century, you—the individual investor—stand at a crossroad. You can continue as an everyday investor stuck in the twentieth century, or you can take control of your investment life by diving head-first into the information age. More than ever before, non-professional investors have the opportunity to emulate professional investors with very little effort and very little cost.

Today, for only the cost of an initial Internet connect charge, investors have instant access to up-to-the-minute economic, financial, and investment information, as well as analysis and commentary from market and industry analysts. This wide array of market information enables everyday investors to base their investment decisions on information that was thought to be unattainable by nonprofessionals just two or three years ago. A cursory glance at the contents (as of this writing) of www.Bloomberg.com (a nationally known financial information provider) demonstrates the breadth of information available to investors on the Internet at no additional cost:

Bloomberg.com

News:
Top Financial News
Top World News
Stock Market Update
Technology Update
U.S. Economy
Columns (market commentary from nationally known analysts)
Special Report

Stocks:
Technology Stocks
Chart Builder (provides user with ability to chart virtually any investment)
World Indices
Movers by Exchange (identifies stock market movers in each major exchange)
Stocks in the Dow (Dow Jones Industrial Average Index)
S&P 500 Index Snapshot
Industry Movers (identifies market movers by industry)
Most Active Options (identifies most active stock options)
IPO center (initial public offerings)
Regional Indices (tracks selected regional stock indices)

Rates and Bonds: Key Rates (provides yield curve information)
U.S. Treasuries
International Bonds (e.g., Japanese and French bonds)
Municipal Bond Yields

Currencies: Currency Rates
Cross Currency Rates
Currency Calculator (permits investors to calculate any exchange rate)
EMU Update (European Monetary Union update)

Commodities: Most Active Futures (volume on commodity futures contracts, such as soybeans)
Commodity Movers (tracks movements in commodities)
Energy

Money: Mutual Funds
Portfolio
Loan Center
Mortgage Calculator
Investing (provides daily investment strategies)
Retirement [provides retirement strategies in retirement accounts such as 401(k)s]

Each item listed above generates its own contents for that particular area. Suffice it to say that the information available on the Internet is more than ample for information-starved investors. Bloomberg.com is just one of literally thousands of market information providers available to individuals. The Federal and local governments, Wall Street investment banking companies, brokerage houses, commercial banks, mutual funds, insurance companies, retirement associations, and countless other organizations offer a wide array of financial and economic information that is useful in developing well-informed investment strategies. As of this writing, some of the more popular investment sites offered on the Internet are: TheStreet.com; PowerStreet (Fidelity); DLJDirect; Datek Online; Ameritrade; Dreyfus; E*Trade; Charles Schwab; Suretrade; and Investor Network.

Perhaps the primary motivation for using the Internet for investing is the fact that the information is so well organized that most individual investors can do one-stop shopping. For example, investors who use

Bloomberg.com would probably need to go no further. Almost everything required for the development of intelligent investment strategies is there. The ease of access and the efficient organization of the information at the site make it increasingly common for novice and intermediate investors to get "hooked." But it is important to note that investors could misuse the financial information that is handed to them. Giving them too much investment data could lead them down troubled roads. The core value of this book is that it provides investors with a structure for organizing and interpreting all of this information. It creates a better understanding of how to gather, sort, and simplify all of the information available on the Internet so that intelligent investment decisions can be made.

Furthermore, because most Web sites that disseminate financial information offer direct links to the primary electronic trading companies, executing most stock and bond transactions is simplified. Companies such as Ameritrade, DLJDirect, E*Trade, and Waterhouse are usually associated with most of the financial information Web sites. In addition, companies such as Merrill Lynch, Fidelity Investments, and so many others, now offer electronic trading within their own Web sites. Of course, investors can continue to trade through an individual broker and seek his or her advice on what has been learned from the Internet sites.

Looking to the future, most individual investors will need only this one-stop investment shopping list:

1. Go to one or more Internet investment sites.
2. View your investment and retirement portfolios' performance.
3. Gather pertinent market information on the economic and investment environments.
4. Develop an investment strategy (sometimes with help from market commentary or from the analysts hosting particular Web sites, and/or your stockbroker).
5. Click your mouse and execute a buy or sell transaction via one of the electronic trading Internet companies.

(A more complete list of information resources is provided in Part Three.)

The great boom of the 1990s created a lot of money for a lot of people, but what will happen when the U.S. economy slips and the long bull market stops roaring? Can today's investors continue to earn double-digit returns with their eyes closed, ignoring the stream of investment information crossing their computer screens daily? The simple answer is: No. Investors need to learn how to use this information to take advantage of market and investment opportunities. If history repeats itself in the twenty-first century, uninformed investors will struggle to maintain adequate returns when the good times turn bad. Today's Internet-driven world of information gives you, the individual investor, opportunities to keep pace with professional investors. But it is up to *you* to learn how to use timely market information wisely and avoid the mistakes of the past.

To grow your money and experience financial success, you need a good map of how the economy works. Just as a hiker needs a good topographic map of the terrain selected for a journey, so does an investor need an equivalent map of the economy. The countryside is full of peaks and valleys, but if you know how to read the map, you can navigate successfully and get to your destination. The economy will always have expansions (peaks) and recessions (valleys), but you can make money in both situations, provided you know what you are doing.

Although the U.S. economy is complicated and can change in unpredictable ways, if you spend some time getting to know it (it won't bite) and follow a few general rules on how to anticipate and respond to these changes, financial rewards will come your way. For example, in the final stages of an economic expansion, housing construction usually turns down, indicating that a recession, a slumping stock market, and falling interest rates are on the horizon. Some investors take this as a signal to reduce their equity holdings and invest in bonds. Others believe, based on the past 70 years of investment experience, that a portfolio of equity investments will almost always outperform other investments (e.g., bonds), if the investment horizon is 20 years or longer. Thus, as a rule, long-term investment portfolios are dominated by equity investments.

The keys to successful investing are: Utilize your knowledge of the economy via Internet-driven investment information, and understand historical economic relationships. A better understanding of how changes in the economy (i.e., business cycles and economic indicators) impact the value of investments is one of the goals of this book. The economy can certainly be intimidating, and the financial markets, with all their computer screens, financial instruments, and financial wizardry, can be mesmerizing. However, the Internet provides average investors with great investment opportunities that did not exist before. The contents of this book will provide you with the guidance necessary to utilize and simplify all of the information offered on the Internet, placing you firmly on the road to growing your money.

Building a Bridge to Success

Before you begin to take advantage of a changing economy by employing rule-of-thumb strategies, you must first look at your personal financial situation. Building a bridge usually begins with a desire to cross a body of water, or a need to reach a desired destination. Similarly, building and learning to use strategies for taking advantage of market opportunities will be more effective if you know your personal financial situation and have a well-thought-out plan for meeting your financial and retirement objectives. Here are some suggested steps that you may want to follow.

STEP 1 Define Your Investment Goals

Is your objective to become rich by age 40, or are you willing to wait until retirement age to cash in on your investments? Whenever you hope to reach your investment goals, this book will assist you in developing sensible investment strategies that will lead to informed investment decisions.

STEP 2 Establish Your Investment Priorities

Up front, you have to decide on the composition of your investment portfolio. There are basically three components: (1) a cash account, (2) a retirement account, and (3) an investment account.

1. The cash account should contain the amount of cash and/or cash equivalents (i.e., low-risk, short-term securities such as certificates of deposits) needed to meet unforeseen emergencies (e.g., paying the bills if you lose your job). This account should be established before any other portfolio accounts. The size of your cash account should probably total between three and six months of your annual income.

2. The retirement account should be your second priority. For most people, the strategy for retirement is actually a no-brainer: Invest,

long term, in the equity market. (However, as your retirement date approaches, safer investments such as bonds should play a more crucial role.) Numerous rule-of-thumb strategies for the retirement account are discussed in Chapter 11.

3.   The investment account should be your most aggressive account. The goal is to make money in the near term, and your success in this account will probably determine how "rich" you will become. Turn toward building your investment account only after you have achieved some comfort level with the cash and retirement accounts.

STEP 3   Determine Your Investment Time Horizon

How many more working years do you have until retirement? Or, how long do you want to wait until you begin using your accumulated wealth? These questions need answers when you are determining your investment horizon. For your cash account, the investment horizon needs to be relatively short because you need easy access to these funds in case of emergency. Also, the price fluctuations in these funds need to be less volatile than for other investments (e.g., the stocks and long-term bonds). Your retirement account's time horizon should be somewhat in line with the number of years remaining until retirement. If you are 20 years away from retirement (you are 45 years old and plan to retire at 65), your investment horizon is about 20 years. Thus, whatever stocks you purchase at age 45 should stay in your portfolio until age 65. Your investment account's time horizon is more difficult to set and may need some flexibility, depending on the nature and quality of certain investment vehicles.

STEP 4   Determine Your Level of Risk Taking

Most investors want to avoid risk. Unfortunately, in the real world, risk is positively correlated with return. The higher the level of risk you are willing to assume, the greater the potential return on your investment. With regard to investments, risk is a volatility measure; it shows how much the value of an investment could change from one period to another. Simply stated, when you are making decisions about your investment portfolio, you need to designate the level of risk you can take on.

Remember, risk should be looked at from both a short-term and a long-term perspective. For example, over the short term, investing in the stock market could be an extremely volatile and choppy ride. The value of your stock portfolio could drop by 40 percent in one year, but may rise in value by 30 percent in the next year. Over the longer term, however, investing in the stock market has not been highly volatile. When stocks are compared with bonds and cash-equivalent investments, risk (volatility) diminishes with time. The investment time horizon is an important factor when determining how much risk you are willing to accept.

For the cash account, I recommend assuming as little risk as possible. The funds in this account are merely a buffer for emergencies (e.g., job loss). Put these funds into relatively short-term, riskless instruments such as commercial bank CDs (under $100,000 deposit insurance coverage), Treasury bills, and bonds. For the retirement account, assume greater risk but extend the investment horizon to your remaining years until retirement. In this way, you can invest in equities that present a significant price risk in any one year but have a diminished risk over the longer run. Acceptable investment vehicles for the retirement account and the investment account are listed in Step 6 below. For the investment account, I recommend taking on as much risk as you can comfortably assume.

STEP 5 Determine Your Level of Diversification

Everyone knows the expression "You don't put all your eggs in one basket." If the basket falls and all your eggs break, you will probably have to go without breakfast, and being hungry at the beginning of the day is never a good idea. Similarly, you don't put all your hard-earned money into one investment. If the investment turns sour, you could lose all your money, which is a worse alternative than losing your breakfast.

Suppose, instead of one basket, you have 100 baskets of eggs. You ship them from Wisconsin to Virginia on one truck, and that truck crashes into the Mississippi River. You still lose all your eggs, even though you have diversified across baskets. The lesson you learn is to have more than one truck transporting your valuables. The key to diversifying is to invest in a mix of investments whose values differ from each other (like different trucks moving in different directions). Diversification is a must in any comprehensive investment strategy.

STEP 6 Determine Your Acceptable Investment Vehicles

Once you develop an investment strategy, make sure the vehicles you choose don't leave you stranded in the middle of the road. Depending on your investment focus (the cash, retirement, or investment account), determine which investment vehicle is best suited for your needs. The most constructive strategy is to make a list of the acceptable investment vehicles available for your investment portfolio. Here are some examples:

1. *The cash account.* Use short-term, high-quality instruments that are easily redeemable for cash: 90-day Treasury bills, commercial bank certificates of deposit (CDs), or commercial paper (short-term borrowings by large corporations). The easiest and most effective way to invest in these instruments (and diversify among them) is to place your cash account in a money market account or a mutual fund that invests only in cash-equivalent instruments that can provide quick and easy access to your funds.

2. *The retirement account.* Invest in equity securities (choose small and large corporations that are publicly traded on the major U.S. stock exchanges), U.S. Government Treasury bills and bonds, government agency bonds (e.g., Fannie Mae mortgage-backed securities), AAA-rated corporate bonds, highly rated municipal bonds, guaranteed investment contracts (sometimes called stable value arrangements), and a variety of mutual funds that encompass any combination of the acceptable investment vehicles mentioned above. These instruments provide solid, long-term returns that are appropriate for retirement investment strategies.

3. *The investment account.* Here you have the greatest number of options, including all of the financial instruments identified for the cash and retirement accounts. Invest in all of the above plus lower-rated corporate and municipal bonds, collateralized mortgage obligations, initial public offerings of equity securities, real estate investment trusts (REITs), other limited partnerships, precious metals (including gold), commodities, futures, and option contracts. Some of these investment vehicles require somewhat more sophisticated investment strategies and personal attention

than do others. The level of risk involved with each of these as-sets is addressed in later chapters.

STEP 7 Determine a Method of Investing

Whom will you blame or pat on the back if you lose your shirt or come out ahead on your investments? Essentially, you have four options available for investing:

1. Take sole responsibility for your portfolio by making all the investments yourself. This option leans heavily on your ability to understand and monitor the economic and investment environments.

2. Utilize the services of a discount broker or an online broker. You would still need to understand and monitor the economic and investment environments.

3. Utilize the services and advice of a full-service broker, permitting him or her to choose and place all of your investments. This more traditional approach may have its limitations in an Internet/information-driven world.

4. Invest your funds in a mutual fund and either condemn or praise the portfolio manager of that fund for the failures and successes.

Investing through mutual funds appears to be most popular among today's investors. Placing your funds in a mutual fund utilizes the expertise of professionals while permitting you to be partially involved in the decision making (the decision comes when you move funds from one mutual fund to another). Cash accounts are usually in no-load mutual funds (which are cheaper than load funds) that invest only in high-quality cash-equivalent instruments. However, some investors prefer to purchase their own commercial bank certificates of deposit (CDs). For managing retirement accounts, either a full-service broker or a mutual fund vehicle is acceptable. You are dealing with a substantial amount of funds, and your retirement needs depend on making the right investment decisions, so ask a professional to help you choose the appropriate investment vehicles, methods, and instruments. For the investment account, any of the above methods of investing are acceptable. Of course, with the advent of the Internet and the greater accessibility to investment information, investors, in increasing numbers, are making independent investment decisions.

The Payoff

Learning how to make the economy work for you is a matter of personal economic survival. If you choose to remain economically ignorant, you are limiting your options for growing your money and, more importantly, you are more likely to get stepped on. Only after you acquire some economic savvy will you be able to go on the offensive and begin maneuvering your way through the varying roads to financial success.

This book offers investors the opportunity to invest successfully in the new information economy. The primary focus is on teaching investors how to gather and use, in a simple and nontime-consuming manner, the investment information that is available on today's Internet. *Investment rules* will be developed to guide investors on how to invest in the new information economy. Particular attention is paid to specific investments that may be materially impacted by today's technological revolution. Just follow a handful of the 150-plus investment rules offered in the remaining chapters of this book, and you'll almost live happily ever after.

2

MONITORING
TODAY'S ECONOMY

K eeping abreast of changes and movements in the U.S. economy on a daily basis used to be complicated and burdensome for most professional and nonprofessional investors. The advent of the Internet has changed all that. Up-to-the minute investment data on virtually every aspect of the economy are available with a click of a mouse. The difficult part for investors is knowing what to do after receiving the investment information. This chapter will help investors to better understand (1) changes in the U.S. economy and (2) how to track economic information that is pertinent to successful investment strategies.

Monitoring the economy is like keeping track of weather. If you know a blizzard is coming, you make proper preparation. Without the right information, you might drive off at the beginning of the day in what appears to be a light snowfall, and get stuck later in several feet of accumulation.

The economy, like the weather, behaves in erratic and sometimes unpredictable ways. Unexpectedly, the economy could grow too fast and generate unwanted inflation that would eat into the purchasing power of our earnings. Conversely, like a heart that stops beating, economic activity could stall, placing hardship on people who lose jobs, income, and pride. We are all subject to the swings of the economic pendulum.

If we could anticipate swings in economic activity, we could then place a greater emphasis (via increased investments) on specific financial assets that would likely increase in value in response to certain economic events. The economy can either harm you or help you. Because you cannot control its movement, your only choice is to understand and respond to what is happening. The process has four quite simple steps:

1. Identify the business cycle—the regular cyclical movements in the economic and financial markets.

2. Identify reliable indicators of economic activity that reflect changes in the business cycle.

3. Evaluate how changes in these indicators influence the value of financial assets.

4. Develop investment rules to respond to and take advantage of these movements.

Identifying Business Cycles

Growing up in New York City, I remember hearing about the biggest and the scariest roller coaster in the world—"The Cyclone" at Coney Island amusement park. There were apocryphal stories about little children who rode the Cyclone and never returned to their families. And I remember, as if it were yesterday, the moment at age seven when my eyes first beheld the mammoth coaster. The coaster's rail cars and the people riding on her back were an astonishing sight. I had marveled at the way some of the older kids were able to ride the waves of the coaster, up and down, moving gently up the steep slope and then free-falling toward a seemingly bottomless pit until the cars were jerked back up again. People who garnered the courage to ride the beast—especially the teenagers, who rode with seemingly reckless abandon—earned my respect.

Moving from the adventurous ride of the Cyclone to the coasterlike ride of the economy is a surprisingly easy transition. Like the Cyclone, which is known for its peaks and troughs—the steepness of a climb and the danger of a fall—the U.S. economy is subjected to the almost predictable whims of the business cycle, with its more or less regular upward and downward movement of economic activity over a period of years. A business cycle has five roller coasterlike phases: (1) downturn (recession), (2) trough, (3) recovery, (4) expansion, and (5) peak.

Although we all want to live happily ever after, the economy won't let us. Business conditions never stand still. Economic expansions give way to recessions, which, in turn, give way to expansions again. And to make matters worse, the U.S. Government, via fiscal policy (government spending and taxing) and monetary policy (the Federal Reserve), participates in and disrupts the business cycle, sometimes reducing and sometimes aggravating its fluctuations.

The biggest swing of our economic pendulum occurred between 1929 and 1945. The economy first plunged into the Great Depression and then experienced a robust expansion when production levels increased during World War II. Between 1929 and 1933, real gross domestic product (GDP) fell by more than 30 percent. This literally crippled U.S. economic activity and devastated most American families. Not until the later years of World War II, when manufacturing met the excessive demands for military support and munitions, did the U.S. economy fully recover.

Since World War II, the average length of U.S. economic expansions has been about 50 months, and the average length of the economy's contractions has been only 10 months. Prior to today's record-setting expansion, the longest expansion (106 months) occurred during the 1960s. The third longest expansion (92 months) took place during Ronald Reagan's presidency in the 1980s. The current expansion, now in first place and running strong at 111 months as of this writing, is shattering all previous records, as shown in Table 2–1.

Someone once defined a recession as a period in which you tighten up your belt. In a depression, you have no belt to tighten up; and when you have no pants to hold up, you're in a panic. Today, a recession is defined as two consecutive quarters (or about six months) of negative growth in our real (adjusted for inflation) GDP. There is no commonly accepted definition of a depression, but believe me, we'll all be painfully aware of one when it arrives.

Why do business fluctuations occur? A host of factors cause changes in economic activity: wars, business failures, fluctuating interest rates, inflation, weather, changing tastes, and government policy. Some of these factors are very real; for example, rising interest rates could choke an economic expansion by making the cost of borrowing prohibitive, and a spate of business failures could certainly do some damage to an expanding economy. On the other hand, business fluctuations sometimes occur for reasons that are not so readily apparent. Intangible factors could include just

		Number of Months in Recession	Number of Months in Expansion
Peak	Trough		
February 1945	October 1945	8	79
November 1948	October 1949	11	36
July 1953	May 1954	10	44
July 1957	April 1958	9	37
April 1960	February 1961	10	23
December 1969	November 1970	11	106
November 1973	March 1975	16	36
January 1980	July 1980	6	57
July 1981	November 1982	16	11
July 1990	March 1991	8	111

Table 2–1   Business Cycles Since World War II

a change in tastes and/or consumer behavior. For example, consumers could wake up one day and decide to keep their automobiles a year longer rather than purchase the new models. This could significantly reduce the demand for new automobiles, and a cutback in the production of automobiles could pose a serious threat to the economy's overall expansion.

Among all the different factors that contribute to business fluctuations, there is one constant—the same fluctuations keep coming back every decade. The duration and magnitude of the cycles may differ from decade to decade, but the shape and form of the cycles remain intact. So, after a while, we all grow accustomed to the business cycle. We learn to understand it, and we know what to expect when it arrives. It is analogous to the teenagers who rode the Cyclone every Friday night. With each ride, they experienced and reexperienced the same ups and downs. Their confidence grew, and by the end of the summer, their hands were no longer tightly clutching the handrails of their seats; instead, they were pointed toward the sky, waving frantically toward the clouds. Similarly, after years of experiencing business cycles, most of us know what to expect, decade in and decade out. Although we are never comfortable when the economy experiences a recession, there is some comfort in knowing that it will probably be short-lived.

Phases of the Business Cycle

To take advantage of a changing economy, we must first be able to identify the regular cyclical movements of business. Usually, the business cycle is measured by noting the peaks in the real gross domestic product (GDP), and measuring the changes that occur from peak to peak. The cycle's phases—downturn, trough, recovery, expansion, and peak—occur with regularity, which heightens the importance of understanding the characteristics of each phase. For instance, today's business cycle is pleasantly stuck in an expansion phase. Our last downturn was a very brief recession during 1990 and 1991. It lasted about eight months before hitting a trough in March 1991. For all of us, and particularly for investors, the trillion-dollar question is: When will the economy hit the peak phase and transition into the downturn phase? As will be apparent later in this book, monitoring and anticipating the different phases of the business cycle will have serious implications for your investment decisions.

1. *Downturn.* Starting from a peak, the first phase of a business cycle is the downturn or recession. Officially, it lasts as long as changes in GDP are negative; two successive declines in GDP growth make a downturn "official." Most indicators of economic activity (e.g., consumer spending) lose value during a downturn. Most investments that ride on the high tide of an expanding economy will begin to lose value during a downturn. It is important to note, however, that toward the end of a downturn some indicators may begin to show some strength, which of course is a precursor for an expanding economy and rising investment values.

2. *Trough.* The trough represents the end of the downturn; GDP is then at its lowest level within the cycle. Some indicators begin to show signs of strength when the economy has fallen to its trough. Housing starts (i.e., construction activity) usually turn upward, signaling a recovery on the horizon.

3. *Recovery.* Recovery officially begins when GDP growth becomes positive, and it officially ends when the GDP level exceeds the previous peak (which is the start of an expansion). A mixed bag of economic indicators appears throughout this period. Some will usually exhibit a good deal of strength (e.g., the housing sector); others may continue to display weakness (e.g., job gains and retail sales).

The recovery period may be the most sensitive period for investments and may also offer the greatest opportunity for market timing of certain investments. Knowing when the recovery is coming has substantial implications for a successful investment strategy.

4. *Expansion.* A recovery changes into an expansion when the economy reaches a new cyclical high, as measured by GDP. Most economic indicators are displaying building strength during an expansion. However, toward the end of the expansion, some indicators, such as housing and interest rates, may begin to deteriorate, signaling that a peak is near. With regard to investment strategies, an expanding economy usually means expanding values for most investments.

5. *Peak.* The *peak,* the highest level of economic activity, offers the greatest change in economic growth (GDP). However, today's investors tend to have a "What have you done for us lately?" mindset. As they perceive that the economy is approaching peak performance, they are already anticipating a fall from the top, and are looking for other economic indicators that suggest a worsening in economic activity. Thus, when economic activity is peaking, some sectors of the economy may already be moving into the next phase of the cycle—downturn (recession). The ability to identify and anticipate a peak offers investors an opportunity to anticipate when good investments turn into bad investments.

Tracking the Economy

The ability to monitor a changing economy and to anticipate its impact on the value of financial assets is crucial in any credible investment strategy. The lessons of the Great Depression still linger. Conversely, the current prolonged expansion (1991–the present) is an excellent example of how an expanding and healthy economy can create additional value for most financial assets. The value of the U.S. stock market, as measured by the Dow Jones Industrial Average (DJIA), rose about 334 percent during the 1990s expansion and crossed the 11,000-point barrier in 1999 (although with some fluctuations).

The general movements in the economy are best judged by applying three important economic measures: (1) GDP, (2) inflation, and (3) interest rates. Investors can monitor changes in the nation's GDP by reviewing the GDP Report, which is released three times during each quarter by the Department of Commerce. Inflationary pressures can be monitored by focusing primarily on the monthly release of the Consumer Price Index (CPI). Interest rates can best be tracked by looking at movements in the interest rates for 30-year Treasury bonds (although the 10-year Treasury bond is becoming increasingly popular).

Economic Measures and the Business Cycle

Changes in the three economic measures are often influenced by the phase of the business cycle, as well as by their own direction and magnitude. For example, rising interest rates can influence the value of financial assets differently, depending on the phase of the business cycle. Rising interest rates during a recovery usually mean that momentum is building in the housing market (more households are buying homes); thus, the value of housing-related stock investments is increasing in spite of rising interest rates. On the other hand, rising interest rates toward the end of an expansion will usually inhibit home-buying activity by raising borrowing costs and depressing the value of housing-related stock investments. One observable primary economic measure—rising interest rates—generates two different effects on the value of financial assets, depending on the phase of the business cycle while the changes are occurring. In short, utilizing changes in indicators without knowing the phase of the cycle could be very misleading.

It is equally important to know that the primary indicators are interdependent with one another, and that their performances should be viewed collectively rather than independently. For example, if the economy is close to full employment and is experiencing a robust expansion, each indicator will be influencing the others. GDP growth will be rising, which exerts upward pressure on inflation—which, in turn, exerts upward pressure on interest rates. However, higher interest rates will eventually inhibit GDP growth, which eases inflationary pressures, which, in turn, lowers interest rates, and so on.

Changes in the primary economic measures may sometimes impact the value of financial assets (e.g., bonds) differently from the value of economic assets (e.g., wages, prices of goods and services). For example, if the economy is experiencing strong GDP growth, the unemployment rate will be low. The value of economic assets most assuredly will rise, but the value of some financial assets may fall. In a robust and growing economy, household wages and wealth usually rise, raising the standard of living for most of us. In contrast, the value of financial assets may actually fall in response to stronger economic news. To participants in both the bond (fixed-income securities) and stock (equity) markets, strong economic growth usually signals rising inflationary pressure, resulting in rising interest rates. This would send bond prices down; in some cases, stock prices would fall as well. Although it may not sit well with your common sense, what is good news for the economy may not necessarily be good news for the financial markets.

Each of the three economic measures can be easily found, and the value of each is monitored on most Internet investment sites. The following brief descriptions of the economic measures include discussions of the factors that influence their behavior.

Gross Domestic Product

The gross domestic product (GDP) is a dollar-value measure of all goods and services produced in the United States during a given time period. GDP, the broadest measure of economic activity, includes individual consumption expenditures, business investment in structures and equipment, residential investment, inventory investment, net exports (exports minus imports), and government expenditures. The largest component of GDP is personal consumption (i.e., consumer spending), which comprises about two-thirds of the total. Other sectors of the economy (e.g., residential investment, inventories, net exports) tend to be more volatile and, thus, more frequently have a greater influence on quarterly GDP growth patterns.

The GDP Report is released three times during a quarter. First, the prior quarter's GDP is released in the first month of the current quarter. A preliminary report is released in the second month, and a final and revised report is released in the final month of the quarter. Although the advance report released in the first month is not as accurate as the later two reports, it probably has greater influence on investments because it provides investors with their first information about overall economic growth for the prior quarter. Investors should focus most attention on two areas of the report:

1. *Quarterly growth rate* in real GDP (adjusted for inflation). The magnitude of the growth rate indicates the health of the

economy. If real GDP is growing by 4 percent, the economy is very healthy. Conversely, if real GDP is growing by a scant 0.5 percent, the economy is weak. A 2 to 2½ percent growth rate is normal for the U.S. economy. (As of this writing, there is a debate as to whether the economy's normal, noninflationary growth pace has been elevated by a full percentage point in recent years, due to productivity gains.)

2. *Final sales* (GDP minus the change in business inventories). This is a broad measure of the demand for goods and services in the economy.

Movements in GDP measure the business cycle. Thus, GDP levels rise during recovery and expansion periods, and fall during downturns (see Figure 2–1). Both the quarterly growth and final sales measures can assist investors in identifying the general direction of the stock and bond markets, as well as other broad market indexes. Projections for robust GDP growth are usually associated with a rise in the broad stock indexes (e.g., S&P 500 Index) and, if near full employment, a drop in the major bond market performance measures. Conversely, modest or negative GDP

Figure 2–1   Real Gross Domestic Product (GDP). By definition, GDP rises during expansions and falls during downturns. Notice the particularly sharp and long fall during the 1974/75 recessions.

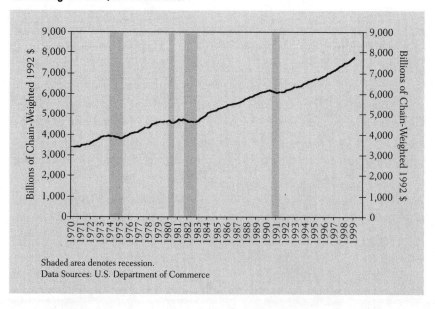

Shaded area denotes recession.
Data Sources: U.S. Department of Commerce

growth is usually associated with a fall in equity prices relative to other assets. However, it may be a stretch to say which specific sector of stocks or bonds will also rise. The key to projecting changes in specific sector financial assets is to identify a handful of monthly indicators that are directly related to future changes in GDP, but can also be tied closely to changes in more specific sectors of the economy (e.g., the housing sector).

Vital Information

Source: Department of Commerce, Bureau of Economic Analysis.

Timing: Quarterly data, but revised and released, on a monthly basis, at 8:30 A.M. on a business day near the end of each month.

Where to Find: All major Internet investment sites, including Bloomberg.com, TheStreet.com, CNN-FN, CNBC, *Wall Street Journal* (next day), Reuters, Telerate News Services, and Department of Commerce's Stat-usa/Internet service @ http://domino.stat-usa.gov/econtest.nsf.

Cyclical Behavior: A coincident indicator: negative growth in downturn, positive growth in recovery and expansion.

Key Financial Assets: S&P 500 Index; DJIA; bonds; other broad market indexes.

Inflation (Consumer Price Index)

Inflation is a general rise in the prices of goods and services. There is no single measure of inflation; the most generally accepted measure is the Consumer Price Index (CPI), and investors should monitor its monthly movements. Other measures of inflation can also be useful: the Producer Price Index, the Employment Cost Index, and the average hourly earnings component reported in the Department of Labor's monthly Employment Report.

Compiled monthly by the Bureau of Labor Statistics, the CPI measures price changes for a fixed basket of goods and services purchased by all urban consumers and wage earners. The CPI has seven major categories: (1) food and beverages, (2) housing, (3) apparel, (4) transportation, (5) medical care, (6) entertainment, and (7) other goods and services. Inflationary pressures, as measured by the CPI, ease during a downturn, moderately rise during a recovery, and rise in expansion periods (see Figure 2–2). However, price pressures tend to ease (the CPI falls) just before the expansion peaks and transitions into a downturn.

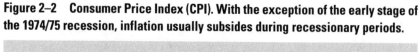

Figure 2–2 Consumer Price Index (CPI). With the exception of the early stage of the 1974/75 recession, inflation usually subsides during recessionary periods.

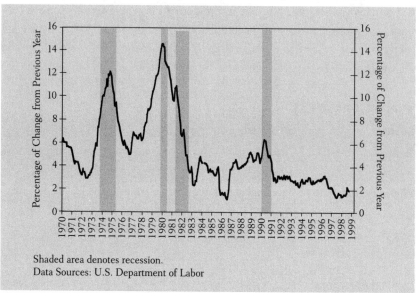

Shaded area denotes recession.
Data Sources: U.S. Department of Labor

Professional investors tend to focus on the monthly changes in the core CPI, which excludes the two most volatile components—food and energy prices. The bond, equity, and foreign exchange markets react adversely to dramatic increases in the monthly core CPI. Bond prices will fall (i.e., interest rates will rise); the value of a large number of stocks will fall; and the U.S. dollar will lose value in the foreign exchange markets when there is an increase in the CPI. Commodity prices will usually rise and fall in conjunction with increases and decreases in inflation. Real estate values may also rise and fall (more indirectly) with changes in inflation.

Significant and prolonged bouts of inflation are damaging to the economy, to business productivity, and to the fixed-income security markets. A rise in general prices distorts relative prices throughout the economy, and sends false signals to consumers and producers. Inflation also distorts economic decisions by helping people who borrow money and hurting people who loan money. Thus, investors (people who loan money) will attach an inflation premium to their investments (sending interest rates upward), to ensure that their return on investment will be close to inflation-proof. In general, the broad measures of equities and bonds will drop, in response to serious inflationary pressures.

Vital Information

Source:	Department of Labor, Bureau of Labor Statistics.
Timing:	Released monthly at 8:30 A.M., two to three weeks after the previous month ends.
Where to Find:	All major Internet investment sites including Bloomberg.com, TheStreet.com, Department of Commerce's Stat-usa/Internet service @ http://domino.stat-usa.gov/econtest.nsf, CNN Business News, CNN-FN, CNBC, Internet, *Wall Street Journal* (next day), Reuters, and Telerate News Services.
Cyclical Behavior:	Slow or negative growth in downturn, slow or rising growth in recovery, rising growth in expansion.
Key Financial Assets:	Interest rate-sensitive stocks; inflation-sensitive stocks; bonds and other fixed-income investments; real estate; commodities; gold and foreign exchange rates.

Interest Rates

Interest rates are the single most important economic variable in any investment decision. For equities, interest rates represent the "alternative" investment (via bonds) to purchasing stocks. Higher-yielding bonds make equity investments less attractive. Interest rates also represent the cost of borrowing for businesses, and a rise in borrowing costs could inhibit profit margins and depress stock prices. For bonds, interest rates represent the return on the investment. Before committing large amounts of funds to any investment, the investor should know which way interest rates are heading.

Literally hundreds of different interest rates are floating in the financial markets at any given time. There are short-term and long-term interest rates; interest rates on Treasury bonds, corporate bonds, municipal bonds, and mortgage-backed securities; interest rates on commercial bank certificates of deposit, savings accounts, and business accounts (the prime lending rate). There are international rates (e.g., LIBOR) and domestic rates. To keep the discussion simple, we will focus on the 30-year Treasury bond yield, to which professional investors pay particular attention. It is the bell-wether of interest rates, the most watched rate in the economy. It has the same importance to the bond markets that the Dow Jones Industrial Average (DJIA) has to the stock market.

The U.S. Treasury borrows a lot of money every week, when it issues Treasury bonds, notes, and bills. Treasury bills are short-term borrowings (a three-month Treasury bill is typical); Treasury notes have an intermediate term (a two-year Treasury note is common). The longer-term borrowings involve, usually, the 10-year and 30-year Treasury bonds. In general, the interest rates paid on Treasury bonds are greater than the rates paid on Treasury notes, which, in turn, are greater than the interest paid on Treasury bills. Borrowers have to pay more (a higher interest rate) if they want to borrow funds for a long period of time (i.e., long-term bonds). A lower rate is paid for borrowing funds for a short period of time (via bills and notes). The short-term versus long-term interest rate relationship among fixed-income securities is represented by a yield curve (an academic term) in which the rate paid on short-term borrowings is less than the rate paid on long-term borrowings.

The interest rate relationship between long-term borrowings and short-term borrowings could change (i.e., the yield curve might be inverted), depending on specific economic conditions. If inflation flares up but investors expect inflation to be a short-term problem that will cool down in the longer run, the interest rate on short-term borrowings could actually be greater than the long-term interest rates. Investors would demand a greater return on their loanable funds in the short term, due to high inflation rates (they don't want to be burned by inflation), but they would accept a lower long-term return on the loanable funds because they do not expect inflation to continue to be a major factor. The bottom line: A host of investment strategies are available, and investors can take advantage of changes in the 30-year Treasury bond rate as well as changes in the relationship between short- and long-term interest rates (Figure 2–3). In general, interest rates rise toward the end of an expansion (thereby choking the expansion with prohibitive borrowing costs) and continue to rise and then fall throughout the downturn period. Rate-sensitive financial assets are most highly influenced by changes in interest rates; these include financial services companies (their profit margins depend on the level of interest rates) and the primary stock indexes (e.g., the S&P 500 Index), because changes in their interest rates influence the direction of the stock market.

Figure 2–3   30-Year Treasury Bond Yield. Movements in the 30-year Treasury Bond Yield have been volatile since the mid-1970s, but usually fall, although erratically, during recessions.

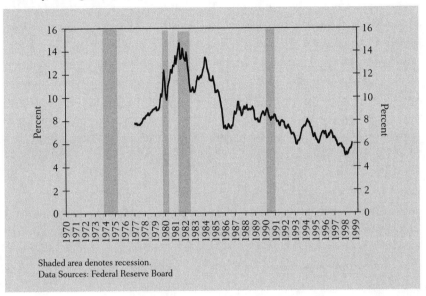

Shaded area denotes recession.
Data Sources: Federal Reserve Board

Vital Information

Source:	U.S. Treasury.
Timing:	Daily quotes; Treasury bonds are market-determined.
Where to Find:	All major Internet investment sites, including Bloomberg.com,The Street.com, Department of Commerce's Stat-usa/Internet service @ http://domino.stat-usa.gov/econtest.nsf, CNN Business News, CNN-FN, CNBC, Internet, *Wall Street Journal* (next day), Reuters, and Telerate News Services.
Cyclical Behavior:	Rising and then falling in downturn, rising toward end of expansion.
Key Financial Assets:	Interest rate-sensitive stocks; inflation-sensitive stocks, bonds, and other fixed-income assets/investments; broad stock market indexes; real estate; commodities; gold; and foreign exchange rates.

Putting the Economic Measures to the Test

Let's put to the test what we have learned up to now. Changes in GDP, inflation, and interest rates influence the values of major investments in the financial markets. For example, there is a strong positive relationship between economic growth and the success of the stock market. Recall that equity prices usually reflect the market's expectations of future company profits. According to Figure 2–4, economic growth, as measured by changes in GDP, is strikingly coincident with advances in the stock market, as measured by the S&P 500 Index. In general, if the economy is growing, so is the stock market. However, it is also clear from Figure 2–4 that the stock market is influenced by the duration of the economic expansion, as well as by other factors. During the 1983–1997 period, the stock market climbed to record highs because of the almost uninterrupted strength of the economy. As we will see below, both inflation and interest rates were kept at relatively low levels during that period. However, during the 1970–1982 period, the stock market's performance was relatively flat, for two obvious reasons: (1) the economy did not grow consistently

Figure 2–4   Real Gross Domestic Product vs. the S&P 500. Movements in GDP and the S&P 500 are highly correlated, although the stock index is somewhat more erratic.

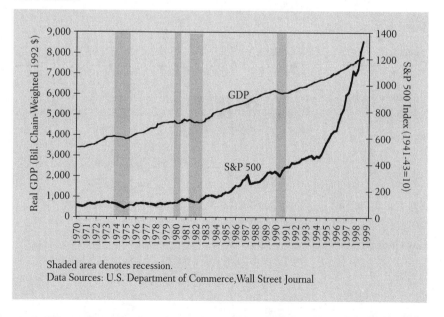

Shaded area denotes recession.
Data Sources: U.S. Department of Commerce, Wall Street Journal

(recessions occurred during 1974, 1980, and 1982), and (2) both inflation and interest rates were relatively high throughout the period.

Consistent, prolonged economic growth with a backdrop of relatively low inflation and interest rates is an ideal environment for the stock market. These factors are most definitely the fuel that generated the record-breaking stock market performance of the 1990s.

Figure 2–5 shows that, in general, relatively high inflation is bad for the stock market, and relatively low inflation is good for the stock market. From 1970 to 1982, inflation, as measured by the CPI, was extremely volatile, but it stayed within a relatively high range (5 percent to 15 percent). Meanwhile, the S&P 500 Index was relatively flat. However, when the inflation rate dropped considerably during the 1982 recession, and then hovered within a relatively tight low-level range (about 1 percent to 5 percent) from 1983 to 1997, the stock market (i.e., S&P 500) experienced solid and consistent advances. With regard to the impact of interest rates on the stock market, Figure 2–5 suggests that, like the effects of inflation, higher interest rates are associated with a flat-to-dismal stock

Figure 2–5   Consumer Price Index vs. the S&P 500. With the exception of the early stage of the 1974/75 recession, inflation has usually subsided during recessionary periods.

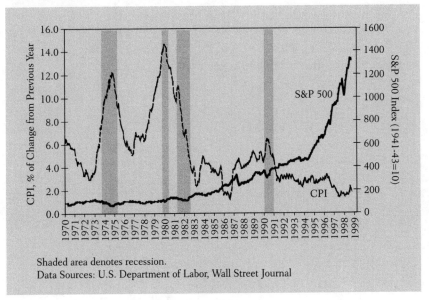

Shaded area denotes recession.
Data Sources: U.S. Department of Labor, Wall Street Journal

market performance, and lower interest rates are associated with solid stock price advances.

It's worth repeating: When interest rates rise, bond prices fall. Similarly, when inflation rises, interest rates rise (due to the inflation premium embedded in rates), and, in turn, bond prices fall. Thus, both inflation and interest rates move the bond markets in very direct ways. The impact of changes in GDP on bond values depends on whether the economy is operating close to full capacity. If so, a robust rise in GDP growth would generate upward pressure on inflation, which, in turn, would exert upward pressure on interest rates, causing bond prices to fall. If the economy is operating at less than capacity, solid growth in GDP could be neutral for bond values.

In summary, three economic measures—GDP, inflation, and interest rates—directly influence investment values, and close monitoring of their movements in today's always changing economy is crucial for any successful investment strategy. These economic measures have a highly influential effect on the broad financial asset indexes, such as the DJIA and the bond market. If we desire to invest in particular sectors of the economy (e.g., the housing market, or manufacturing companies), or if we need to anticipate movements in the three economic measures *before* they move, then we need to utilize other economic indicators offered in the markets. These *secondary* market indicators are crucial for developing any investment strategy. Investors must anticipate movements in the three primary indicators, and that can only be accomplished by employing the secondary indicators. In the next chapter, I present the most influential economic reports (secondary indicators) available in the markets today.

3

INFLUENTIAL
ECONOMIC REPORTS

Changes in the economy and in the three primary measures of economic activity—GDP, inflation, and interest rates—can be measured and anticipated through the hundreds of economic reports
released every month by the U.S. Government and by other nonprivate
and private organizations. Like the primary measures, all of these reports
can be tracked at all of the major Internet investment sites.

Every business day, professional traders, investment bankers, and
private investors wait nervously to view the important daily economic reports. As soon as the reports are released, they carefully evaluate their
content and anticipate how these fresh data will impact GDP, inflation,
and interest rates—and, in turn, investments. In the 1970s and early
1980s, by far the most influential report was the Federal Reserve's release of the monetary aggregates (i.e., the money supply—M1, M2, and
M3). Every Thursday, traders and investors alike would hold their collec-
tive breath, awaiting the release of these numbers. Seconds after the report's release, it was not unusual for interest rates to move ⅛ to ¼
percentage point in either direction.

In recent years, the Department of Labor's monthly Employment
Report has become the most popular and most widely anticipated economic release. The employment numbers are released at 8:30 A.M. on
the first Friday of every month, and all financial market participants

await, and react to, this important economic information. Like the money supply numbers during the 1970s and 1980s, the employment data can, from time to time, move the markets by a relatively large magnitude (e.g., interest rates have moved by about $\frac{1}{8}$ to $\frac{1}{4}$ percentage point in either direction).

Included with the Employment Report are other economic reports that seem to always command attention from financial market participants. In fact, during the 1990s, a handful of reports stood out as the most influential economic releases. They were either widely anticipated by the major players (e.g., traders and professional investors) or they were widely known as "market movers" because they influenced the value of financial assets as soon as they were released (see Appendix A).

Listed below are the economic reports I have selected as being influential in the markets today. Three of these reports are clearly "market movers." The other reports are highly popular among professional investors and traders. Monitoring all or some of these reports will be valuable in anticipating changes in GDP, inflation, and interest rates, as well as changes in the value of financial assets. Even though the indicators point to a sector (e.g., manufacturing) as a good general investment opportunity, exercise caution when investing in a specific company. Carefully evaluate the company's performance through information services like Value Line, or through various Internet online information services, or go directly to the company's published reports. Look at the stock price indicators, such as the price–earnings ratio, dividend payout ratio, and earnings per share, to gain a better appreciation for a specific company's history. (See Chapter 6 for more details.)

The influential economic reports I recommend are:

1. The Employment Report.
2. Retail Sales.
3. Consumer Confidence Index.
4. Capacity Utilization.
5. National Association of Purchasing Managers Index.
6. Housing Starts.
7. Merchandise Trade Balance.
8. Durable Goods Orders.

1. The Employment Report

For investors, the release of the Employment Report is critical because, every month, it is the first piece of information that signals how much and how fast the gross domestic product (GDP) is growing. It is a proxy for GDP growth estimates. The Employment Report is derived from two surveys: (1) a household survey based on personal interviews of about 50,000 people, and (2) an establishment survey that compiles statistics on employment, hours worked, overtime, and hourly wages, based on payroll data from more than 390,000 business establishments.

For investment purposes, attention is focused on just three pieces of information released in this report: (1) *nonfarm payrolls,* (2) *the unemployment rate* (taken from the household survey), and (3) *hourly wages.* The nonfarm payroll component (Figure 3–1) tells investors that the employment sector is either expanding or contracting, which suggests that the GDP may be either expanding or contracting as well. If the economy is operating close to full employment, increases in nonfarm payrolls will

Figure 3–1 Nonfarm Payroll Employment. Nonfarm payrolls are coincident with the economy's growth. They advance during expansions and contract during recessions.

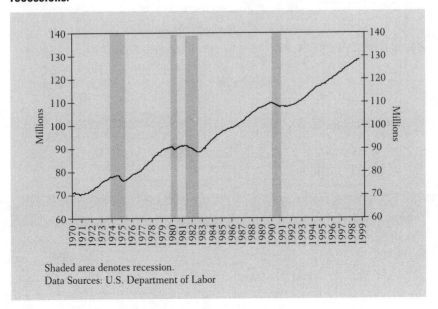

Shaded area denotes recession.
Data Sources: U.S. Department of Labor

also result in upward pressure on inflation and, thus, on interest rates. Bond prices on fixed-income securities will be lower. Given the broad economic implications of the Employment Report, movements in non-farm payrolls directly impact the broad measures of financial assets, such as the Dow Jones Industrial Average, the S&P 500, and some broad bond market indexes. The unemployment rate is just a very popular measure of the "pain or gain" of the economy, because it tells how many workers have jobs. The hourly wages component of the report is a reliable leading indicator of wage inflation, which is on every investor's radar screen. In general, the Employment Report is a coincident indicator with GDP (i.e., it moves in the same direction). Employment rises in an expansion and falls during a contraction. However, payrolls are slow to grow during the recovery phase because companies may delay hiring workers until they are assured that the increased demand for their products and services will be long lasting.

Vital Statistics

Source:	Department of Labor, Bureau of Labor Statistics.
Timing:	First Friday of every month, released at 8:30 A.M.
Where to Find:	CNN Business News, CNN-FN, CNBC, Internet, *Wall Street Journal* (next day), Reuters, Telerate, Bloomberg News services, and Department of Commerce's Stat-usa/Internet service @ http://domino.stat-usa.gov/econtest.nsf.
Cyclical Behavior:	A coincident indicator exhibiting negative growth in downturn and positive growth in expansion, but a lagging indicator exhibiting negative and then positive growth in the recovery period.
Key Financial Assets:	S&P 500 Index; bonds; other broad market indexes.

2. Retail Sales

The Retail Sales report is a good proxy for consumer spending. It provides investors with information on the demand for goods and services during the previous month. This feedback is critical for monitoring the month-by-month spending patterns of consumers. Consumer spending comprises about two-thirds of the GDP, and any change in this component will seriously impact changes in the economy, and, in turn, the profit performance of businesses.

The report is first released as an "advance" estimate, based on a small sample of about 2,000 retailers. Eventually, it is revised to include a much larger sample of about 30,000 retailers. Thus, the first monthly Retail Sales report is likely to undergo a significant revision when the next month's report is released. For this reason, when we evaluate the Retail Sales report for June, we are equally concerned about the reported revisions for April and May. The largest move in the stock market (as measured by the S&P 500 Index) during the 1990s was a 2.73 percent drop in the S&P 500 Index on April 11, 1997, caused primarily by the release of the Retail Sales report. Some sharp upward revisions in some prior months' Retail Sales reports unnerved the stock market.

It is important to note that automobile sales comprise about 20 percent of all retail sales. However, because the auto sales component has been historically volatile (erratic from month to month), economists usually focus attention on retail sales, excluding auto sales. This gives investors a better sense of the true spending behavior of consumers.

The Retail Sales report includes both nondurable and durable goods. Spending on nondurable goods, which occurs in food stores, gasoline stations, apparel shops, department stores, and drug stores, appears to be fairly steady through the business cycle. An increase in nondurable goods sales, compared to the prior month, portends favorably for apparel retailers, nondurable household product companies, and the entertainment and leisure industries. Leading companies in these categories include Clorox Company, Colgate-Palmolive, James River Corporation, Kimberly-Clark, Procter & Gamble, The Gap, Inc., Nordstrom, Inc., King World Products, and Time Warner, Inc.

Retail spending on durable goods is highly interest-rate-sensitive because consumers usually purchase durable goods on credit, making the interest rate an important factor. Furniture, automobiles, building materials, personal computers, and refrigerators are major items in this category. A positive monthly change in the durable goods spending component of the report portends favorably for durable household product companies, computer/information companies, furniture/appliances, electronics, and automotive-related companies. Among the well-known companies in these categories are Newell Company, Premark International, Rubbermaid, Inc.,

Figure 3–2   Retail Sales. Retail sales are subject to wide swings throughout a business cycle, but they generally fall during the early stages of a recession.

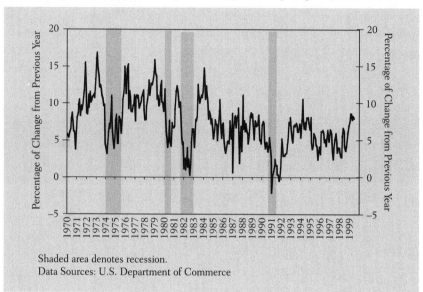

Shaded area denotes recession.
Data Sources: U.S. Department of Commerce

Black & Decker, Maytag Corporation, Whirlpool Corporation, Circuit City, IBM, Apple Computer, Ford, Chrysler, and General Motors.

In summary, the Retail Sales report is highly influential because the direction and magnitude of total retail sales serve as reliable proxies for consumer spending (Figure 3–2). By distinguishing nondurable and durable goods spending, the report helps investors gain better insight into their general investment strategy. They can track the overall stock market (e.g., the S&P 500 Index) and the overall bond market (e.g., a Treasury bond fund) as well as sector stocks in consumer-related companies. The Retail Sales report is a coincident indicator—retail sales figures increase during expansions and drop off during contractions.

Vital Statistics

Source:	Department of Commerce, Bureau of the Census.
Timing:	Released at about mid-month at 8:30 A.M.
Where to Find:	CNN Business News, CNN-FN, CNBC, Internet, *Wall Street Journal* (next day), Reuters, Telerate, Bloomberg News services,

and Department of Commerce's Stat-usa/Internet service @ http://domino.stat-usa.gov/econtest.nsf.

Cyclical Behavior: A coincident indicator: negative growth in downturn, positive growth in recovery and expansion.

Key Financial Assets: S&P 500 Index; bonds; other broad market indexes.

3. Consumer Confidence Index

Monitoring and measuring consumer sentiment became almost a fad during the 1990s. Literally hundreds of consumer sentiment surveys are conducted annually by a wide variety of government agencies and private corporations. Questions range from how consumers feel about current and future economic conditions to whether they favor the Big Mac over the Whopper. On top of the pile of consumer surveys stands the Conference Board's consumer sentiment survey, *Consumer Attitudes and Buying Plans,* which is the wellspring of the Board's Consumer Confidence Index, perhaps the most popular index in the nation.

The Consumer Confidence Index reflects how consumers feel about the present economic situation and how they expect to feel about economic prospects six months in the future. The Consumer Confidence Index basically rises during expansions and falls during downturns (Figure 3–3) and is a leading indicator just before downturns and just before recoveries. Historically, consumer confidence plunges just before a recession (usually with about three months' lead time). Consumers usually regain confidence toward the end of a recession, providing a valuable signal of when the economy is about to enter a recovery period.

Not surprisingly, the Consumer Confidence Index soared to new heights during the amazing 1990s expansion. The strength in the index provides comfort to investors: Households will continue to spend money on goods and services (particularly the big-ticket items—homes and automobiles). Gains in consumer confidence make investors feel more secure with their equity investments because more consumer spending usually means higher corporate profits. On the other hand, a drop in consumer confidence signals a weaker economy ahead, suggesting lower interest rates (or rising bond prices). After a prolonged period of expansion, if the index drops for more than two months consecutively, it may be time to pull out of stocks.

Figure 3–3 Consumer Confidence. Consumer confidence usually falls just before a recession and rises in advance of a recovery period.

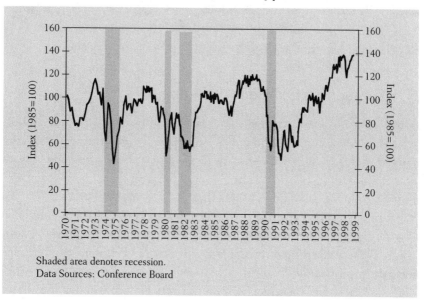

Shaded area denotes recession.
Data Sources: Conference Board

Vital Statistics

Source:	Conference Board.
Timing:	Released on the last Tuesday of each month, at 10:00 A.M.
Where to Find:	CNN Business News, CNN-FN, CNBC, Internet, *Wall Street Journal* (next day), Reuters, Telerate, and Bloomberg News services.
Cyclical Behavior:	A coincident indicator: negative growth in downturn, positive growth in recovery and expansion.
Key Financial Assets:	S&P 500 Index; bonds; other broad market indexes.

4. Capacity Utilization

The Capacity Utilization report, a monthly release from the Federal Reserve, measures the percentage of productive capacity in the manufacturing, mining, and utility sectors of the economy. It provides investors with a sense of how much slack remains in the goods-producing sectors of the economy: how much more the economy can produce (grow) before inflationary pressures begin to build.

The capacity utilization rate is a coincident indicator; a rising rate signals more economic growth, and a falling rate signals slower economic growth (Figure 3–4). However, the utilization rate usually turns down just before a recession, and it stays down until the recession ends.

If the economy is operating dangerously close to full capacity—for example, around 84 percent—any further rise in the capacity utilization rate could be inflationary. Bond investors view a rise in the capacity utilization rate as a signal that inflationary pressures may build, causing interest rates to rise. Investors in the stock market favor increases in the utilization rate because they signal greater economic strength and higher corporate profits. Because gains in utilization rates usually result in higher interest rates (at least when the economy is operating close to capacity), the U.S. dollar gains in value and becomes relatively more attractive.

Released with the capacity utilization rate is an Index of Industrial Production. It covers manufacturing, mining, and utilities, and it measures the production of consumer durables and business equipment. This index

Figure 3–4   Capacity Utilization. The capacity utilization rate drops precipitously during recessions.

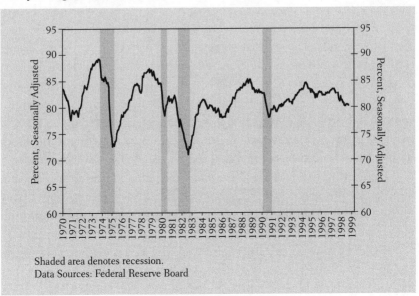

Shaded area denotes recession.
Data Sources: Federal Reserve Board

is coincident; it gains value during expansions and loses value during contractions. A rise in the index usually is a negative for the bond markets and a positive for the equity markets, because the index is coincident with the economy. More specifically, for investors in the stock market, a rise in the Index of Industrial Production usually points to increases in corporate earnings, which bolster equity values.

Vital Statistics

Source:	Federal Reserve.
Timing:	Released about the middle of every month, at 9:15 A.M.
Where to Find:	CNN Business News, CNN-FN, CNBC, Internet, *Wall Street Journal* (next day), Reuters, Telerate; Bloomberg News services, and Department of Commerce's Stat-usa/Internet service @ http://domino.stat-usa.gov/econtest.nsf.
Cyclical Behavior:	A coincident indicator: negative growth in downturn, positive growth in recovery and expansion.
Key Financial Assets:	S&P 500 Index; bonds; other broad market indexes.

5. National Association of Purchasing Managers Index

The National Association of Purchasing Managers (NAPM) Index is usually the first piece of economic information released to the financial markets each month. The NAPM surveys more than 250 purchasing agents regarding new orders, production, employment, and supplier deliveries. The NAPM Index measures the percentage of purchasing agents reporting greater activity in each area. An index reading of 50 percent or greater indicates that the manufacturing sector is expanding; a reading of less than 50 percent indicates that the manufacturing sector is contracting. If the index drops below 44 percent, it is a signal that the economy is in recession.

The NAPM Index is usually a reliable leading indicator of economic activity (lead time is about three months). The Index usually drops below 50 just before a downturn period, and begins to rise in value toward the end of a downturn (Figure 3–5).

Investors have taken a fancy to the NAPM Index, not only for its content, but because Federal Reserve Chairman Alan Greenspan has praised it as a reliable indicator of economic activity. The NAPM Index is

Figure 3–5 NAPM Index. The NAPM Index, although erratic at times, stays primarily at about 50 percent throughout expansions, and drops well below 50 percent during recessions.

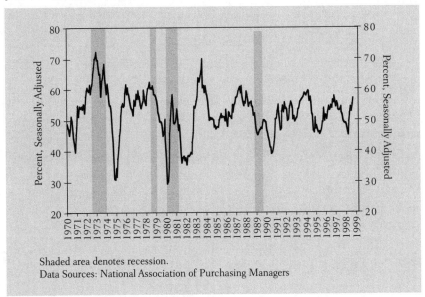

Shaded area denotes recession.
Data Sources: National Association of Purchasing Managers

a mix of a leading and a coincident indicator, because of its new orders component. When the index exceeds 50 percent, it bodes well for future economic activity. A reading below 50 percent suggests that the manufacturing sector may experience slower or negative growth. Any reading above 50 percent receives applause from equity investors; readings below 50 percent usually result in bond prices' rallying.

Vital Statistics

Source: National Association of Purchasing Managers.

Timing: Released on the first business day of the month, at 10:00 A.M.

Where to Find: CNN Business News, CNN-FN, CNBC, Internet, *Wall Street Journal* (next day), Reuters, Telerate, Bloomberg News services, and Department of Commerce's Stat-usa/Internet service @ http://domino.stat-usa.gov/econtest.nsf.

Cyclical Behavior: A coincident indicator: negative growth in downturn, positive growth in recovery and expansion.

Key Financial Assets: S&P 500 Index; bonds; other broad market indexes.

6. Housing Starts

From a pool of about 19,000 places (i.e., towns, cities, and metropolitan statistical areas) in the United States, the Commerce Department collects figures on housing starts and permits. The Housing Starts report includes single-family and multifamily units and is the most reliable indicator for residential investment. Because a home purchase usually results in further spending in other sectors of the economy (landscaping, appliances, and so on), the housing sector is considered a leading sector of economic activity. Thus, the Housing Starts report can provide an investor with a fairly reliable indicator of future economic (GDP) activity.

Residential investment is sensitive to both the business cycle and interest rates. Housing starts usually rise during expansions and fall during downturns (Figure 3–6). However, investors regard them as leading indicators because they fall about three to six months before a recession and rise toward the end of a recession (signaling a recovery). Historically, when the housing sector shows signs of life (via growth in starts and permits), the economy becomes poised for a transition from

Figure 3–6 Housing Starts. Housing starts drop off consistently before every recession, but they gain momentum throughout most of the recession.

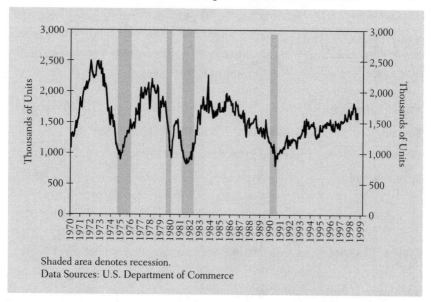

Shaded area denotes recession.
Data Sources: U.S. Department of Commerce

recession to recovery. Thus, investors pay particular attention to the housing starts at the turning points of the business cycle.

When the economy is strong, generating jobs and income, households have the financial ability to purchase homes. Conversely, when the economy is experiencing a downturn, jobs are lost and so is the demand for home buying. Similarly, when interest rates are falling, the cost of borrowing falls, making homes more affordable. Rising interest rates increase the cost of borrowing, and the demand for housing goes down. Popular companies in the homebuilders category include: Centex Corporation, Clayton Homes, Kaufman & Broad, Lennar Corporation, MDC Holdings, Pulte Corporation, and Walter Industries.

Vital Statistics

Source: Department of Commerce, Bureau of the Census.

Timing: Released at 8:30 A.M. about two to three weeks after the previous month ends.

Where to Find: CNN Business News, CNN-FN, CNBC, *Wall Street Journal* (next day), Reuters, Telerate; Bloomberg News services, and Department of Commerce's Stat-usa/Internet service @ http://domino.stat-usa.gov/econtest.nsf.

Cyclical Behavior: A coincident indicator: negative growth in downturn, positive growth in recovery and expansion.

Key Financial Assets: S&P 500 Index; bonds; other broad market indexes.

7. Merchandise Trade Balance

The best measure of changes in our net export sector is the Merchandise Trade Balance report, released by the Commerce Department six weeks after each month ends. The report presents the growth trends for U.S. exports and imports of goods and services. It is usually the last report released by the Commerce Department for each month, so it is not very timely. However, it does provide investors with a sense of our "international situation."

Net exports are the total exports of goods and services, less the total imports of goods and services. Data for both exports and imports are given in six categories: (1) foods, feeds, and beverages; (2) industrial supplies and materials; (3) automobiles, including parts and engines; (4) capital goods (excluding autos); (5) nonfood consumer goods; and (6) other merchandise. The net export component of GDP is growing in importance and is sensitive to the business cycle. As the economy gains strength, imports of foreign goods and services rise because U.S. households have more money to spend. Conversely, as the economy contracts, imports fall. Similarly, our exports grow when other countries' economies are growing, but the demand for exports falls when other countries' economies are contracting. Moreover, imports and exports are sensitive to movements in the value of the U.S. dollar. As the dollar rises in value relative to other currencies, imports rise (they are now relatively cheaper) and exports fall (they are now relatively more expensive). Conversely, a weaker dollar suggests falling imports and rising exports.

At present (and for some time now), the U.S. trade balance is expressed as a deficit. The United States imports more goods and services every year than it exports. Running a trade deficit is a drag on GDP because when we import more than we export, we spend more money on other nations' goods and services than those nations spend on our goods and services. If the trade balance report shows that our trade deficit has

Figure 3–7   U.S. Trade Balance. The U.S. trade balance narrows a bit during recessions, as consumer appetites for foreign goods and services are dampened.

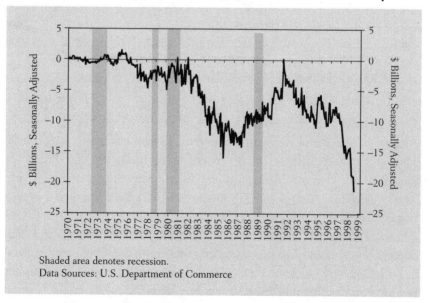

Shaded area denotes recession.
Data Sources: U.S. Department of Commerce

widened, investors will view this as inhibiting our GDP growth. Conversely, if the trade deficit has narrowed, they will view it as a positive development for GDP growth.

Even though the release of trade balance data is not very timely, investors do pay some attention to the widening or narrowing of the trade deficit. However, as Figure 3–7 shows, changes in our trade balance are somewhat choppy throughout the business cycle. During an expansion, the deficit trends downward (widens). During recessions, there are forces that positively influence the trade balance (e.g., import demand weakens). Investors are also focused on the major nations that are our trading partners in imports and exports. A widening trade balance is favored by bond investors because it suggests a weakening economy. A narrowing deficit is favored by equity investors. As of this writing, the United States is running an extremely large negative trade balance, and any rise in imports weakens the exchange value of the U.S. dollar. Strong export growth and weak import growth portends healthy growth in profits/earnings for U.S. domestic companies.

Vital Statistics

Source: Department of Commerce, Bureau of the Census.

Timing: Released about six weeks after month-end, at 8:30 A.M.

Where to Find: CNN Business News, CNN-FN, CNBC, Internet, *Wall Street Journal* (next day), Reuters, Telerate; Bloomberg News services, and Department of Commerce's Stat-usa/Internet service @ http://domino.stat-usa.gov/econtest.nsf.

Cyclical Behavior: A coincident indicator: negative growth in downturn, positive growth in recovery and expansion.

Key Financial Assets: S&P 500 Index; bonds; other broad market indexes.

8. Durable Goods Orders

The Commerce Department releases an advance report of orders placed by manufacturing companies for durable goods (i.e., good with a life expectancy of at least three years). The report includes information about companies' shipments, new orders, and unfilled orders of durable goods.

The Durable Goods Orders report serves as a proxy for estimating business fixed investment, which covers the investment expenditures by businesses in the United States, including spending on office buildings, factories, plant and equipment, computer systems, and trucks. These are big items, and their acquisition is highly dependent on fluctuations in corporate profits. Corporate profits rise in an expanding economy, and decline in a contracting economy. In an expanding economy, corporations will spend some of their increased profits to enlarge their operations or to meet a greater demand for their product and services by investing in new plant and equipment. Conversely, when the economy is contracting, the demand for product/services subsides. Corporate profits are low, so companies cut back their investment in plant and equipment.

Although the Durable Goods Orders report does not directly survey business fixed investment, it is a leading indicator of production, which is highly correlated with businesses' fixed investment expenditures. The report is divided into several categories, such as defense and nondefense goods, and capital and noncapital goods. Durable goods orders rise in an expanding economy and fall in a contracting economy (Figures 3–8). Thus, a positive Durable Goods Orders report portends favorably for future corporate profits which can boost equity prices. A

Figure 3–8   Durable Goods Orders. Although durable goods orders exhibit erratic behavior, they consistently drop off just before a recession begins.

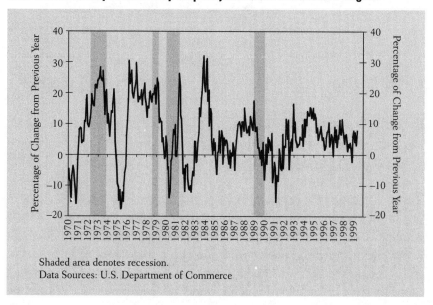

Shaded area denotes recession.
Data Sources: U.S. Department of Commerce

negative report suggests falling corporate profits and lowered equity prices, particularly for manufacturers. Company categories include heavy machinery, factory equipment, transportation equipment, electrical components, and building materials. Among the well-known companies in these categories are: Cummins Engine, Eaton Corporation, Navistar International, Giddings & Lewis, AGCO Corporation, Caterpillar Inc., Deer & Company, Avnet Inc., Emerson Electric, Honeywell Inc., and Vulcan Materials. For bond investors, an increase in durable goods orders signals economic strength. Upward pressure is applied on rates (and downward pressure on bond prices).

Because of its "new orders" and "unfilled orders" categories, this report is a leading indicator of *future* economic activity. Because the report is somewhat choppy from month to month, investors should look at three- to six-month trends instead. Orders are usually up in expansions and down during recessions. Orders may drop just before a recession and rise slightly just before the recovery period.

Vital Statistics

Source: Department of Commerce, Bureau of the Census.

Timing: Released about three to four weeks after the previous month ends, at 8:30 A.M.

Where to Find: CNN Business News, CNN-FN, CNBC, Internet, *Wall Street Journal* (next day), Reuters, Telerate, Bloomberg News services, and Department of Commerce's Stat-usa/Internet service @ http://domino.stat-usa.gov/econtest.nsf.

Cyclical Behavior: A coincident indicator: negative growth in downturn, positive growth in recovery and expansion.

Key Financial Assets: Manufacturing companies; S&P 500 Index; bonds; other broad market indexes.

Appendix A

ECONOMIC REPORTS:
MOVING THE MARKET

A ccording to a study conducted by Goldman Sachs,* a prestigious Wall Street investment banking company, a handful of reports has been highly influential in "moving the markets" in recent years. The Goldman Sachs study looked at all the major economic data reports that were released during 1992–1997 and identified the reports that "moved" the market. "Moving" the market was defined as changing the S&P 500 and the 30-year Treasury bond's basis points (25 basis points equals a quarter of a percentage point) from the close of the previous New York business day to the close of the announcement day. Other market factors, apart from the economic releases, could also have influenced the equity and bond markets during those days, but there is little reason to believe those factors would all occur on a particular day of the month.

The Goldman Sachs study found that, at some point during the 1992–1997 period, reports on employment, retail sales, capacity utilization, the Employment Cost Index (a quarterly release), and the GDP (already identified in the previous chapter as a "must monitor" report) "moved" the market in a meaningful manner. On the top ten data release

---

* *Understanding U.S. Economic Statistics,* Third Edition, Economic Research, Goldman Sachs, November 1997.

days during this period (see pages 49 and 50), the 30-year Treasury bond and the S&P 500 Index were moved, and all five of these reports are associated with the outcomes.

Not surprisingly, some of these reports were associated with more than one top ten day, which bolstered their reputation as market movers. For example, the Employment Report earned five of the top ten spots in the 30-year Treasury bond market and four of the top ten spots in the S&P 500 market. For the 30-year Treasury bond market, the largest single-day move was a gain of 25 basis points (i.e., a quarter of a percentage point) on July 5, 1996, triggered by the release of the Employment Report. At that time, the economy was thought to be operating dangerously close to capacity, suggesting that any sign of strong economic growth would be inflationary. On the equity side, the largest market move

Top Ten Data Release Days, 1992–1997
Treasuries (30-Year Bond Yield)

Day	Move (basis points)	Report	Analysis
1. July 5, 1996	+25	Employment	Strong earnings and payroll growth result in market plunge.
2. May 6, 1994	+20	Employment	Payroll growth is very strong.
3. July 29, 1994	−16	GDP	Bond yields fall on very weak final sales and building inventories.
4. August 1, 1997	+16	Employment	Strong payroll growth heightens market sensitivity toward Fed tightening.
5. February 3, 1995	−15	Employment	Unemployment rate rises, easing fears of further Fed tightening.
6. September 16, 1994	14	Capacity Utilization	Increase in capacity utilization rate signals potential Fed tightening move.
7. August 1, 1996	−14	GDP	Strong growth, no inflation, ease Fed fears.
8. July 14, 1994	−14	Retail Sales	Signs appear that the economy is slowing down.
9. August 5, 1994	+14	Employment	Higher payroll and earnings growth bring back fears of Fed rate hike.
10. May 2, 1996	+14	GDP	Strong GDP data send 30-year bond yields over 7 percent.

Source: Understanding U.S. Economic Statistics, Third Edition, November 1997, Goldman Sachs, Ne York, NY.

Top Ten Data Release Days, 1992–1997 S&P 500			
Day	Move (%)	Report	Analysis
1. April 29, 1997	+2.73	Employment Cost Index	Fears of Fed tightening drop on weak compensation costs news.
2. April 11, 1997	−2.73	Retail Sales	Sharp upward revisions in retail sales frighten markets.
3. July 5, 1996	−2.22	Employment	Strong earnings and payroll growth revive fears of weak economy.
4. April 2, 1993	−1.98	Employment	Lower-than-expected payroll growth.
5. August 2, 1996	+1.92	Employment	Drop in hourly earnings eases fears of tight labor markets.
6. March 13, 1997	−1.83	Retail Sales	Upward revisions to recent retail sales data indicate strong growth.
7. June 6, 1997	+1.73	Employment	Weaker-than-expected payroll growth lifts the market.
8. May 2, 1996	−1.71	GDP	30-year Treasury yield hits 7 percent on strong GDP data.
9. October 28, 1994	+1.70	GDP	Price deflator comes in lower than expected, despite strong GDP growth.
10. June 12, 1997	+1.60	Retail Sales	Retail sales (excluding autos) drop, indicating slowing economy.

Source: Understanding U.S. Economic Statistics, Third Edition, November 1997, Goldman Sachs, New York, NY.

was a 2.73 percent drop in the S&P 500 Index on April 11, 1997, caused primarily by the release of the Retail Sales report. Some sharp upward revisions in retail sales in some prior months unnerved the stock market, implying that current economic growth might be stronger than anticipated. Because the economy was perceived to be operating close to full capacity (in business cycle jargon, the economic expansion was approaching its peak phase), investors believed that strong growth numbers could trigger the Federal Reserve to raise interest rates and slow the economy down in an effort to avoid unwanted inflation.

For each release, there is an explanation of why the report impacted the value of bonds and/or equities on that particular date. Usually, the economic release either unnerved investors or comforted them into believing that the economy was overheating (causing inflation worries and exerting upward interest rates) or that economic growth was moderating (easing inflation worries and exerting downward pressure on interest rates).

4

KNOWING WHAT'S
IMPORTANT FOR GUIDING
INVESTMENT STRATEGIES

I f you are over 40 years old and you're like me, it's getting increasingly easy to be forgetful. But in the investment game, forgetfulness can be very costly. Ignoring important factors and/or developments in the economy can result in following a misguided investment strategy and realizing lower-than expected returns or outright financial loss. This chapter covers the "other factors" that you should not ignore when developing a winning investment strategy.

So far, our recipe for investing is a pretty simple one. We begin with three economic measures (GDP, inflation, and interest rates), then monitor the influential economic reports and mix them together in a business cycle. To complete this recipe, we need to add several other ingredients to the mixing bowl—Federal Reserve policy, Federal budget/tax policy, market psychology, demographics (baby boomers), company-specific activities, and noneconomic factors. Fortunately, the impact of and the changes in most of these ingredients are also monitored and/or analyzed at most Internet investment sites by professional analysts/economists for all nonprofessionals to view.

Federal Reserve Policy

I recently heard a rather biting remark from a nationally prominent economist about Federal Reserve Chairman Alan Greenspan: "Every time
Chairman Greenspan walks into a room and smells flowers, he looks for
a coffin." The impression many have is that the Federal Reserve always
views the glass as half-empty. The Fed is always looking for ways to spoil
the fun, to remove the punch bowl from the party. The reality, however, is
far from this perception. The Federal Reserve plays an important role in
protecting the value of our investments.

Granted, when the economy and the financial markets are involved,
the Federal Reserve's influence is everywhere. Most of the time, the Fed
has to play the role of good cop/bad cop. When the economy is in the doldrums—when it's experiencing sluggishness and workers are losing jobs
and investors are losing money in the stock market—the Fed is there to
bail us out by lowering interest rates and reducing borrowing costs in an effort to stimulate economic activity. For example, toward the end of 1998,
the Fed lowered the federal funds rate three times (for a total of ¾ of a percentage point) to keep the U.S. economy from falling prey to the world
economic slowdown. In bad times, the Fed is like a friend—or better yet,
like a protective family member. In good times, the Fed is no longer seen
as a big brother to lean on. It is viewed as a parent or a teacher, telling its
charges that they are too loud and should stop having fun and get down to
business. For example, the Fed may view the economy as growing too rap-
idly, so that rising inflation may result. In an attempt to slow a runaway
economy, the Fed may raise interest rates, causing chagrin among many
(especially bond) investors.

The Federal Reserve is an extremely important player in the economy
and in the financial markets, and its actions from time to time are bound
to upset the investment community. The Fed's greatest power is in its
control over the direction of interest rates (i.e., the Federal funds rate) via
open market operations [the purchase (or sale) of government securities
by the Federal Reserve on the open market]. The Fed increases and decreases the money supply by buying and selling U.S. government securities on the open market, thereby influencing the direction of interest
rates. It's easy to see why professional investors keep a very careful eye on
the Federal Reserve and monitor its behavior on a daily basis.

At the Federal Reserve, who actually makes the decisions to remove
the punch bowls and spoil the economic party? Primarily, a group of

underpaid (compared to their Wall Street counterparts) economists who form the Federal Open Market Committee (FOMC). The FOMC is comprised of the seven governors of the Federal Reserve Board, appointed by the President of the United States, plus five of the twelve Presidents of the regional Federal Reserve Banks across the country. Eleven of them rotate to serve on the FOMC for a given year; the President of the New York Federal Reserve Bank is a permanent member of the FOMC. As of this writing, the committee is chaired by Chairman Alan Greenspan. The FOMC meets about every six weeks and is considered by investors to be the most powerful committee in the world.

In summary, the Fed is the 800-pound gorilla all investors have to tolerate and deal with in the financial markets every day. Most professional investors see the Fed Chairman (Alan Greenspan, until his term expires) as the second most powerful person in the world, just behind the President of the United States. The more one participates in investments in the financial markets, the more one realizes how much truth there is in that statement. In fact, every time I look at a one-dollar bill, George Washington looks more and more like Chairman Greenspan . . . no kidding.

Federal Funds Rate

Source: Federal Reserve Board.

Timing: Daily quotes of federal funds are market-determined but are highly influenced by the actions of the Federal Reserve.

The federal funds rate is the interest rate at which commercial banks borrow from each other on a daily basis. The Federal Reserve controls this interest rate to implement monetary policy by attempting to influence the direction of other interest rates. Usually, the Federal Reserve will make a public announcement, via the FOMC, when it decides to change this rate, and it is critical for investors to know that this is happening. The financial markets, including both the bond and equity markets, have experienced wide swings in value, in anticipation of a Fed rate hike or drop. Financial assets that are highly influenced by Fed rate changes include fixed-income securities, the S&P 500, and financial services companies, such as BankAmerica, Bankers Trust, Chase Manhattan, Citicorp, First Chicago, Norwest, American Express, Fannie Mae, Dean Witter, and Merrill Lynch. It is not uncommon for the entire bond and equity markets to experience a significant change in values upon an announcement of a change in Federal Reserve policy regarding the federal funds rate.

When planning a strategy, investors need to be able to evaluate the current Fed behavior and anticipate its future behavior. Critical in all of this is the Fed's influence over the direction of interest rates. For example, consider a situation where the Fed has been following a restrictive monetary policy, exerting upward pressure on interest rates. Knowing that the Fed needs to calm inflationary pressures before it can reverse policy, investors will favor bonds over stocks, reasoning that higher interest rates will slow economic activity and, in turn, corporate earnings and stock prices. What should investors be monitoring in a situation like this? They should be focused on the inflation indicators—Consumer Price Index (CPI), Producer Price Index (PPI), and hourly earnings, from the Employment Report—and on evaluating and anticipating Federal Reserve behavior. A calming of the inflation indicators would signal an opportunity for the Fed to become less restrictive (i.e., more accommodative) and to lower interest rates, thereby stimulating economic activity, corporate earnings, and stock prices. In this scenario, investors would be wise to place greater emphasis on equities in their investment portfolio. We need only observe what happened in the latter half of the 1990s to see the wisdom in this approach. The primary inflation indicators—CPI and PPI—trended downward during the 1994–1998 period. And because of a neutral Fed monetary policy, interest rates remained near cyclical lows throughout this period. It was not surprising to see the stock market post solid gains throughout the period as well.

Federal Budget/Tax Policy

Every hour of each day of every year, the U.S. government is spending money or raising money via collecting taxes or issuing bonds. And every month, the U.S. Treasury Department releases a budget report, stating the receipts and outlays incurred by the federal government. Receipts are comprised of all federal taxes. (The individual income tax is the largest source of revenue.) Outlays include total government spending. Investors are not really concerned with the details of the federal budget. They need to know only whether the budget deficit (surplus) has widened or narrowed. During the past several decades (since 1969), the federal budget has been running a deficit, exerting some upward pressure on interest rates. The government has been borrowing (i.e., selling government bonds) more than it takes in, and government borrowings are competing against private corporate borrowings, exerting upward pressure on interest rates. A widening of the budget deficit is a negative for the bond market; bond prices fall when interest rates rise. A widening budget deficit also negatively impacts the stock market. Corporations' borrowing costs rise when interest rates rise, and their profit margins are squeezed. A wider budget deficit that raises U.S. interest rates may be a positive factor for the foreign exchange markets. Higher U.S. interest rates attract more foreign capital into the United States, bidding up the value of the U.S. dollar.

In 1998, the U.S. experienced its first federal budget surplus in almost 30 years. As the budget deficit fell dramatically from the $200 billion area in the early 1990s to the $50 to $100 billion surplus experienced toward the end of the decade, interest rates fell and the stock market rose, providing further evidence of the positive effects of a narrowing budget deficit and/or a widening budget surplus.

For investors, monitoring the federal budget on a monthly basis makes little sense. What does make sense is gaining an appreciation of whether the federal budget is running a large deficit, which would provide a negative environment for interest rates (apply upward pressure), or a slight deficit or even a surplus, which would suggest that the government spending and taxing policies are neutral for the investment marketplace.

Market Psychology

Sometimes, in the heat of competition, a competitor does something outside the realm of his or her normal pattern. In basketball, a seven-foot center may take an unexpected three-point shot from 23 feet out; in baseball, a powerful home run hitter may try to bunt down the first-base line; and in a poker game, a desperate card player (facing huge losses) may go for broke by doubling his bet on a losing hand, in an attempt to bluff his opposition. We have all learned that a human element in competition generates a degree of unpredictability, and the game of investing is no exception.

Investors can learn the rules of investing, understand the investments they have made, read the economy correctly, predict the Federal Reserve's next interest-rate move, and still miss the boat on the future value of a particular investment in the short term because they did not read other investors' psychological behavior correctly. For example, the price of IBM stock may go down in the near term—not for purely economic reasons, but because a rumor that the current Chairman of IBM may resign has spurred a mass selling of IBM stock.

Monitoring and evaluating market psychology are musts for any serious investor. If inflation is running at a relatively tame 3 percent pace, but investors believe that inflation will eventually rear its ugly head at a 5 percent pace, the yield on a 30-year Treasury bond may be at 8 percent rather than at 6 percent. As an investor, you need to understand when market psychology is dominating a particular market. For example, if you're investing in the bond market and you know that the current mood of investors can be characterized by a fear that inflation may flare up in the not-too-distant future, you will be more cautious in your investment approach toward fixed-income securities (e.g., you may require a higher return on your loanable funds).

From time to time, there are glaring examples of how market psychology dominates financial market outcomes. In the greatest stock market collapse in U.S. history—the Crash of 1929—investors and consumers simply went bonkers. The Crash began with investors' bailing out of stocks because of rumors surrounding the Smoot–Hawley Act, which was an attempt by the U.S. Congress to impose tariffs on a host of goods and services imported into this country. All havoc broke loose, and every psychological hang-up known to humans surfaced and stayed. The stock market plunged, bringing the economy to its knees. (GDP dropped by over 33 percent!) In addition, for no economic reason, consumers took their money out of banks. The bank run reduced the money supply by almost 33 percent, and interest rates dropped to almost zero. Thousands of banks failed, and the U.S. economy went into a decade of depression.

More recently, the U.S. stock and bond markets were victims to the psychological whims of investors. During the summer of 1998, the world feared financial and economic collapse in a number of nations, including Russia, the emerging Asian nations, Japan, and Brazil. Russia began the chaos by defaulting on some very large loans. Japan was mired in a deep recession; its banking system was overleveraged and plagued with about $500 billion of problem loans. The trouble in Russia, combined with Japan's economic woes and the distressed economies of the emerging Asian nations, sent shock waves to investors throughout the world. A negative psychology of investing began to dominate the financial markets.

When investors around the world got anxious or nervous about another nation's financial crisis, they sought a safe haven for their funds in the United States. The demand for U.S. Treasury securities soared and U.S. interest rates hit historical lows. With investors around the world panicking, most of the world's capital flowed into the "safe" U.S. Treasury markets, no matter what a particular investment was returning. Money was even withdrawn from the world's stock markets, including the U.S. stock market. At its worst moment, the Dow Jones Industrial Average dropped by almost 20 percent, a large stock market correction. As a result, U.S. investors incurred substantial losses on values in most non-U.S. Treasury financial assets. Ironically, the U.S. economy was in wonderful shape at the time; GDP growth was averaging a robust 3.6 percent for the year. But because of the uncertainty of world events, investors could not overcome their psychological barriers. Safety was a number-one priority, no matter how high the return on other financial assets.

Other examples of psychology moving the markets are plentiful. One of the most obvious continuous examples is an unanticipated Federal Reserve policy announcement. In September 1998, the Fed announced that the central bank was lowering the federal funds rate by ¼ percentage point. Usually, when the Fed lowers interest rates, both bond and equity markets respond in a positive manner, believing that lower rates will improve economic conditions. However, in September 1998, investors expected the Fed to lower rates by at least ½ percentage point—not, as they perceived it, a measly ¼ percentage point. The disappointment was expressed by the stock market's falling by about 100 points (as measured by the Dow Jones Industrial Average).

At other times, key economic releases may report favorable news when investors anticipated even better results. For example, if nonfarm payrolls (from the Employment Report) are strong—say, about 200,000 job gains—but the market is anticipating 300,000 job gains, stock market values may actually go down rather than up, even though the 200,000 job gains are good for the economy.

Market and investor psychology has strange outcomes. Good news for the economy could actually be bad news for the financial markets. And bad news for the economy could be good news for the financial markets. Black is not always black, and white is not always white, in the investment business. Successful investors usually are schooled well in Investment Psychology 101.

Demographics: Riding the Baby Boomer Wave

Imagine taking 9 to 12 million American men, in the prime years of their lives, out of their homes and neighborhoods and sending them overseas to spend four long years with only other men. And then imagine sending these same men back to the United States and into their home neighborhoods, which happen to be inhabited by a large number of very impatient young women. What would you get? How about 76.7 million baby boomers!

Perhaps the most interesting fact about boomers, people born between the years 1946 and 1969, is that they tend to do things together in a big way. When the boomer generation decided that golf was not just for older gentlemen wearing plaid pants and green blazers, golf became big business. Millions of boomers spent gobs of money on titanium golf clubs, hoping to hit the ball farther and, perhaps more importantly, straighter. Everything boomers do as a group has a significant impact on the economy, businesses, and the financial markets. Boomers are a highly influential group in today's economy, and financial markets and investors need to monitor boomers' living and spending habits as they develop investment strategies. Most research and observation has concluded that boomers have a different set of spending and behavior patterns than previous generations. Boomers spend more money today than the World War II generation's households spent twenty years ago. Boomers' households have substantially lower savings rates; they range from as high as 6 percent to as low as 0 percent, compared with a historically high 8 percent gross savings rate.

Although population growth and household formation rates are projected to slow during the first decade of the new millennium, led by aging baby boomers, population growth within the peak earning groups—ages 45–54 and 55–64—is projected to surge. According to the U.S. Census Bureau, the 45–54 and 55–64 age groups are projected to grow by 9.2 percent and 8.2 percent, respectively, during 2000–2010, and the 25–34 and 35–44 age groups are projected to contract by 4.1 percent and 1.1 percent, respectively. The economy, and particularly the housing markets, will be dominated by the boomer generation during the next 10 years.

The aging baby boomers, now in the 35–44 and 45–54 age ranges, are adding 1.5 million people per year to these groups. These two middle-age groups are in the peak home-buying years. The economy and particularly the housing markets (and health services) can expect a rise in trade-up home buying, renovations, jumbo lending, and home equity lending. The 55–64 age group is projected to add 566,000 people per year, spurring demand for second homes as well as renovations, trade ups, and home equity lending. And finally, the 65+ age group is projected to add 235,000 people per year, which portends favorably for retirement housing.

To see how the "boomer effect" can be put to use in developing an investment strategy, consider the following stock market plays. For equity investors, because boomers will be spending a good deal of their money on health care as they age, health care sector stocks would be a relatively safe long-term (10–20-year) investment. Similarly, as the boomers enter their peak earning years, they will require more financial services, bolstering the prospects of the financial services sector as an equity investment play. And there is no question that aging boomers are behind the success of Viagra, the wonder drug. Viagra has been hailed as the cure for impotence, a saving grace for men entering their 50s and 60s (and even 70s). Viagra even improves the sexual drive in women. So how did the financial markets react when Pfizer, Inc. introduced Viagra to the marketplace in March 1998? The stock climbed over 80 percent in the 12 months after the announcement before flattening out in 2000.

Company-Specific Activities

Perhaps the most important factors directly influencing the value of equity investments are the activities of companies themselves. A surprise announcement of layoffs usually results in a drop in a company's stock price. If investors are aware that a company needs to reduce expenses, an announcement of layoffs may result in a rise in the company's stock price because reducing labor costs is seen as a step in the right direction.

Rumors of an acquisition and/or merger almost always seem to boost stock prices. A technological breakthrough, à la Viagra, moves stock prices as well. A management change at a large corporation could also move a company's stock price. In addition, a company's announcement of a large debt offering or an additional equity offering usually influences the direction of its stock price.

Investors need to monitor several pieces of company-specific financial information that highly influence the value of company stock. The release of a company's quarterly (and sometimes monthly) earnings reports affects the direction of its stock price. Monitoring a company's dividend payout policy, and its earnings per share, debt equity, and price–earnings ratios also helps investors better anticipate the direction of its stock price (More on this subject in Chapter 8.)

Noneconomic Factors

If you are a living, breathing, rational human being, you realize that there is more to life than just the U.S. economy. Not everything revolves around the principles of supply and demand. Other events in life exert a great deal of influence over how we think and behave, and they can heavily influence the values of our investments.

The most obvious example is war. Declaring war on another country immediately presents an economic challenge. The demand for munitions, ships, planes, and tanks when the United States entered World War II lifted the U.S. economy (as well as the U.S. stock market) from the depression years of the 1930s. Changes in the weather also create havoc with economic activity and the value of investments. Snow or below-freezing temperatures can destroy Florida's plentiful citrus crop. I knew someone whose investment more than paid for a vacation in Florida. He sold futures contracts on oranges (anticipating a price drop on oranges) after he saw snow while vacationing in Florida during a Christmas holiday break. The unusual weather patterns of El Niño, during 1998, heavily influenced economic activity and investment values. Weather conditions in certain regions of the country provided a more favorable backdrop for construction activity (aiding housing and construction-related investments).

Amazingly, other noneconomic factors may move the markets, even though they appear to have nothing to do with anything. The annual Super Bowl, at the end of the professional football season, is an excellent example. With only one exception, every time a team from the National Football Conference defeats an American Football Conference team in the Super Bowl, the Dow Jones Industrial Average rallies. It has nothing to do with anything, but would you purchase any new stocks the day after an NFC team wins the Super Bowl?

5

INVESTING IN GOOD
TIMES AND BAD TIMES

The goal of investing is to protect your principal and make it grow in both good times and bad times, and some of the times in between. The first step is to identify the current economic environment. Are you investing during a downturn, a recovery, or an expansion? Next, determine whether the investment climate is characterized by high inflation and high interest rates or low inflation and low interest rates. If, for example, the current economic environment is a recession and interest rates are falling, you would be better off choosing bonds rather than stocks. Bond values are likely to rise, but most stocks (particularly industrial and durable goods-related stocks) are likely to fall in value. Conversely, if the economy is expanding and interest rates are rising, you would be better off favoring stocks over bonds.

Think how useful it would be if you could anticipate when you are making a transition from one environment to another. Perfect anticipation of environmental transitions is far-fetched; no one can predict with consistent accuracy the turning points of business cycles. However, if you are currently in an expansion and your investment strategy is to purchase stocks rather than bonds, eventually your strategy will fail because expansions usually give way to recessions. Anticipating, well in advance, a transition from an expansion to a downturn environment may help you avoid getting caught holding too many stocks and too few bonds. For example, if the monthly Housing Starts report begins to show that housing construction activity is falling, it is probably signaling a transition from an expanding economy to a contracting economy. Several months of falling housing starts numbers toward the end of an expansion period is a strong signal to turn bearish on stocks. Economic downturns usually result in disappointing profit performance for most companies.

We will focus our attention on investing in bad times (economic downturn or recession) and in good times (recovery and expansion). From our experiences in these environments, we will identify general investment principles that will be useful when developing investment strategies. To provide a historical perspective on the changes in investment values over a complete business cycle (the 1990s), we offer two tables, 5–1 and 5–2, entitled "The Most Recent U.S. Business Cycle Experience" and "Selected Monthly Indicators/S&P Indexes," respectively. The business cycle represented is the 1990s, including the late stages of the 1980s expansion (1988–1990); the 1990–1991 recession; the 1991–1992 recovery; and the later 1990s expansion.

The Table 5–1 contains information of the levels or rates for GDP, CPI, 30-year Treasury yields and the S&P 500 Index for the pre-recession (1988 to 1990), recession (1990:Q3 to 1991:Q1), recovery (1991:Q2 to 1992:Q1), and expansion (1992:Q2 to 1998:Q4) periods.

Table 5–1	The Most Recent U.S. Business Cycle Experience (1988 to 1999)			
		GDP (%)	CPI (%)	30-Year Treasury	S&P 500
Pre-Recession	1988:Q1	2.44	3.04	8.63	258.12
	1988:Q2	4.12	4.67	9.06	263.14
	1988:Q3	2.40	4.96	9.17	266.92
	1988:Q4	5.14	4.56	8.97	274.98
	1989:Q1	3.97	4.62	9.04	290.50
	1989:Q2	3.00	6.50	8.71	313.41
	1989:Q3	2.16	3.27	8.12	342.01
	1989:Q4	0.36	4.02	7.93	345.55
	1990:Q1	3.94	7.06	8.44	336.41
	1990:Q2	1.24	4.12	8.65	349.59

Table 5–1 (Continued)

		GDP (%)	CPI (%)	30-Year Treasury	S&P 500
Recession Period	1990:Q3	−1.90	7.08	8.80	335.35
	1990:Q4	−4.05	6.96	8.55	317.05
	1991:Q1	−2.06	3.02	8.20	353.57
Recovery	1991:Q2	1.81	2.39	8.32	378.66
	1991:Q3	1.02	3.08	8.18	385.61
	1991:Q4	1.00	3.36	7.85	387.10
	1992:Q1	4.69	2.74	7.80	412.00
Expansion	1992:Q2	2.52	3.11	7.90	410.16
	1992:Q3	3.03	3.09	7.44	417.15
	1992:Q4	4.31	3.55	7.53	423.66
	1993:Q1	0.05	2.84	7.08	442.36
	1993:Q2	2.04	3.01	6.86	445.46
	1993:Q3	2.13	1.86	6.32	453.55
	1993:Q4	5.32	3.26	6.13	464.25
	1994:Q1	2.97	2.12	6.56	469.46
	1994:Q2	4.73	2.29	7.36	450.99
	1994:Q3	1.78	3.75	7.59	460.87
	1994:Q4	3.61	2.35	7.96	460.00
	1995:Q1	1.74	2.97	7.64	480.11
	1995:Q2	0.40	3.22	6.96	523.69
	1995:Q3	3.33	2.12	6.71	565.08
	1995:Q4	2.76	2.37	6.23	597.67
Expansion	1996:Q1	3.33	3.33	6.30	637.01
	1996:Q2	6.06	3.66	6.93	658.61
	1996:Q3	2.08	2.32	6.97	660.54
	1996:Q4	4.23	3.26	6.61	726.79
	1997:Q1	4.22	2.54	6.82	785.59
	1997:Q2	3.95	1.17	6.93	824.44
	1997:Q3	4.19	1.93	6.53	930.02
	1997:Q4	2.95	1.84	6.14	950.82
	1998:Q1	5.55	0.99	5.88	1021.31
	1998:Q2	1.83	1.82	5.85	1109.67
	1998:Q3	3.67	1.65	5.47	1083.95
	1998:Q4	6.01	1.72	5.11	1122.32

Table 5–2 Selected Monthly Indicators/S&P Indexes

	Housing Starts (mil.)	Durable Goods (mo. chg. %)	CPI (mo. chg. %)	30-Year Treasury	S&P 500	S&P Homebuilding	S&P Mfg.	S&P Financials	S&P Industrials	S&P Cons. Cyclicals	S&P Cons. Staples	Fed Funds
8801	1.27	1.7	0.3	8.83	250.48	36.42	210.98	22.47	288.49	N.A.	N.A.	6.83
8802	1.47	1.1	0.1	8.43	258.13	39.44	215.30	23.32	297.61	N.A.	N.A.	6.58
8803	1.53	−0.7	0.3	8.63	265.74	37.80	234.54	23.30	308.04	N.A.	N.A.	6.58
8804	1.57	0.1	0.5	8.95	262.61	37.05	236.52	22.37	305.74	N.A.	N.A.	6.87
8805	1.42	1.4	0.3	9.23	256.12	37.10	232.10	22.28	297.39	N.A.	N.A.	7.09
8806	1.48	2.6	0.4	9.00	270.68	40.69	247.22	24.48	312.82	N.A.	N.A.	7.51
8807	1.47	−0.5	0.4	9.14	269.05	40.17	237.90	24.57	311.02	N.A.	N.A.	7.75
8808	1.49	1.0	0.3	9.32	263.73	38.12	216.40	25.00	303.12	N.A.	N.A.	8.01
8809	1.49	−0.1	0.5	9.06	267.97	38.75	216.69	25.75	307.40	N.A.	N.A.	8.19
8810	1.52	1.1	0.3	8.89	277.40	39.12	217.83	26.05	319.04	N.A.	N.A.	8.30
8811	1.57	−0.9	0.3	9.02	271.02	37.89	206.20	24.85	311.84	N.A.	N.A.	8.35
8812	1.56	9.8	0.3	9.01	276.51	42.18	212.12	24.79	319.07	N.A.	N.A.	8.76
8901	1.62	−2.9	0.4	8.93	285.41	44.30	220.92	25.51	330.17	N.A.	N.A.	9.12
8902	1.43	−3.0	0.3	9.01	293.38	44.93	221.16	26.63	338.95	N.A.	N.A.	9.36
8903	1.42	−0.2	0.5	9.17	292.71	44.55	213.04	26.96	337.74	N.A.	N.A.	9.85
8904	1.34	0.9	0.7	9.03	302.58	48.76	215.41	28.33	348.82	N.A.	N.A.	9.84
8905	1.33	−5.0	0.5	8.83	313.93	55.52	229.18	29.10	360.88	N.A.	N.A.	9.81
8906	1.40	2.6	0.2	8.27	323.73	64.76	231.52	30.85	370.36	N.A.	N.A.	9.53
8907	1.43	−1.8	0.4	8.08	331.92	62.87	232.94	31.70	379.45	N.A.	N.A.	9.24
8908	1.33	−1.1	0.0	8.12	346.61	65.20	251.97	33.16	396.85	N.A.	N.A.	8.99
8909	1.28	2.5	0.2	8.15	347.50	63.41	248.31	33.30	397.22	N.A.	N.A.	9.02
8910	1.41	−3.5	0.5	8.00	347.40	64.07	240.94	33.76	396.34	N.A.	N.A.	8.84

8911	1.35	6.6	0.3	7.90	340.69	54.14	224.34	32.49	388.68	N.A.	N.A.	8.55
8912	1.25	2.2	0.4	7.90	348.57	47.19	231.77	31.14	398.44	N.A.	N.A.	8.45
9001	1.55	−7.7	0.9	8.26	339.97	47.84	234.05	29.68	390.58	N.A.	N.A.	8.23
9002	1.44	2.6	0.4	8.50	330.80	46.63	232.60	28.25	381.45	N.A.	N.A.	8.24
9003	1.29	6.2	0.4	8.56	338.47	48.63	248.89	28.47	391.71	N.A.	N.A.	8.28
9004	1.25	−5.4	0.3	8.76	338.18	51.11	250.83	27.53	393.17	N.A.	N.A.	8.26
9005	1.21	3.3	0.2	8.73	350.25	50.71	264.01	28.73	408.10	N.A.	N.A.	8.18
9006	1.18	−2.0	0.6	8.46	360.35	51.06	272.04	29.80	421.54	N.A.	N.A.	8.29
9007	1.17	2.1	0.5	8.50	360.03	46.48	273.08	28.46	425.76	N.A.	N.A.	8.15
9008	1.12	−2.8	0.8	8.86	330.61	38.24	237.67	24.85	390.61	N.A.	N.A.	8.13
9009	1.11	0.8	0.7	9.03	315.41	32.56	221.39	22.57	372.81	N.A.	N.A.	8.20
9010	1.01	1.8	0.7	8.86	307.12	28.01	205.09	20.05	361.00	N.A.	N.A.	8.11
9011	1.15	−9.3	0.2	8.54	315.29	29.56	207.95	21.52	369.35	N.A.	N.A.	7.81
9012	0.97	4.1	0.4	8.24	328.75	39.01	227.26	23.53	384.75	N.A.	N.A.	7.31
9101	0.80	−2.9	0.4	8.27	325.49	41.11	230.65	23.20	382.78	49.65	47.16	6.91
9102	0.97	0.5	0.1	8.03	362.99	51.16	263.02	27.83	428.91	57.41	53.30	6.25
9103	0.92	−6.0	0.0	8.29	372.23	53.28	270.53	28.66	441.75	59.76	55.86	6.12
9104	1.00	4.3	0.2	8.21	379.71	57.16	269.15	30.27	450.21	62.23	57.18	5.91
9105	1.00	2.6	0.4	8.27	377.99	57.97	269.67	29.81	450.06	62.22	56.10	5.78
9106	1.04	−3.2	0.3	8.47	378.28	54.88	287.40	30.14	450.85	64.44	55.05	5.90
9107	1.06	13.9	0.1	8.45	380.23	50.94	277.19	29.89	453.38	64.94	55.68	5.82
9108	1.05	−5.4	0.3	8.14	389.40	49.19	273.94	31.48	263.26	67.23	58.80	5.66
9109	1.02	−2.6	0.3	7.95	387.20	50.28	273.85	31.43	459.11	65.78	57.80	5.45
9110	1.08	1.1	0.1	7.93	386.88	55.02	270.63	31.27	457.39	64.62	57.68	5.21
9111	1.10	1.8	0.4	7.92	385.92	57.11	259.51	31.22	454.97	63.89	57.97	4.81
9112	1.08	−6.5	0.3	7.70	388.51	62.25	249.71	31.21	458.00	64.41	60.14	4.43

(continued)

Table 5-2 (Continued)

	Housing Starts (mil.)	Durable Goods (mo. chg. %)	CPI (mo. chg. %)	30-Year Treasury	S&P 500	S&P Homebuilding	S&P Mfg.	S&P Financials	S&P Industrials	S&P Cons. Cyclicals	S&P Cons. Staples	Fed Funds
9201	1.18	4.3	0.1	7.58	416.08	77.38	290.04	34.36	493.37	71.76	65.15	4.03
9202	1.25	0.3	0.2	7.85	412.56	88.69	291.18	34.34	490.89	74.35	64.97	4.06
9203	1.30	2.4	0.4	7.97	407.36	85.38	287.82	34.29	484.86	74.14	64.40	3.98
9204	1.10	2.2	0.2	7.96	407.41	72.33	284.94	33.94	484.53	73.68	64.51	3.73
9205	1.21	-1.4	0.2	7.89	414.81	68.45	286.49	35.17	490.72	73.41	65.51	3.82
9206	1.15	2.3	0.3	7.84	408.27	63.50	278.04	34.90	481.96	72.85	63.85	3.76
9207	1.14	-2.4	0.3	7.60	415.05	67.40	271.14	36.18	487.16	73.35	66.07	3.25
9208	1.23	-1.2	0.2	7.39	417.93	69.79	273.47	35.78	490.88	74.26	67.09	3.30
9209	1.19	1.6	0.2	7.34	418.48	66.71	282.70	35.22	493.56	74.86	68.39	3.22
9210	1.24	2.3	0.4	7.53	412.50	73.06	281.63	36.13	483.32	74.87	67.50	3.10
9211	1.21	-1.9	0.3	7.61	422.84	82.17	288.38	38.03	496.09	79.11	69.72	3.09
9212	1.23	7.3	0.1	7.44	435.64	87.21	289.89	39.98	509.50	82.00	70.99	2.92
9301	1.21	-3.9	0.3	7.34	435.23	92.09	300.60	41.34	504.96	83.30	69.12	3.02
9302	1.21	3.6	0.3	7.09	441.70	88.91	309.05	42.88	508.91	85.22	69.03	3.03
9303	1.08	-3.1	0.1	6.82	450.16	89.29	308.99	44.51	517.24	87.02	69.62	3.07
9304	1.26	0.8	0.3	6.85	443.08	83.38	308.01	44.55	505.00	83.26	63.35	2.96
9305	1.26	-2.3	0.3	6.92	445.25	88.54	308.35	42.82	513.68	84.45	64.67	3.00
9306	1.28	3.2	0.1	6.81	448.06	94.23	315.16	43.22	515.73	83.14	63.90	3.04
9307	1.25	-2.2	0.1	6.63	447.29	92.46	310.66	45.50	508.10	82.70	63.22	3.06
9308	1.30	0.9	0.2	6.32	454.13	106.96	323.51	46.64	514.17	85.17	63.38	3.03
9309	1.34	1.0	0.1	6.00	459.24	109.15	334.82	47.55	517.37	84.66	64.64	3.09
9310	1.39	2.1	0.4	5.94	463.90	112.80	334.07	46.88	527.13	88.28	66.44	2.99

9311	1.38	2.7	0.2	6.21	462.89	106.91	342.52	43.54	534.92	93.71	67.63	3.02
9312	1.53	0.7	0.3	6.25	465.95	111.79	344.22	44.37	538.37	93.20	69.24	2.96
9401	1.27	4.2	0.0	6.29	472.99	113.93	358.16	44.84	550.53	93.37	69.40	3.05
9402	1.34	-1.8	0.3	6.49	471.58	115.52	370.87	44.57	551.04	95.40	69.45	3.25
9403	1.56	2.1	0.3	6.91	463.81	99.77	370.79	43.28	543.71	94.77	67.73	3.34
9404	1.47	-0.9	0.1	7.27	447.23	84.25	351.01	43.46	520.36	89.54	65.62	3.56
9405	1.53	1.6	0.2	7.41	450.90	78.66	345.25	44.40	526.27	88.38	66.05	4.01
9406	1.41	2.1	0.3	7.40	454.83	73.10	349.17	45.80	528.76	87.88	66.24	4.25
9407	1.44	-2.4	0.3	7.58	451.40	71.03	349.36	44.70	525.88	87.52	65.41	4.26
9408	1.45	3.2	0.4	7.49	464.24	72.22	361.59	45.61	542.48	88.85	68.50	4.47
9409	1.47	0.7	0.2	7.71	466.96	72.01	357.68	44.79	551.48	88.37	69.60	4.73
9410	1.45	-0.6	0.1	7.94	463.81	64.72	357.93	42.89	551.09	86.37	72.30	4.76
9411	1.51	3.9	0.3	8.08	461.01	59.93	351.66	42.06	548.99	84.68	73.11	5.29
9412	1.46	2.3	0.2	7.87	455.19	63.49	350.03	41.43	540.89	81.51	73.33	5.45
9501	1.41	0.8	0.3	7.85	465.25	65.41	363.76	42.77	551.94	82.80	73.74	5.53
9502	1.32	-0.2	0.3	7.61	481.94	68.66	375.58	45.50	569.24	84.24	77.03	5.92
9503	1.25	0.7	0.2	7.45	493.15	68.08	387.28	45.84	586.43	85.07	79.74	5.98
9504	1.27	-4.9	0.3	7.36	507.91	65.32	406.40	47.51	603.65	87.50	80.86	6.05
9505	1.31	3.0	0.3	6.95	523.81	76.70	426.85	49.90	622.95	89.82	83.62	6.01
9506	1.28	-1.6	0.2	6.57	539.35	80.68	431.79	51.81	641.45	93.19	86.01	6.00
9507	1.46	-1.5	0.1	6.72	557.37	80.18	465.41	52.56	665.69	96.75	87.16	5.85
9508	1.42	4.9	0.2	6.86	559.11	77.22	471.45	53.82	664.37	95.88	87.70	5.74
9509	1.37	2.4	0.1	6.55	578.77	78.00	475.53	57.94	682.86	97.79	90.66	5.80
9510	1.37	-1.8	0.3	6.37	582.92	79.54	459.85	59.63	682.81	94.27	93.71	5.76
9511	1.45	0.9	0.1	6.26	595.53	87.11	474.73	59.86	700.14	97.27	97.47	5.80
9512	1.43	3.1	0.2	6.06	614.57	92.15	492.25	61.97	721.39	99.49	100.78	5.60

(continued)

Table 5-2 (Continued)

	Housing Starts (mil.)	Durable Goods (mo. chg. %)	CPI (mo. chg. %)	30-Year Treasury	S&P 500	S&P Homebuilding	S&P Mfg.	S&P Financials	S&P Industrials	S&P Cons. Cyclicals	S&P Cons. Staples	Fed Funds
9601	1.47	−0.6	0.4	6.05	614.42	88.81	497.13	61.42	720.07	98.56	101.34	5.56
9602	1.49	−2.5	0.3	6.24	649.54	85.29	546.87	66.24	763.18	103.16	105.82	5.22
9603	1.42	2.0	0.3	6.60	647.07	82.21	556.87	66.23	764.51	108.45	105.45	5.31
9604	1.52	−2.6	0.4	6.79	646.09	77.16	560.78	65.58	767.08	109.03	101.74	5.22
9605	1.50	4.7	0.3	6.93	661.23	80.05	576.34	65.85	786.77	115.03	105.14	5.24
9606	1.47	−1.0	0.1	7.06	668.50	83.15	563.54	66.99	797.05	116.93	108.77	5.27
9607	1.47	0.8	0.3	7.03	644.07	77.13	550.98	65.24	763.59	108.76	106.16	5.40
9608	1.56	−2.5	0.1	6.84	662.68	79.12	579.95	69.17	783.07	112.61	107.78	5.22
9609	1.48	3.8	0.3	7.03	674.88	77.54	587.65	70.50	798.57	112.50	108.95	5.30
9610	1.39	0.4	0.3	6.81	701.46	81.69	605.54	74.93	827.47	115.19	111.23	5.24
9611	1.49	−0.1	0.3	6.48	735.67	86.32	661.51	81.11	863.12	116.87	117.45	5.31
9612	1.37	−2.5	0.3	6.55	743.25	82.53	666.23	82.05	872.97	115.56	116.90	5.29
9701	1.37	4.3	0.2	6.83	766.22	84.12	671.58	84.53	900.97	115.97	120.53	5.25
9702	1.53	1.6	0.3	6.69	798.39	87.08	694.91	92.68	932.40	119.48	128.09	5.19
9703	1.47	−2.5	0.1	6.93	792.16	86.70	717.90	92.32	924.49	123.22	128.88	5.39
9704	1.49	1.3	0.1	7.09	763.93	79.75	703.02	85.90	898.02	119.81	126.92	5.51
9705	1.43	−0.8	0.0	6.94	833.09	86.51	754.33	93.54	981.62	126.59	136.19	5.50
9706	1.50	2.8	0.1	6.77	876.29	93.02	801.57	100.32	1030.40	132.08	139.95	5.56
9707	1.44	−0.1	0.2	6.51	925.29	103.53	851.32	105.44	1090.21	139.97	145.32	5.52
9708	1.40	2.9	0.2	6.58	927.74	112.04	830.89	106.58	1091.76	144.66	141.53	5.54
9709	1.53	0.0	0.2	6.50	937.02	112.67	815.33	109.54	1097.81	148.61	138.06	5.54
9710	1.52	−0.1	0.1	6.33	951.16	117.99	821.56	113.75	1109.20	149.56	142.61	5.50

9711	1.50	4.4	0.1	6.11	938.92	120.39	777.74	111.38	1095.70	148.68	144.94	5.52
9712	1.53	-4.6	0.1	5.99	962.37	128.65	778.47	117.92	1113.48	151.99	152.75	5.50
9801	1.53	1.3	0.1	5.81	963.36	132.44	773.13	114.44	1121.68	152.96	154.54	5.56
9802	1.64	-0.5	0.1	5.89	1023.74	144.10	829.57	122.37	1193.25	165.61	159.81	5.51
9803	1.58	0.0	0.0	5.95	1076.83	158.38	885.71	130.79	1251.57	179.85	168.28	5.49
9804	1.54	1.6	0.2	5.92	1112.20	157.10	910.55	136.95	1290.17	182.89	170.66	5.45
9805	1.54	-3.3	0.2	5.93	1108.42	148.49	903.78	133.54	1294.30	185.25	170.92	5.49
9806	1.63	0.1	0.1	5.70	1108.39	150.13	864.43	133.76	1292.63	192.98	174.83	5.56
9807	1.72	2.0	0.2	5.68	1156.58	166.11	874.99	142.23	1346.41	198.83	180.48	5.54
9808	1.62	2.0	0.1	5.54	1074.62	159.82	789.10	124.17	1266.95	186.04	168.91	5.55
9809	1.58	1.3	0.1	5.20	1020.64	N.A.	N.A.	N.A.	N.A.	N.A.	N.A.	5.51
9810	1.70	-2.2	0.2	5.01	1032.47	N.A.	N.A.	N.A.	N.A.	N.A.	N.A.	5.07
9811	1.65	0.4	0.2	5.25	1144.43	N.A.	N.A.	N.A.	N.A.	N.A.	N.A.	4.83
9812	1.75	3.4	0.1	5.06	1190.05	N.A.	N.A.	N.A.	N.A.	N.A.	N.A.	4.68

Table 5–2 contains monthly information on the levels and/or changes in housing starts, durable goods orders, the Consumer Price Index, the 30-year Treasury yield, and the federal funds rate. It also provides the monthly values of the S&P 500 Index as well as the values of the S&P indexes for the homebuilding, manufacturing, financial, industrial, consumer cycle, and consumer staples sectors.

From this historical information, we can infer a great deal about how investments behave in bad times and in good times. The environment scan presented for each investment era is based on the real economic/investment experiences during the 1989–1999 business decade.

Investing in Bad Times—Recession

Environment Scan

Indicator	Likely Direction
GDP	Falling
CPI	Falling
30-year Treasury yield	Falling
S&P 500	Falling
Market psychology	Bearish
Federal funds rate	Falling
Federal Reserve	Accommodative
Federal budget	Neutral

Perhaps the most dangerous time for investment is during an economic downturn. Most indicators of economic activity are usually declining; consequently, most investments begin to lose value. Equity investors who find themselves in a recession need to proceed with caution. Generally, they can expect to observe negative GDP growth, falling interest rates, negative market psychology, and an accommodative Federal Reserve Board. In this environment, most companies and industry sectors are struggling to survive, and profits are falling. Some sectors, such as financial services and homebuilding, may fare better than others during a recession. Further, there are strategies that favor some company types over others. Investors in a bearish stock market seem to favor blue-chip companies over small-cap companies.

Real GDP fell in the third and fourth quarters of 1990 and in the first quarter of 1991. Consumer prices (measured by the CPI) rose throughout the recession, a hangover from the upward price pressures of the previous expansion. Following the inflationary pressures, interest rates, as measured by the 30-year Treasury bond yield, also began rising. Leading up to the recession, the market's psychology could be characterized as bearish for stocks. Prior to the beginning of the recession (i.e., in the third quarter of 1990), the S&P 500 Index fell dramatically from a second-quarter high of 349.59 to 335.35 in the third quarter of 1990, and to a low of 317.05 during the fourth quarter of 1990.

Federal Reserve monetary policy was accommodative in the markets leading up to and through the recession. The federal funds rate peaked at 9.85 percent in March 1989, and fell to an 8.11 percent monthly average in October 1990. Thus, the Federal Reserve was investor-friendly in this environment. The federal budget deficit was rising out of control in 1990; it climbed to $236 billion from the $155 billion deficit posted in 1989. A high budget deficit applies upward pressure on interest rates and is not a friend to most investments.

Good Times—Recovery and Expansion

Although both recovery and expansion are characterized as good times, there are important distinctions between them. A recovery begins as the GDP starts growing out of a recession, and it ends when the GDP reaches the level it had attained before the recession began. The economy is officially in the expansion phase when the GDP grows above prerecession levels, and that phase ends when a recession begins. The investment environment during the early stages of recovery is somewhat different from the environment during robust expansions. Some sectors of the economy are sluggish during the early stages of recovery, while most sectors of the economy are running on all cylinders throughout the expansion period. Furthermore, the direction of interest rates during the early stages of a recovery is usually just the opposite of the direction of interest rates during later stages (when the economy operates close to full capacity). For these reasons, we will evaluate the recovery and expansion environments independently. Our goal is to paint a realistic picture of the "good times" environment so that we can develop successful rules for investing during the good economic times.

Investing in Good Times—Recovery

Environment Scan

Indicator	Likely Direction
GDP	Moderately rising
CPI	Falling or rising
30-year Treasury yield	Falling or rising
S&P 500	Rising
Market psychology	Bullish
Federal funds rate	Falling
Federal Reserve	Accommodative
Federal budget	Neutral

We noted earlier that a recovery begins as the GDP starts growing out of a recession, and it ends when the GDP reaches the level it had attained before the recession began. A cursory scan of the recovery environment would usually reveal that GDP growth is positive and climbing, interest rates and inflation are most probably flat or falling, market psychology is likely to be improving, and the Federal Reserve is expected to continue to be accommodative in the markets.

Generally, when they invest during a recovery, investors are hopeful that momentum will build and they will witness a transition into an expansion. During recovery, many companies and industry sectors shed the weaknesses that were exposed during the recession. They grow profits and earnings per share, creating many interesting and profitable investment opportunities.

Real GDP growth rose throughout the recovery period, but at a less-than-robust pace (i.e., below 2.5 percent). Inflationary pressures, as measured by consumer prices, began to ease somewhat throughout the recovery, giving investors a more favorable environment. Interest rates, as measured by the 30-year Treasury bond yield, fell throughout the period as well. The market's psychology could be characterized as mildly bullish for stocks. Prior to the beginning of the recovery (which began in the second quarter of 1991), the S&P 500 Index rose dramatically (from a low of 317.05 in the fourth quarter of 1990 to 353.57 in the first quarter of 1991). The index continued to rise and reached 378.65 during the second quarter of 1991. Federal Reserve monetary policy remained accommodative throughout the recovery period; the federal funds rate continued to drop almost one full percentage point. However, the federal budget deficit continued to rise. From the $236 billion deficit posted during the recession, it climbed to $267 billion.

In summary, both stocks and bonds were in favor during the recovery period. The broad stock indexes, such as the S&P 500, performed well, rising by almost 17 percent throughout the recovery. However, during the early stages of recovery, some sectors of the economy fared better than others. For example, the homebuilding, manufacturing, industrial, and consumer cyclical sectors did not perform as well as the financial and consumer nondurable sectors, as measured by movements in their respective S&P indexes.

Investing in Good Times—Expansion

Environment Scan

Indicator	Likely Direction
GDP	Rising
CPI	Falling or rising
30-year Treasury yield	Falling or rising
S&P 500	Rising
Market psychology	Bullish
Federal funds rate	Falling or rising
Federal Reserve	Accommodative or restrictive
Federal budget	Neutral

Equity investors during an expansion period are like children in a candy store—everywhere they look, there is something that they like. Just as a rising tide raises all boats, an economic expansion raises earnings growth prospects for companies in virtually every sector of the economy. The key to investing during an expansion is to make the most of your investments. Why earn a 10 percent return on your investments when, by using a little economic savvy, you can earn 20 percent? Another key is to monitor the upward pressures on inflation and interest rates throughout the expansion period. Depending on the stage of the expansion (early, middle, or late), inflation and interest rates could be falling, stable, or rising, resulting in either a favorable or an unfavorable bond market.

Real GDP growth rose at a robust pace (greater than 2.5 percent) throughout most of the expansion period. Inflationary pressures, as measured by the CPI, remained relatively subdued. Interest rates, as measured by the 30-year Treasury bond yield, fell rather substantially throughout most of the expansion. The market's psychology might have been characterized as bullish for both stocks and bonds. All the major stock indexes climbed rather substantially throughout the expansion period. The Federal Reserve had been accommodative during the early stages of expansion but then tightened its policy. Interest rates were raised about 2 full percentage points during 1994, in a successful attempt at orchestrating a soft landing for the economy. The central bank first eased monetary policy (by lowering rates) and then tightened monetary policy (by raising rates) in what can be characterized as a roller-coaster ride leading to the year 2000. The federal budget deficit turned into a surplus during the late 1990s, providing a more favorable backdrop for both stock and bond investments.

Investment Principles in Good Times and Bad Times

Given the above characterizations of the investment environments for good times and bad times, the following list of ten investment principles can be useful for developing successful investment strategies in a recession, a recovery, and an expansion. Attention to these principles will go a long way toward creating savvy investors. Most of the specific investment rules presented in this book are based on the principles identified for the recession, recovery, and expansion environments. Some of these principles are simple and may be obvious to most investors, but they need to be stated nonetheless.

PRINCIPLE 1:

> Recession creates a negative (bearish) investment environment for stocks. Recovery and expansion create a more favorable (bullish) investment environment for stocks.

Sometimes it's necessary to state the obvious. The economy contracts during a recession. Corporate earnings are lower for most companies. Stock prices reflect future corporate earnings, and most stock indexes are down during downturn periods. Economic growth turns positive during recovery, and so do most stock values. It is important for investors to adapt their overall investment strategies, from a negative (bearish) perspective to a positive (bullish) one, when they are operating in a recovery environment. Economic growth, although somewhat erratic, is usually more robust during expansions than during recovery periods, which provides more ammunition and evidence for the stock market bulls.

PRINCIPLE 2:

Expect the broad stock market indexes to fall throughout the early and middle stages of a recession. They will rise throughout the recovery period and during the early and middle stages of the expansion.

Historically, the broad stock indexes lose value during the early and middle stages of economic downturns. For example, the S&P 500 Index fell 9.2 percent, from a high of 349.59 in the second quarter of 1990 to a low of 317.05 in the fourth quarter of 1990. Investors who shy away from these broad stock indexes during the early and middle stages of a recession will eventually reap big dividends. Economic growth improves during recoveries, and so do the broad stock market indexes. For example, the S&P 500 Index climbed almost 17 percent, from a low of 353.7 in the first quarter of 1991 to a high of 412 in the first quarter of 1992. During the early and middle stages of an expansion, most sectors of the economy are building growth momentum, to generate value gains in the broad stock indexes. For example, the S&P 500 Index rose by over 10 percent from the beginning of the expansion to November 1993 (our arbitrary investment date).

PRINCIPLE 3:

Throughout the recession and recovery periods, expect the Federal Reserve to provide accommodation by exerting downward pressure on interest rates.

During recessions and recoveries, the Federal Reserve is usually accommodative. It lowers the federal funds rate, which, in turn, lowers other interest rates. Monitoring the Fed's behavior during recessions and recoveries is critical to developing successful investment strategies. Investors who know the future direction of interest rates have an advantage with both bond investments and certain interest-rate-sensitive stocks.

PRINCIPLE 4:

Expect market psychology to be bearish for most stocks throughout most of a recession, and bullish for most stocks throughout the recovery period and during the early and middle stages of the expansion period.

Investor psychology plays an important role during bad economic times. During recessions, a scare mentality usually sets in, making investors nervous and anxious in the marketplace. Historically, the stock market is bearish during economic downturns. Investors need to be reminded not to bet against the momentum of market psychology. Usually, when the economy reverses direction, investor psychology plays an important role. Recoveries give birth to bull stock markets, and the early stages of expansion are usually associated with favorable growing pains for the economy and for investors. Confidence builds throughout the early stages of expansion. Investors believe that corporate earnings growth will exceed prior expectations (when the economy is thought to still be in the recovery stage). As a consequence, the market's psychology is usually bullish for stocks.

PRINCIPLE 5:

A decline in housing starts is usually the most reliable leading indicator of a recession.

It is important for investors to note that the monthly Housing Starts report signals a transition from good times to bad (i.e., from an expansion to a recession). Housing starts began to fall during the late stage of the expansion, in February 1990, five months before the recession officially started. Investors monitoring these monthly releases knew, well in advance of the GDP reports, that a recession was coming.

PRINCIPLE 6:

A recovery, in general, prolongs the positive investment environment for bonds, which is established during the recession.

Recessions are usually associated with falling interest rates, which create a favorable backdrop for bond investments. Recovery periods are associated with continuation of the Fed's accommodative posture, established during the prior recession. An accommodative Fed creates a positive environment for interest rates. Rates are usually flat or falling during recoveries. Either status is favorable for bond investing.

PRINCIPLE 7:

> Throughout a recession and during the early stages of recovery, most sector stocks drop in value. During the early and middle stages of expansion, most sector stocks rise in value almost coincident with the broad market indexes.

It is important to identify which sectors of the economy—and thus, which sector stocks—will lose the most during recessions and recoveries, and will gain the most during expansions. In advance of and during the early stages of the 1990–1991 recession, the value of the S&P indexes for the homebuilding, manufacturing, financial, and industrial sectors fell at greater rates than for other sectors of the economy. In addition, the S&P indexes for the homebuilding, manufacturing, industrial, and consumer durables sectors all exhibited flat to weak performance during the early and middle stages of recovery, while the S&P indexes for the financial and consumer nondurables sectors exhibited solid performance throughout the recovery period. The S&P indexes for the homebuilding, manufacturing, financial, and industrial sectors all rose at greater rates than for other sectors of the economy during the early stages of the 1990s expansion.

PRINCIPLE 8:

> Expect the broad stock market indexes to exhibit some volatility throughout the late stages of expansion.

During the late stages of an expansion, some sectors of the economy begin to show signs of weakening, and interest rates are usually rising significantly. As a result, the values of the broad stock indexes vary widely, compared with the earlier stages of expansion.

PRINCIPLE 9:

> As the economy approaches capacity during the final stages of expansion, there is likely to be upward pressure on inflation and

interest rates. This pressure creates a negative environment for investing in both stocks and bonds.

As the economy approaches capacity constraints, wages for workers and prices of goods and services usually rise in response to excess demand, which, in turn, puts upward pressures on inflation. In this environment, the Federal Reserve is likely to raise interest rates in an effort to slow a runaway economy (which might generate unwanted inflation). The economy is likely to exert its own upward pressure on interest rates. Investors' demands for higher-risk premiums on their loanable funds (in anticipation of higher future inflation) may create a negative investment environment for both stocks and bonds.

PRINCIPLE 10:

An expansion, combined with falling inflation and interest rates, creates an excellent investment environment for both stocks and bonds.

This is perhaps the most compelling principle for investing in the U.S. economy. During the post-WWII period, historically low inflation and interest rates have provided excellent investment opportunities for both stocks and bonds. For example, during the last 50 years of the twentieth century, whenever inflation and interest rates were historically low for at least a three-year period, the S&P 500 Index steadily rose.

Developing Specific Rules

Having gained a better understanding of how to invest in good times, bad times, and in-between times, we are now able to develop specific investment rules for making money and growing rich. In Part Two, we will focus on investing in stocks, bonds, real estate, options and futures, international assets, and retirement assets in good and bad times. Some investment rules work, regardless of whether the environment is a recession, a recovery, or an expansion. All rules for investing, regardless of their environment, will be based on the lessons and investment principles presented in Part One of this book.

PART TWO

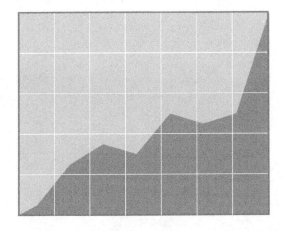

THE TOOLS FOR GROWING RICH

6

INVESTING IN STOCKS

Michael Jordan, formerly of the Chicago Bulls, and probably the greatest basketball player of our time, had a reputation for being the most prepared player on the court. With all his God-given talents (he could jump, shoot, and defend better than any other player, not to mention hit a 20-foot jump shot when the game was on the line), Jordan earned respect around the National Basketball Association for his preparation to be the best he could be. Before the basketball season began, he worked out and stayed in top physical condition. And throughout the season, Jordan was the consummate professional—practicing hard, studying other players, and executing his team's game plans.

Investing in today's equity (stock) markets requires a good deal of preparation. Knowing who the players are, understanding basic concepts about the stock market, monitoring a changing economy, and reviewing some investment rules—these are the preparations I recommend for the game of equity investing. Virtually all of the Internet investment sites offer comprehensive information on equity investing, including specific company information and stock market commentary and coverage. Today's information marketplace offers excellent opportunities for individual investors to participate successfully in the stock market.

The Players

Professional investors come in all ages, genders, shapes, and sizes. Some look to make money today, rather than waiting until tomorrow. Others have longer-term investment horizons. Some are risk-averse; others are risk seekers. It is important to understand that most professionals are investing for reasons quite different from yours. Some financial institutions invest in bonds and equities just as you do, but they are also managing a business for a large clientele. Some investors are speculators; their activities include arbitraging excessive price variations of securities (i.e., assuring that market prices stay competitive). Other investment companies have large portfolios of bonds and equities, many of which are issued by private companies. The government, at the local, state, and federal levels, also issues securities.

There are also professional traders who buy or sell for their own account or purchase equity for their inventory, which eventually gets sold to investors. The common thread among professional investors is that they use economic and market data in a way that helps them formulate effective investment strategies. They are market animals; they may commit millions or even billions of dollars to split-second decisions based on market events. Consequently, professional investors react sensitively and quickly when new economic data are released.

As an individual investor, you have access to an abundant amount of economic and market information via the Internet and other information sources. You can use the same information the pros use to astutely develop successful investment strategies. But compared to the professionals, individual investors are like minnows in the Pacific Ocean; the big fish have them for breakfast, lunch, and dinner. Professional investors are hooked into all sorts of information services: economic databases, news wire services, and sophisticated investment computer programs. They are in this for the long haul; their livelihood depends on it.

Abraham Lincoln once said, "If you have an elephant by his tail and he wants to get to his food, it might be best to let him go." That's good advice for you as an individual investor. Let the big investors go on ahead; let them make the investment decisions. If you follow some key economic indicators (you can access the same information they do) and observe a few general investment rules, you will essentially be following the big players' lead. The hungry elephant will be crushing bushes and trees in its path to carve out a road to financial success, and you will be right on its tail.

A Stock Market Primer

There are two primary methods for evaluating stocks: fundamental analysis and technical analysis. Information and analyses for both methods are available on most Internet investment sites. Fundamental analysis focuses on evaluating the financial performance of a company, as well as the economic/market developments that influence the financial successes and/or failures of that company and of the stock market as a whole. Not surprisingly, this book's primary focus is on fundamental analysis. Technical analysis leans heavily on historical stock price patterns as a way of anticipating future stock prices. Both methods are followed by market participants in today's marketplace and provide meaningful contributions to evaluating equities.

Fundamental Analysis

Investors using fundamental analysis focus their attention on the basic underlying reasons for movements in the value of a particular stock and/or the stock market. For the stock market as a whole, particular attention should be given to identifying the phase of the business cycle, the interest rate direction, and the level of inflation. For a particular company, investors analyze its financial condition, performance statistics, efficiency of operations, and management effectiveness. Described below are some of the financial ratios and performance measures that can help investors evaluate the current and future performance of companies' stock values. Keep in mind that these measures are influenced by and reflect changes in the economy, but they are also affected by performance-related activities, such as a corporate acquisition, a company's strategic business plan, or an announcement of employee layoffs.

1. *Earnings per Share (EPS)*. This figure is the total amount of after-tax profits divided by the number of shares of common stock that have been issued. This measure of the profitability of a company is usually compared with specific EPS goals. Investors look for a consistently increasing EPS. A typical company, posting

an EPS of 95 cents in the current year, may project an EPS of 98 cents for the next year.

Earnings per share ratios vary widely, and investors need to put a company's EPS in the proper context. For example, a growth company with good earnings will usually have a good EPS, but a growth company with poor earnings will usually have a poor EPS. Established companies with strong earnings and dividend payouts will post a respectable EPS. For example, in 1999, Gillette paid a $0.59 dividend, had a strong price/earnings ratio (described later) of 31.85, and posted a respectable $1.15 EPS. Other established companies that are struggling to maintain their earnings performance may have a low or even a negative EPS. For example, in 1998, Motorola had a poor EPS of − $1.64, reflecting its negative earnings. However, its annual dividend remained a healthy $0.48 per share.

2. *Dividends.* Dividends are the returns that shareholders of common stock receive from a company after various expenses have been paid out of after-tax profits. Usually, young companies must cover a host of expenses, including debt and capital investments. Dividends are usually paid by more established companies— those with a steady and stable cash flow built up over the years. Relatively new companies are still trying to break even and are not able to pay dividends. Stockholders in these "young growth" companies are looking for stock price appreciation rather than dividend income from their investments.

Good examples of companies that usually pay dependable dividends are electric utilities, the regional Bell companies ("Baby Bells"), and Real Estate Investment Trusts (REITs): In 1999, Dominion Resources (a utility) paid an annual dividend of $2.58 per share, well above the market. Microsoft, on the other hand, paid no dividend in 1999. Investors who desire dividend income from a stock purchase need to consider both the dividend payout and the price appreciation when they compare the stock investment to other nondividend stock investments. One helpful measure is the dividend yield, the dividends divided by the stock price.

3. *Debt-to-Equity Ratio.* The debt-to-equity ratio expresses a company's long-term debt as a percentage of the total value of its

common stock. This measure gives investors a sense of how leveraged the company is in the marketplace. The higher the ratio (i.e., the greater the debt), the more the company is leveraged. A highly leveraged company is operating on funds other than its own, so it is burdened with high debt obligations. A company's long-term debt usually should be no higher than the total value of its common stock.

Be careful when you evaluate the appropriate amount of leverage for a company. Leverage ratios may differ, depending on the type of company. Companies that use a lot of equipment are generally well leveraged; they are able to borrow against the assets they own. Examples include transportation stocks (e.g., airlines) and utility stocks (including the Baby Bells). Companies that rely on technology generally are not very well leveraged because their existence depends on an intangible idea or a software package. These companies usually have a very large number of outstanding shares that provide equity for growth. The recent merger of At Home and Excite illustrates the fact that billions of shareholders' dollars can be used to fund growth rather than leveraging through bond issuance. At Home, a provider of high-speed Internet services delivered over cable TV, purchased Excite, an Internet search and directory company, by mostly exchanging equity rather than taking on debt.

Some companies that are highly leveraged do not offer great growth potential because they are servicing large amounts of debt. The airline industry is a prime example. It is a mature industry that services a good deal of debt to pay for the heavy cost of equipment. American, United, and Delta are good examples of companies that use their equipment as collateral for their debt issuance. Their performance in terms of price-to-earnings (P/E) ratios (explained below) usually is below that of other industries, because of the airlines' limited growth potential.

Another important leverage ratio is the current ratio: current assets divided by current liabilities. This measure helps investors ascertain a company's ability to pay its current debt obligations.

4. *Price-to-Earnings Ratio (P/E).* This ratio measures a company's current stock price as a percentage of its most recent 12 months

of earnings per share. Historically (i.e., before the 1990s), typical price/earnings ratios were in the 12 to 18 range, but because the dispersion of typical price/earnings ratios has widened substantially, the range is now from about 15 to an unthinkable 400. Comparing today's P/E multiples with those of the past can be misleading, particularly for the major stock indexes. For example, the composition of the S&P 500 Index has changed to include about 70 percent growth-oriented companies today, compared to about 25 percent 20 to 30 years ago. Thus, the index should have higher P/E multiples. Furthermore, today's lower interest rate environment provides a favorable backdrop for higher multiples.

What were some of the significant recent changes to the major indexes? The Dow Jones Industrial Average (DJIA) added several companies in 1997, including Hewlett-Packard, Johnson & Johnson, and Wal-Mart. According to Roxbury Capital Management, LLC, if these stocks had been added in 1980, the DJIA would be around 20,000 today. As evidence of today's high P/E multiples, the S&P 500 Index had a P/E multiple of 32.3 in the fourth quarter of 1999 versus a multiple of 11.7 in the fourth quarter of 1989.

Companies with price-to-earnings ratios well above 32 can be viewed as expensive, but caution should be advised. America Online (AOL) during 1999 had a P/E ratio exceeding 400 and was viewed as a long-term investment play by many astute stock analysts. However, after the Time Warner merger announcement the P/E ratio tumbled to the 130s in early 2000. Companies like AOL are viewed as large speculative plays. Another example is Nokia's P/E hovering around 300 in 1998 and early 1999. Investors impressed by Nokia's aggressive product development and marketing had compared it to Motorola, with a P/E ratio well below 35 at the time. Motorola's stock price has moved modestly during the past six years. It traded at 51⅝ in January 1994 and climbed to only 69½ in January 1999. During the same time period, Nokia's stock price skyrocketed. It traded at 12⅝ in January 1994 and boomed to 142 in January 1994. Today's relatively high P/E ratio of about 90 for Nokia reflects an optimism that is only partly justified by past performance.

Although it is difficult to know whether a company's P/E ratio is high or low, there are some factors to consider. Most importantly, you need to focus on a company's earnings growth (past and future). It is also important to compare a company's P/E ratio to its industry's sector. For example, low growth industries, such as retail are associated with lower P/Es than Internet companies.

5. *Price-to-Book Ratio.* Book value represents a company's assets less its liabilities. The price-to-book ratio is calculated by dividing the company's stock price by its book value—another term for stockholders' equity. This ratio indicates how the market views the current value of the company. A high price-to-book ratio indicates that the market has high hopes for the company. A low price-to-book ratio may indicate that the market is skeptical about its future performance prospects.

6. *Return on Equity (ROE).* The ROE measure is perhaps the most important measure to a company's board of directors. ROE measures how well a company's management is utilizing the retained capital in the company. ROE is usually in the 10 to 20 percent range. An ROE that exceeds 20 percent consistently is viewed favorably by investors. An ROE consistently below 10 percent raises investors' alarm.

7. *Market Value.* A company's market value, or market capitalization, is calculated by multiplying its current share price by the latest available common shares outstanding. When they know a company's market value, investors have a sense of whether the company has a minor or a major role in the stock market. Companies with large market values tend to be more liquid and are usually associated with large trading volume, which gives investors a comfort level. The technology giant, Nokia, has a total market capitalization of $225 billion (as of early 2000) and its 30-day average trading volume is a high 3.8 million shares. Advocat, Inc., a health care company based in Franklin, Tennessee, has a total market value of only $9.4 million, and its 30-day trading volume averages only 50,000 shares (as of early 2000).

8. *Beta.* Beta is a measure of the sensitivity of a stocks' returns to the returns on a market index (e.g., the S&P 500 Index). If a stock's beta is equal to 1 then its returns move in line with the market (as measured by a market index). If a stock's beta is less than 1, then its returns are assumed less volatile (less risky) than the markets'.

If a stock's beta is greater than 1, the company's returns are considered more volatile (risky) than the overall markets'. Investors use a company's overall investment portfolio for diversification purposes.

Technical Analysis

Investors who use technical analysis are usually sold on its merits as a reliable predictor of future stock price movements. The technical approach is based on the high correlation of stock price and volume movements with historical trends. Technical analysts evaluate the historical price and volume series of stocks and use their movements to forecast future price changes. Charting—placing the historical price series on charts—makes it easier to identify points of reference for future stock price movements.

Because stock price movements have daily volatility, technical analysts smooth out the day-to-day variations by calculating moving averages. For example, on nine successive business days, the stock price of Company A is $5, $10, $6, $6, $12, $9, $7, $13, and $10. An investor might conclude that the stock price has a great deal of volatility. However, calculation of a three-day moving average for the stock would result in a $7, $9, and $10 stock price series—a nice upward pattern. A three-day moving average is calculated by totaling the stock prices for the first three days—$5 + $10 + $6 = $21—and dividing by 3 to get the average ($21/3 = $7). The same calculations are then performed for the next two three-day sets of prices.

Identifying patterns in individual stock price series, or even in the broad stock price indexes, helps investors to see formations that may indicate when a particular stock or index is nearing its resistance level or approaching a support level. For example, if we know that over the past 12 months the stock price of Company A has continually approached a $5 stock price low, but has never fallen below this level, the $5 price is said to be a resistance level. An investor actively using technical analysis may conclude that when the stock price of Company A posts a $5 low, it may be an excellent buying opportunity because he or she will expect resistance to any descent below this level. But if the stock price breaks through the $5 resistance level and goes to $4, it may be signaling a sell-off strategy.

Some technical analysts subscribe to what is called stage analysis. It is a theory that stock price movements go through four stages. Stage 1 is a period where a stock price moves in a narrow range across a 200-day moving average. Stage 2 is when a stock price moves above the 200-day moving average. Stage 3 is when the stock definitely crosses the 200-day moving average and is the time to sell and take profits. Stage 4 is when the stock price begins its descent.

Technical analysts utilize a varied menu of identification patterns every day in trading stocks. Technical analysis is complicated, and investors should consult professional technical analysts (e.g., investment brokers) for direction. Investors can also gather technical information from the charting programs offered by personal finance/stock market Internet sites.

Stock Exchanges and Types of Stocks

The United States is home to a number of stock exchanges that permit trading of U.S. equities. Among the many exchanges are the big three: the New York Stock Exchange, the American Stock Exchange, and the National Association of Securities Dealers (NASDAQ). Among the many local exchanges are the Arizona Stock Exchange, the Boston Stock Exchange, the Chicago Stock Exchange, the Cincinnati Stock Exchange, and the Philadelphia Stock Exchange, to name a few. A wide variety of companies offer stock (equity) to the public (investors) via these exchanges. The companies range from well-established, large multinationals traded on the New York Stock Exchange to relatively small start-up companies traded on the NASDAQ and other smaller stock exchanges. The main function of these secondary markets is to provide liquidity to individuals who acquire securities. Once issued, a security may be traded on the floor the New York Stock Exchange or any other organized security exchange. The New York Stock Exchange is the largest and most important organized exchange in the United States. NASDAQ trades securities not listed on the organized exchanges. In contrast to the organized exchanges, dealers and brokers do some trading directly with one another in the over-the-counter markets, which do not have a central location but are connected via an elaborate communications network throughout the United States and the world.

What types of stocks are available? The most popular categories are: income stocks, growth stocks, large-cap stocks, blue-chip stocks, small-cap stocks, and penny stocks.

Income stocks are shares in companies that maintain a relatively stable stock price over the years, and follow a consistent dividend payout policy, year in and year out. Public utilities and Real Estate Investment Trusts (REITs) are the most popular types of income stocks. Dominion Resources and Carolina Power & Light are good examples of electrical utilities; Indy Mac is a good example of a mortgage REIT. Investors usually treat income stocks as a close substitute for bond investments because they have a consistent annual return.

Growth stocks are issued by relatively young, start-up companies that do not yet have dividend payout policies. Investors usually hope that these young growth stocks will eventually experience significant price appreciation. As they mature, growth stocks can become more mature companies but still retain their favorable growth prospects. Today, growth stocks are best associated with the high-technology industry and with biochemical companies. Examples of growth stocks that became successful are plentiful; they include Disney, Gillette, Procter & Gamble, Merck, and Schering Plough. These companies usually pay low dividends, but their earnings growth is reflected in their solid price appreciation.

Large-cap stocks are the large (in terms of market capitalization) and financially strong companies in the United States. They are considered relatively safe investments compared to other equities. Because of their size and capitalization, large caps have a built-in advantage over other equity investments. Many of them are multinational companies that enjoy the diversification benefits of a global scope of operations. They also benefit from disinflation; they can take advantage of low inflation by controlling their costs more effectively than smaller domestic companies can. Large-cap companies can force some of their suppliers to lower their prices; smaller companies usually have little clout with their suppliers. Large-cap companies usually benefit from economies of scale—bigger is better or is at least less costly to operate. Finally, large-cap stocks are usually relatively safer when the economy is expected to slow appreciably or to go into recession. Examples of large-cap companies today are Intel, Pfizer, and Microsoft. The S&P 500 is probably the most popular large-cap index among investors today.

Blue-chip stocks, a subset of large-cap stocks, are the largest and financially strongest companies in the United States. Blue chips are considered relatively safe investments, in contrast to other equities. Blue-chip companies are well-established financial giants such as IBM,

Microsoft, General Motors, Philip Morris, General Electric, AT&T, and Coca-Cola. Investors know that blue-chip stocks will almost always pay dividends (Microsoft does not pay dividends), even in bad times, and that their stock prices usually appreciate in good times and fall in bad times. These stocks are the most highly capitalized companies, and investors have the comfort of trusting that the stocks will probably outlive their owners. The Dow Jones Industrial Average is the most followed blue-chip index offered in today's marketplace.

Small-cap stocks are small (in terms of market capitalization) companies that are either growth-oriented or are not fully established but show signs of promise. The Russell 2000 Index is the most popular index that tracks small-cap companies. Compared to the large-cap companies, these companies have greater growth potential over the longer term. For example, the return on investment during the 1920–1999 period (according to Ibbotson Associates) was 12.6 percent, compared to 11.3 percent return for large-cap companies. Historically, small-cap companies are better investments relative to large-cap companies when an economy comes out of a recession. For example, according to Ibbotson Associates, the Russell 2000 Index surged to 46 percent in 1991 (when the 1990–1991 recession transitioned into a recovery), compared to only a 30.5 percent return for the S&P 500 companies.

Penny stocks are a risky subset of small cap stocks and are considered growth companies that are essentially long shots. They are typically very small companies that are high-risk investments, but there is a likelihood that if the company succeeds, the stock price will experience a substantial price appreciation. Most "pennies" are undercapitalized and rely on "fad" growth (i.e., favorable market psychology). Most penny stocks stay penny stocks or go bust, but a few do pay off in big ways.

To illustrate a pennies-to-riches-to-pennies story, consider the favorable timing for the American Sensors Company. It was the first company to market carbon monoxide detectors, and it was considered a penny stock that hovered at $5 per share for some time. The stock then soared from under $5 per share to $40 per share when Vitas Gerulaitis (the late tennis star) died in his home from carbon monoxide poisoning and the public realized the need for American Sensors equipment. The company then underwrote a secondary offering to fund future growth, but First Alert, Inc. entered the market with a decided competitive advantage over American Sensors and crushed it into oblivion. Another example is

Gandalf, Inc. The company was at the forefront of ISDN (integrated services digital network) technology and was well on its way. Then the Baby Bells (the original AT&T breakup companies) decided that they could develop the technology without outside help. The stock rose from $4 to $18 per share before disappearing.

To be fair, there are some pennies-to-riches stories. Amgen Company was the first to develop a marketable biotech drug (e.g., human growth hormone). Food and Drug Administration (FDA) test results were positive and fueled the growth of a very successful company. The stock price hovers at well over $100 per share.

Selling Short

Investors who desire an opportunity to earn money when stock prices go down rather than up can take the more nontraditional and risky road of selling short: temporarily borrowing a stock that is owned by someone else, and selling it to a buyer at the market price. The seller is obligated to buy it back sometime in the future (this is called *covering a short position*), so that it can be returned to the original owner. To sell short, an investor need only call a broker and indicate which stock is to be sold short. The broker does all the rest and the investor never meets the original owner of the stock.

Why do some investors "short" stocks? It's a way of taking advantage of a bear market or some negative news about a specific company. Basically, they are betting on the downside. For example, suppose the pilots for US Air go on strike and the short-term prospects for a labor settlement are dim. Your gut tells you that a prolonged labor dispute could hurt the company's next quarterly earnings report, which would result in a drop in stock price. To take advantage of the expected drop in stock price, you call your broker and tell him or her to sell short 100 shares of US Air stock at the market price. The broker borrows the stock from someone who owns it, and then sells it, on your behalf, to a buyer, at the market price of $20 per share. On the first Monday of the next month, the company announces a large earnings loss for the fourth quarter. The stock price drops to $15 per share by the end of the week. You then call your broker and tell him or her to close your short position. He or she buys the stock at $15 per share and returns the stock to the original owner. You sold the stock for $20 per share and you bought it back at $15 per share, so you earned $5 per share in just a week's time. If you sold short 100 shares, you earned $500 in a week.

Selling short does have a downside. Unlike a buy-and-sell strategy, in which an investor's losses are limited by the purchase amount (i.e., number of shares × the stock price), potential losses on selling short are virtually unlimited. If the company's stock price rises considerably instead of falling, you lose. To the extent that the company's stock price continues to climb upward, your losses continue to mount. Fortunately, for investors who do not wish to risk the potential downside of short selling, there are other investment vehicles that can accomplish similar financial objectives while limiting downside risk. Among these vehicles are options and futures contracts, which will be presented in a later chapter.

Initial Public Offerings

Perhaps the hottest investment opportunity of the new information age economy has been the initial public offerings, IPOs, of new, hot Internet companies. It was not uncommon during the late 1990s to observe an Internet-based company IPO priced at $15 per share, only to soar to $60 to $70 per share one week later. There have been some significant profits earned by the fortunate investors able to get their hands on an IPO. Unfortunately, IPOs are not made available on a regular basis to ordinary investors. Usually, institutions and large professional investors have direct and first access to IPOs, leaving only a small number of IPO shares for everyone else. Typically, an investor who has a good account and relationship with a major investment bank (stockbroker) would be handed 100 or 200 shares of an IPO. Online brokers are beginning to offer IPO shares but they are yet to bring a significant amount of IPO shares to the table compared to their direct broker counterparts.

When a company that is not publicly traded wants to offer stock to the general public with the help of an underwriter (usually an investment banking company), an IPO is offered. The underwriter may, in turn, put together a syndicate of other investment banking companies. The underwriting syndicate agrees to pay the issuer a certain price for a minimum number of shares and then, resells these shares to the public (often their best clients).

For investment purposes, it is important to distinguish between a good IPO and a poor one. This is not an easy task. There is some research that suggests that the return on IPO's issued during the 1970 to 1990 period generated only a five percent annual return. Remember, for every Qualcom, there is a company that fails to get off the ground. Investors need to be wary and either place a good deal of trust in their stock brokers or online offerings, or they must utilize the fundamental analysis that has been presented throughout this book. Investors need to understand the company's market presence, its future earnings stream and ability to compete in the marketplace.

Why History Makes a Case for Equities

Return Performance

The historical investment performance of the major equity and bond investment vehicles shows that, in the long run, common stocks are the

Table 6–1 Compound Annual Rates of Return, by Decade									
	1920s[1]	1930s	1940s	1950s	1960s	1970s	1980s	1990s	1926–99[2]
Large Companies	19.2	−0.1	9.2	19.4	7.8	5.9	17.5	18.2	11.3
Small Companies	−4.5	1.4	20.7	16.9	15.5	11.5	15.8	15.1	12.6
Long-Term Corp. Bonds	5.2	6.9	2.7	1.0	1.7	6.2	13.0	8.4	5.6
Long-Term Govt. Bonds	5.0	4.9	3.2	−0.1	1.4	5.5	12.6	8.8	5.1
Intermed. Govt. Bonds	4.2	4.6	1.8	1.3	3.5	7.0	11.9	7.2	5.2
Treasury Bills	3.7	0.6	0.4	1.9	3.9	6.3	8.9	4.9	3.8
Inflation	−1.1	−2.0	5.4	2.2	2.5	7.4	5.1	2.9	3.1

[1] Based on the period 1926–1929.
[2] Based on the average rates of return by decade.
Source: Ibbotson Associates

Definitions:

Large Companies are represented by the S&P 500 Index.

Small Companies are represented by the fifth capitalization quintile of stocks on the New York Stock Exchange, 1926–1981, and the performance of the Dimensional Fund Advisors Small Company Fund thereafter.

Long-Term Corporate Bonds are represented by the Salomon Smith Barney Brothers long-term, high-grade corporate bond total return index.

Long-Term Government Bonds are represented by a one-bond portfolio with a maturity of 20 years.

Intermediate-Term Government Bonds are represented by a one-bond portfolio with a maturity of 5 years.

Treasury Bills are represented by a one-bill portfolio containing, at the beginning of each month, the bill having the shortest maturity (not less than one month).

Inflation is represented by the rate of change in consumer prices, as measured by the Consumer Price Index for all urban consumers.

best performers. It's a no-brainer: If your objective is to earn the greatest return over a long period of time (20 years or more), invest in the stock market. Do not waste time investing in fixed-income securities.

Table 6–1 presents almost 70 years of financial market performance and reveals the stock market's long-term superiority over any fixed-income security investment. The investment performance of stocks (represented by both large and small companies) is compared with the performance of long-term corporate bonds, long-term government bonds, intermediate-term government bonds, Treasury bills, and inflation.

Portfolios of large and small company stocks clearly outperformed all types of fixed-income portfolios during these 70 years. The large and small cap company stock portfolios averaged 11.3 percent and 12.6 percent, respectively, during the 1926–1999 period, while long-term corporates, long-term governments, intermediate governments, and Treasury bills averaged only 5.6 percent, 5.1 percent, 5.2 percent, and 3.8 percent returns, respectively. To put the outcome in perspective, a $1 investment in a Treasury bill portfolio in 1925 was worth only $10 in 1995. The same $1 invested in a stock portfolio was worth $975.

Stocks Are Risky Investments in the Short Term

For short-term investors, investing in stocks rather than bonds can be very risky. The volatility of stock and bond returns is shown in Table 6–2, which presents the standard deviations (i.e., variations) of returns for a

Table 6–2 Volatility of Returns by Decade
(Annualized Monthly Standard Deviations)

	1920s[1]	1930s	1940s	1950s	1960s	1970s	1980s	1990s	1926–99[2]
Large Companies	23.9%	41.6%	17.5%	14.1%	13.1%	17.1%	19.4%	13.4%	20.1%
Small Companies	24.7	78.6	34.5	14.4	21.5	30.8	22.5	19.0	33.6
Long-Term Corp. Bonds	1.8	5.3	1.8	4.4	4.9	8.7	14.1	10.2	8.7
Long-Term Govt. Bonds	4.1	5.3	2.8	4.6	6.0	8.7	16.0	12.2	9.3
Intermed. Govt. Bonds	1.7	3.3	1.2	2.9	3.3	5.2	8.8	6.7	5.8
Treasury Bills	0.3	0.2	0.1	0.2	0.4	0.6	0.9	1.3	3.2
Inflation	2.0	2.5	3.1	1.2	0.7	1.2	1.3	1.2	4.5

[1] Based on the period 1926–1929.
[2] Based on the average standard deviations by decade.
Source: Ibbotson Associates.

group of stock and bond portfolios. An investment's standard deviation of return is a measure of its riskiness. For example, the stock market was extremely volatile during the years surrounding the Great Depression. The standard deviation for large company stock returns was 41.6 percent during the 1930s and was 78.6 percent for small company stocks, compared with only a 5.3 percent standard deviation for long-term corporate and government bond returns. Thus, the return on a $1 investment in a large-company stock portfolio during the 1930s could, on average, drop to $0.58 in value, while the return on a long-term government bond portfolio would drop to only $0.95. Obviously, there is a trade-off between return and risk.

Volatility of returns is important to any investor, but the historical performance of stocks reveals that the volatility inherent in a stock portfolio drops considerably as the investment horizon lengthens. As Table 6–3 illustrates, for a one-year holding period, the return on a large companies stock portfolio exhibited a good deal of volatility during the past 70 years. Although the portfolio generated a dramatic 53.99 percent return in 1933, its value had dropped by an astounding 43.34 percent in 1931. For anyone who held on to a large companies stock portfolio for 10 years, the largest drop in value, from 1929 to 1938, was less than 1 percent. When the investment horizon is at least 20 years in length, stock portfolios are superior to bond portfolios. Stock portfolios generated the highest returns in 55 out of a possible 55 20-year investment holding periods during the 1926–1999 period, while the risks were kept at reasonable levels. Even the minimum return of 3.11 percent during the 1929/48 period exceeded the minimum returns of 1.34 percent for long-term corporate bonds and 0.69 percent for long-term government bonds.

Thus, it is safe to assume that if the investment horizon is 20 years or longer, a portfolio fully invested in equities can be expected to generate returns that are superior to those of bond portfolios. However, it is also clear that as the investment horizon diminishes, a fully invested equity portfolio takes on greater risks.

Equity Investing and the Business Cycle

According to fundamental analysis, equity values are directly correlated with changes in economic activity, interest rates, inflation, and company-specific developments. Based on these dynamic factors, we know that the performance of company stocks differs markedly across economic

**Table 6–3   Maximum/Minimum Returns for Differing Holding Periods
(Compound Annual Rates)**

	Maximum Value		Minimum Value		Times	Times Highest
	Return (%)	Year	Return (%)	Year	Positive	Returning Asset
Annual Returns						
Large Companies	53.99	1933	−43.34	1931	54	16
Small Companies	142.87	1933	−58.01	1937	52	32
Long-Term Corp. Bonds	42.56	1982	−8.09	1969	57	6
Long-Term Govt. Bonds	40.36	1982	−9.18	1967	53	6
Intermed. Govt. Bonds	29.10	1982	−5.14	1994	66	2
U.S. Treasury Bills	14.71	1981	−0.2	1938	73	6
Inflation	18.16	1946	−10.3	1932	64	6
5-Year Rolling Periods						
Large Companies	28.55	1995/99	−12.47	1928/32	63	22
Small Companies	45.90	1941/45	−27.54	1928/32	61	37
Long-Term Corp. Bonds	22.51	1982/86	−2.22	1965/69	67	7
Long-Term Govt. Bonds	21.62	1982/86	−2.14	1965/69	64	1
Intermed. Govt. Bonds	16.98	1982/86	0.96	1955/59	70	2
U.S. Treasury Bills	11.12	1979/83	0.07	1938/42	70	0
Inflation	10.06	1977/81	−5.42	1928/32	63	1
10-Year Rolling Periods						
Large Companies	20.06	1949/58	−0.89	1929/38	63	20
Small Companies	30.38	1975/84	−5.70	1929/38	63	35
Long-Term Corp. Bonds	16.32	1982/91	0.98	1947/56	65	6
Long-Term Govt. Bonds	15.56	1982/91	−.07	1950/59	64	0
Intermed. Govt. Bonds	13.13	1982/91	1.25	1947/56	65	2
U.S. Treasury Bills	9.17	1978/87	0.15	1933/42	65	1
Inflation	8.67	1973/82	−2.57	1926/35	59	1
20-Year Rolling Periods						
Large Companies	17.88	1980/99	3.11	1929/48	55	5
Small Companies	21.13	1942/61	5.74	1929/48	55	50
Long-Term Corp. Bonds	10.86	1979/98	1.34	1950/69	55	0
Long-Term Govt. Bonds	11.14	1979/98	0.69	1950/69	55	0
Intermed. Govt. Bonds	9.85	1979/98	1.58	1940/59	55	0
U.S. Treasury Bills	7.72	1972/91	0.42	1931/50	55	0
Inflation	6.36	1966/85	0.07	1926/45	55	0

Source: Ibbotson Associates.

sectors (industries) and by stock type (e.g., large caps versus small caps). During each phase of the business cycle, some sectors of the economy benefit more than others, which boosts the stock values of the companies operating in those sectors. For example, the housing sector performs relatively well when the economy is in the recovery stage (characterized by falling interest rates), so placing greater emphasis on housing-sector stocks during this period will prove fruitful. Similarly, during each phase of the business cycle, some stock company types perform better than others. For example, historically, large company stocks (large caps) have outperformed small company stocks in bear stock markets and/or economic recessions.

Sector Investing

The economy can be divided into two major sectors, manufacturing and services, and most subsectors of activity can be classified into these sectors. For investment purposes, equity investors should categorize companies according to their relevant sectors. Standard & Poor's (S&P) classifies most companies into the following major sectors:

Banks	Energy	Oil
Capital Goods	Financial	Retail Stores
Chemicals	Health Care	Technology
Communication	Homebuilding	Transportation
Consumer Cyclicals	Industrials	Utilities
Consumer Staples	Insurance	

The stock performances of most companies within each sector are usually consistent and highly correlated throughout the business cycle. However, if an investor's objective is to invest in sectors rather than companies, Standard & Poor's has created indexes for each of these sectors. In addition, most mutual fund families offer investors sector funds that usually cover most, if not all, of these sectors.

The performance of the S&P sectors during the past ten years provides an excellent basis for investment strategies by sector. We lean heavily on the most recent ten years of experience—1989 to 1999—because this time period covers a complete business cycle and comes as close as possible to today's economy. Going back 20 to 30 years may not be appropriate because of apples-versus-oranges comparisons in the context of some economic environments. However, basing future investment strategies on just one sample time period (i.e., 1989–1999) may also be questionable. Investment strategies are dependent not only on the events that took place from 1989 to 1999 but on the economic and investment concepts developed throughout the book. Tables 6–4 through 6–6 present the performance of the S&P sector indexes during the 1990–1991 recession, the 1991–1992 recovery, and the 1993–1999 expansion.

Reviewing the 1990–1991 recession (officially, July 1990 to March 1991), it is useful to know whether sector performance deteriorated before the recession actually began or deteriorated during the recession.

Table 6–4   1990/1991 Recession
(July 1990 to March 1991)

Selected S&P Indexes

S&P Sectors	High Value	Low Value	End of Recession (March 1991)	End of Recovery (March 1992)
Banks	190.78 (Aug. 1989)	93.66 (Oct. 1990)	135.47	187.56
Capital Goods	296.33 (Aug. 1989)	241.7 (Oct. 1990)	308.67	317.67
Chemicals	174.77 (June 1990)	138.5 (Oct. 1990)	174.64	205.77
Energy	382.92 (Aug. 1990)	342.87 (Jan. 1991)	376.16	330.52
Financial	33.76 (Oct. 1989)	20.05 (Oct. 1990)	28.66	34.29
Health Care	173.6 (July 1990)	157.81 (Sept. 1990)	202.34	231.36
Homebuilding	65.20 (Aug. 1989)	28.01 (Oct. 1990)	53.28	85.38
Industrials	425.75 (July 1990)	361.00 (Oct. 1990)	441.75	484.86
Insurance	181.22 (June 1990)	130.97 (Oct. 1990)	186.40	184.93
Oil	724.42 (Aug. 1990)	655.65 (Jan. 1991)	716.89	637.01
Retail Stores	224.87 (July 1990)	165.00 (Oct. 1990)	236.48	294.05
Technology	203.69 (July 1990)	157.12 (Oct. 1990)	205.44	208.24
Transportation	315.37 (Sept. 1989)	216.47 (Oct. 1990)	267.7	346.73
Utilities	152.17 (Dec. 1989)	130.33 (Sept. 1990)	142.87	139.45

Leading Indicators	Lead Time to Recession	Coincident Indicators	Lead Time to Recession
Homebuilding	11 months	Chemicals	1 month
Banks	11 months	Insurance	1 month
Capital Goods	11 months	Energy	−1 month
Transportation	10 months	Oil	−1month
Financial	9 months	Health Care	0
Utilities	7 months	Industrials	0
		Retail Stores	0
		Technology	0

Source: Standard & Poor's, NY.

Table 6–5   Recovery
(April 1991 to March 1992)

Selected S&P Indexes and Growth Rates

Sector	Begin (April 1991)	End (March 1992)	Growth Percentage
Bank	145.44	187.58	28.9%
Capital Goods	306.42	317.07	3.7
Chemicals	175.86	205.77	17
Communication	60.87	58.78	−3.4
Consumer Cyclicals	62.23	74.14	19.1
Consumer Staples	57.18	64.4	12.6
Energy	379.62	330.52	−12.9
Financial	30.27	34.29	13.3
Health Care	210.69	231.36	9.8
Homebuilders	57.16	85.38	49.4
Industrials	450.21	484.86	7.7
Insurance	194.69	184.93	−5
Oil	728.2	637.01	−12.5
Retail Stores	255.31	294.05	15.2
Technology	202.33	208.24	2.9
Transportation	274.28	346.73	26.4
Utilities	143.13	139.45	−2.6

Source: Standard & Poor's, NY.

This is critical information; investors need to know at what point their sector and/or company equity holdings will fall in value when economic expansions turn to recessions. According to Table 6–4, the banks, capital goods, financial, homebuilding, transportation, and utilities sectors all began to deteriorate well before a recession actually began. Banks, capital goods, and homebuilding began to display poor stock performance 11 months in advance of the 1990–1991 recession; the transportation, financial, and utilities sectors led the recession by 10, 9, and 7 months, respectively. Conversely, the chemicals, energy, health care, industrials, insurance, oil, retail stores, and technology sectors all began to deteriorate coincident with (i.e., within one month of) the recession.

Table 6–6   Expansion
(April 1993 to March 1999)

Selected S&P Indexes and Growth Rates

Sector	Begin (April 1993)	End (March 1999)	Growth Percentage
Bank	187.31	679.18	262.6%
Capital Goods	312.79	894.33	185.9
Chemicals	211.97	424.06	100.0
Communication	60.88	208.81	242.9
Consumer Cyclicals	73.68	217.09	194.6
Consumer Staples	64.51	184.53	186.0
Energy	341.65	729.88	113.6
Financial	33.94	140.52	314.0
Health Care	226.83	798.50	252.0
Homebuilders			
Industrials	484.53	1537.88	217.4
Insurance	182.56	631.16	245.7
Oil	660.18	1477.66	123.8
Retail Stores	287.61	898.49	212.4
Technology	201.38	1293.80	542.5
Transportation	344.98	704.59	104.2
Utilities	141.61	241.33	70.4
S&P 500	407.41	1300	219

Source: Standard & Poor's, NY.

Tables 6–5 and 6–6 illustrate how well all of the sectors performed (based on their growth percentages) during the 1991–1992 recovery and 1993–1999 expansion periods. Eight of the 17 sectors fared well (posted double-digit growth) during the recovery period: bank, chemicals, consumer cyclicals, consumer staples, financial, homebuilders, retail stores, and transportation. The remaining nine sectors posted either single-digit or negative growth: capital goods, communication, energy, health care, industrials, insurance, oil, technology, and utilities. Notice that there are predictable reasons for some of the observable sector performances. Of the eight sectors that fared well during the recovery period, four sectors—bank, consumer cyclicals, financial, and homebuilders—perform well in a low-interest-rate environment (rates were beginning to fall during the recovery). The remaining four sectors—chemicals, consumer staples, retail stores, and transportation—are *necessity* sectors (e.g., consumers need transportation and they need to purchase consumer staples, regardless of the economy's prospects). Among the nine sectors that did not fare as well, energy and oil posted relatively high negative returns: −12.9 percent and −12.5 percent, respectively. Their demise is more related to energy problems (a struggling energy industry, particularly in Texas) than to general economic conditions.

All sectors generated strong positive growth throughout the 1993–1999 expansion period, but some sectors significantly outperformed others. The 1990s expansion was marked by a technological revolution, and technology sector stocks took advantage of this development. The S&P technology sector index grew by an astounding 542.5 percent during this period. Other sectors that outperformed the 219 percent growth rate of the S&P 500 Index were: financial, 314 percent; banks, 262.6 percent; health care, 252 percent; insurance, 245.7 percent; and communication, 242.9 percent. The financial, banks, and insurance sectors benefited from the low interest rate/low inflation environment, as well as from a successful consolidation that lowered operating costs in their respective industries. The health care sector benefited from an explosion of new health care products and an aging baby boomer generation, and the communication sector benefited from the technology revolution (e.g., cable TV, wireless communications, and the Internet).

Company-Type Investing

Depending on the phase of the business cycle, some company types perform better than others. Earlier in this chapter, the different types of stocks were listed and defined: income stocks, growth stocks, large-cap stocks, blue-chip stocks, small-cap stocks, and penny stocks. Company-type performance varies greatly as the economy moves from recovery to expansion to recession, and investors need to have a comfort level for when to commit funds to certain types of companies.

By their very nature, penny stocks are the riskiest. Investors should consider them cautiously, and probably only in expansion periods. These companies are small and undercapitalized; they could get drowned in a recession and may struggle during a recovery period. A prudent investment strategy is to avoid them during recessions and recoveries. Similarly, growth stocks are relatively young, start-up companies that usually do not pay dividends; investing in them during recessions and recoveries is risky. Today's most popular growth stocks are in the high-flying technological and biochemical sectors. Both have promising futures. Selective investing in growth stocks during recession and recovery periods could be permissible and quite profitable. Income stocks (e.g., electric utilities) provide a stable income flow (dividends) to investors and are popular during recessions and recovery periods. They represent little risk, even in bad economic times, because their products (usually electricity or telephones) are always in demand.

Perhaps the greatest challenge equity investors face is knowing when to invest in large-cap versus small-cap stocks. As defined earlier, large-cap stocks are the large (in terms of market capitalization) and financially strong U.S. companies, and they are considered relatively safe investments, compared to other equities. Small-cap stocks are small (in terms of market capitalization) companies that are either growth-oriented and/or are less well established companies but show signs of promise.

After dominating the large-cap companies in the early part of the 1990s, small caps have underperformed in recent years, and their returns pale in comparison to large caps. Since 1994, robust economic growth, low inflation, low interest rates, and the globalization of the world's economies have combined to boost corporate profits for the large-cap companies. Being "big" was a bonus in the latter part of the 1990s; large U.S. companies competed effectively in a globalized financial marketplace. Short-term investment strategies need to focus on the ability of large-cap companies to generate profits in today's globalized economy.

Over the longer term, small-cap companies provide returns that are superior to those of large-cap companies. For example, during the past 70 years, small-cap companies earned a 12.6 percent average annual return versus 11.3 percent for large-cap companies. In theory, small caps have greater growth potential than large caps, over the longer term.

But across the phases of the business cycle, there are certain times to commit investment funds to small caps, and certain times to commit funds to large caps. Historically, in bear stock markets and/or recessions, large-cap stocks have outperformed small-cap stocks. Large caps usually represent large, well-established companies that give investors a relatively high comfort level in economic bad times and periods of volatility.

In addition, large-cap companies are more liquid (i.e., a higher volume of shares is being traded) than small-cap companies, which makes them more attractive in fragile markets.

On the other hand, small-cap companies are historically better investments when an economy comes out of a recession. For example, according to Ibbotson, Inc., the Russell 2000 Index surged 46 percent in 1991 (when the 1990–1991 recession transitioned into a recovery), compared to only a 30.5 percent return for the S&P 500 companies.

Whenever the U.S. or the world economy is in crisis, investors look for a safe haven for their funds. They usually turn to the U.S. Treasury markets, but if they need to keep funds in equities, U.S. blue-chip stocks represent their safe haven. (Blue-chip stocks, a subset of large-cap stocks, are the largest and financially strongest companies in the United States and are considered relatively safe investments in contrast to other equities.) These stocks are the most highly capitalized companies, and investors have the comfort of knowing that these stocks will probably outlive their owners. The Dow Jones Industrial Average (DJIA) is the most followed blue-chip index offered in today's marketplace.

The Powerful Influence of the Internet

The commercialization of the Internet during recent years has changed forever the landscape of America's financial markets and businesses. The Internet has created and will continue to develop a more efficient and open financial system worldwide. Financial markets stemming from virtually every nation in the world have converged on the Internet. Larger and more liquid financial/investment markets have permitted investors to participate in more diversified financial products and services. Indeed, the Internet may be the primer behind the substantial increase in the trading volumes on the U.S. equity exchanges. According to the National Venture Capital Association, average daily trading volume on the New York Stock Exchange soared from about 45 million shares in 1980 to almost 800 million shares in 1999. And according to Forrester Research, at the end of 1999, 3 million U.S. households had online trading accounts totaling about $375 million in assets. The same source estimates that by 2003, 9.7 million households will have online accounts totaling $3 trillion.

On the business side, companies that had the vision to utilize the fledgling Internet as an electronic vehicle for commerce have reaped impressive rewards. Literally millions of users (customers) are on the Internet every day, boosting online revenue to unprecedented levels with each passing year. Established traditional industries, such as books, music, and travel, have been transformed, literally overnight, into electronic industries that attract online customers to their electronic retail centers. New companies entering old industries—for example, Amazon.com in the book and music business—have experienced sensational market capitalization via initial public offerings (IPOs).

The inevitable transformation of a significant part of the physical business world into the electronic business world has enormous implications for industries just now experiencing this transition, and for other industries that have yet to (but will) experience the Internet impact. However, the very existence of other industries may be threatened by the growth of the Internet.

The reach of the Internet plays a crucial role in most investment decisions. Investors today simply cannot ignore the impact of the Internet on future company profits or even on the future viability of the industries themselves. Industries that depend on Internet commerce to a significant degree are many and varied: the book, music, travel, insurance, and newspaper industries, and, to a lesser extent, the automobile and real estate industries. The main thrust of competition for these industries is between the physical and electronic worlds. For example, Amazon.com created an electronic bookstore and dislodged a significant market share from more traditional booksellers such as Barnes & Noble. Eventually, Barnes & Noble went electronic; barnes&noble.com now competes in the Internet world of commerce. Examples of Internet start-up companies that won market share from the traditional players are numerous. Expedia (owned by Microsoft) took the airline booking business by storm, and Internet insurance companies such as InsWeb have attempted to eliminate the insurance agent business by bringing insurance customers and sellers of property and casualty insurance together on the World Wide Web.

Future investment strategies should include an assessment of whether targeted industries are currently influenced or will become influenced by the long and powerful reach of Internet commerce. Investors need to identify (1) the industries that will prosper via Internet commerce; (2) the start-up Internet-based companies that will eventually gain market share over the traditional companies within these industries; and (3) the traditional companies that are committed to making the transition into the Internet world. Surveys and research conducted by Forrester Research Reports and presented in "Are You Next?" an article edited by Jeffrey Davis in *Business 2.0* magazine (March 1999), made these predictions for 15 industry segments that are expected to be impacted in a meaningful manner by Internet commerce by 2003:

	E-commerce Projection by 2003	
	$ Billions	Percent of Market
Businesses selling to consumers:		
Home electronics	$21 billion	12%
Apparel	13.5	4
Food and beverages	10.8	2
Health and beauty	6.3	5
Housewares	5.7	7
Event tickets	2.6	19
Toys	1.5	5
Businesses selling to businesses:		
Computing and electronics	$395 billion	39%
Auto	213	15
Chemicals	178	14
Utilities	169.5	26
Paper and office	65.2	6
Food and agriculture	53.6	3
Pharmaceutical and medical	44.1	8
Construction	28.6	1

Investment Rules for Equities

Investing in the stock market is a big plunge for most individual investors. The values of equity investments are subject to wider swings than bond investments. Simply stated, stock prices can be volatile over the short term. Investors' objectives should be to avoid, as much as possible, the downswings in stock prices, and to take advantage of the upswings. With these objectives, an investment portfolio grows at a healthy pace—a pace that far exceeds that of inflation.

There are two basic stock investment strategies: (1) buy-and-hold investing and (2) market-timing investing. Buy-and-hold investing is simply purchasing a particular mutual fund, company stock, or stock index, and keeping it in a portfolio. Market-timing investments are attempts to purchase timely investments (e.g., buying low and selling high). Buy-and-hold strategies are generally employed for retirement investing (outlined in Chapter 11). But even for an investment portfolio, investors should take advantage of the superior long-term returns of stocks and utilize buy-and-hold strategies. However, there are times when investors can take advantage of movements in the economy by employing market-timing investment strategies for stocks. The investment rules given later in this chapter reflect both types of strategies.

Most investors panic when the markets go into a tailspin and dump some of their investments, particularly stocks. Panic may possibly be the worst strategy to employ, for two reasons:

1. Stockholders are usually the last to know about (and thus to react to) a large drop in the stock market or bond market.

2. According to historical trends, stock and bond investments usually make their sharpest gains after lengthy slumps.

A buy-and-hold strategy eliminates the problems of market timing. And, as demonstrated elsewhere, if a well-diversified stock portfolio is held long enough, it will return gains that are superior to those of other comparable investments.

The typical investment portfolio is comprised of stocks, bonds, and cash (which includes CDs and money market funds). A real portfolio may also contain real estate, futures/options, metals, and so on, but, for now, we will keep the investment process simple. Stocks and/or mutual funds/stock indexes can be purchased by using a stockbroker, a discount broker, or an online Internet service. Prospects for equity stocks are dependent on the phase of the business cycle and the relative levels of inflation and interest rates. Downturns portend unfavorable stock price performance, and recoveries lift stock price performance. Expansions that have a backdrop of relatively low inflation and interest rates sustain performance.

All the investment rules are meant to be general; that is, there are no specific recommendations for investing in individual stocks. No attempt to recommend individual company purchases is made in this book because up-to-the-minute market and company information is required for informed investment decisions. The investment rules given here are not dependent on current market information. They lean heavily on historical performance, particularly the most recent decade of experience: 1989 to 1999. This time period covers a complete business cycle as well as providing the closest status of today's economy. If an investment rule recommends investing in a particular industry sector, the investor can choose to invest in any of the individual companies that comprise that particular sector. Buying individual stocks entails greater risk, but the rewards could exceed those of sector index buying.

By putting everything we've learned about stocks alongside the basic principles for investing in both bad and good times (Chapter 5), we create an excellent backdrop for developing investment rules for the equities market. The top ten list of "grow-rich" rules that follows is highly recommended. These rules are general in nature, and easy for investors to digest and follow. Hungry investors who wish to expand beyond these ten rules and spend more time and energy with investment strategies are offered "More Grow-Rich Rules for Stocks." These rules tend to be more specific and require more monitoring by investors.

The Top Ten Grow-Rich Rules for Stocks

INVESTMENT RULE 1

An expanding economy that is experiencing prolonged periods of low inflation and low interest rates is the ideal environment for investing in the stock market.

Rationale. Expansions that have a favorable backdrop of relatively low inflation and interest rates are a breeding ground for prolonged "bull runs" in the stock market. In an expansion, the economy is running on all cylinders, and most industries are the beneficiaries of solid demand for their products and services. Low interest rates usually are associated with (1) relatively low company-borrowing costs and (2) widening profit margins. In this environment, company profits rise, suggesting that most company stock prices will exhibit a favorable performance. As soon as this type of market environment is identified, bet heavily in stocks—all types and sizes.

INVESTMENT RULE 2

If the economy is experiencing an expansion and there are substantial upward pressures on inflation and interest rates, reduce your investment emphasis on stocks. Favor shorter-term bonds (and other money market instruments) instead.

Rationale. To investors in the stock market, an expanding economy is only as good as the inflation/interest rate conditions. As we learned in the 1970s, the economy could be expanding, but if there is excessive pressure on inflation and interest rates, the growth in stock values will be somewhat constrained.

INVESTMENT RULE 3

During the late stages of expansion, if monthly housing starts have dropped substantially over a two- to three-month span, avoid investing in the broad stock indexes, and particularly the housing-related sector, immediately following the report's release.

Rationale. Housing starts reflect the construction activity of single-family and multi-family residential homes. Historically, starts plunge just before a recession (usually with three to six months' lead time). Avoid the following categories: home builders, mortgage lending companies, and realtors.

INVESTMENT RULE 4

In the late stages of an expansion, if the Federal Reserve raises the federal funds rate by at least $\frac{1}{4}$ of a percentage point, avoid purchasing stocks (particularly interest-sensitive stocks) in anticipation of or immediately after the policy maneuver.

Rationale. A raise in the federal funds rate reflects a less accommodative Federal Reserve (i.e., it is reducing the money supply). The interest rate rise likely indicates that the Federal Reserve is nervous about inflationary pressures. Investors usually view higher interest rates as a negative development in the markets. Higher interest rates raise the cost of corporate borrowings, eventually choking an expanding economy, which does not bode well for stock prices. Avoid the following categories of interest-sensitive stocks: homebuilders, mortgage lending companies, realtor companies, and financial services companies.

INVESTMENT RULE 5

If you are in a recovery period, focus your equity investments on sectors of the economy that perform well relative to other sectors, such as homebuilders, banks, transportation, consumer cyclicals, chemicals, retail, financials, and consumer staples.

Rationale. Recoveries originate from recessions, and some sectors of the economy continue in recession or in a slow growth phase for some time. Investors need to focus attention on sectors that immediately participate in the economy's recovery. The S&P indexes for the following sectors all posted double-digit growth rates from the beginning to the end of the 1991 recovery period: homebuilders, banks, transportation, consumer cyclicals, chemicals, retail, financials, and consumer staples.

INVESTMENT RULE 6

If the economy is in a recovery period, in general, place a greater emphasis on investing in the broad stock indexes rather than in sector stocks.

Rationale. During a recovery period, the GDP is growing from its recession lows, and prudent investors should avoid choosing sectors that have not yet participated in the recovery. Investing in the broad indexes keeps investors in the stock market while avoiding potentially unpleasant sector plays. The S&P 500 Index rose 16.5 percent from the beginning of the last recovery (first quarter 1991) to the end (second quarter 1992).

INVESTMENT RULE 7

If the economy is in a recession and GDP growth is negative, postpone investing in stocks, particularly the broad stock indexes, until the late stages of the downturn.

Rationale. This is a no-brainer investment strategy. An economy in recession and a quarterly GDP report registering negative growth give stock investments two strikes against them. Keep your money on the sidelines until the late stages of the recession. Also, market psychology is usually very bearish, and it is not safe to go against it. During the economy's 1990–1991 recession, the S&P 500 Index dropped 9 percent, reaching 317.05 in the fourth quarter of 1990. (A 349.59 value had been posted in the second quarter of 1990.) However, during the final quarter of the recession (i.e., the late stage), the stock index came back a remarkable 11.5 percent in anticipation of the recovery period.

INVESTMENT RULE 8

If the economy is in a recession and interest rates are flat or falling, in general, favor interest-sensitive stocks (or sectors) over non-interest-sensitive stocks (or sectors).

Rationale. A weakening economy usually exerts downward pressure on interest rates, favoring interest-sensitive stocks. Companies in the financial services sector and public utilities fare comparably better than companies that do not receive direct benefits from falling interest rates. For example, a bank's profit margin widens when interest rates fall because it immediately lowers the interest rate on its borrowings (CDs), but does not respond as quickly to lowering its loan rates to customers (e.g., the prime lending rate comes down slowly). Thus, the bank's profit margin (loan rates minus borrowing rates) widens in falling-rate environments.

> ## INVESTMENT RULE 9
>
> When the economy is firmly in recession but the stock market is beginning to show signs of turning around, invest in stocks, particularly housing-related and manufacturing (durable goods-related) companies.

Rationale. Stock prices reflect the market's expectation of future corporate earnings. If a bear stock market is showing signs of turning around, investors are signaling their belief that the recession is coming to an end. This represents an excellent buying opportunity for investors. Housing-related (identified by the housing starts release) and manufacturing (identified by the durable goods orders release) companies are prime buying candidates in this market environment because both perform well toward the end of a recession and in the early stages of recovery.

> ## INVESTMENT RULE 10
>
> If the economy has been in a recession and quarterly GDP growth turns positive for the first time, invest in high-quality stocks, such as companies included in the S&P 500 Index.

Rationale. When quarterly GDP growth turns positive for the first time, it signals that the economy has transitioned from a downturn to a recovery period, which usually means rising corporate profits and stock prices. However, until you are assured that the recovery is well on its way (wait until GDP growth is positive for a second consecutive quarter), invest only in high-quality companies (i.e., blue chips).

More Grow-Rich Rules for Stocks

Any stockbroker or stock analyst will tell you that there is an endless list of rules for investing in stocks. The additional list of grow-rich rules presented below represents the best of the rest, taking advantage of the ability to monitor the economic and investment environments via sources such as the Internet. To make these rules easier to follow, they are categorized as: Indicators, Market Psychology, Baby Boomers, The Internet, Company/Industry-Specific Rules, and Other Factors. Some of these rules require monitoring the Internet investment sites on a monthly basis; others require only common sense.

Indicators

INVESTMENT RULE 11

If you can identify that the economy is in the early stages of recession, push your stock investments toward consumer-related stocks and away from housing- and manufacturing-related stocks.

Rationale. If the economy is in the early stages of recession or the late stages of expansion, certain sector stocks will begin to deteriorate in value. For example, the homebuilding, banks, and capital goods sectors all began to drop in value in August 1989, 11 months prior to the beginning of the 1990–1991 recession. It is not a coincidence that these sectors are all interest-sensitive.

INVESTMENT RULE 12

If the economy is in recession and the Federal Reserve cuts the federal funds rate by at least ¼ of a percentage point, direct your stock investments toward interest-sensitive stocks.

Rationale. The decision to lower the federal funds rate comes from an accommodative Federal Reserve (i.e., the Fed is increasing the money supply). Lower interest rates are always viewed favorably by investors because the costs of corporate borrowings are reduced, which helps to boost economic activity and exerts upward pressure on corporate earnings and stock prices. For interest-sensitive stocks, target the following categories: homebuilders, mortgage lending companies, realtor companies, and financial services companies.

INVESTMENT RULE 13

If the economy is in the final stages of a downturn or the beginning of a recovery, you have a green light to fully participate in the stock market, but with caution and with a long-term investment perspective.

Rationale. As the economy is lifted out of recession, company profits begin to pick up and stock prices escalate. Take advantage of the final stages of a recession by purchasing high-quality stock companies (e.g., blue chips) that you know will survive the economic downturn. The broad S&P Index, as well as most sector indexes, began to rise during the late stages of the 1990–1991 recession. Basically, if you take a longer-term investment perspective, you will be buying low and selling high.

INVESTMENT RULE 14

In a recession, news (or anticipation) of a relatively small monthly nonfarm payroll gain (less than 50,000 employees) is likely to be bearish for stocks. News (or anticipation) of a relatively large monthly nonfarm payroll gain (greater than 200,000 employees) is likely to be bullish for stocks.

Rationale. The Employment Report is the first major piece of data on economic activity for the month, so stock investors need to pay particular attention to its contents. If the economy is already in a downturn, a weak nonfarm payroll number helps confirm investors' belief that the economy will continue in the doldrums in the near future. This pessimistic news translates into downward pressure on stock prices. If you are market-timing your investments (that is, looking for a short-term gain), sell stocks (preferably a broad stock index) on a weak nonfarm payroll number, and purchase stocks on a strong nonfarm payroll number.

INVESTMENT RULE 15

In a recession, news (or anticipation) of a drop in the Consumer Confidence Index is likely to be bearish for stocks. News (or anticipation) of, at least, a two-month successive rise in the Consumer Confidence Index is likely to be bullish for stocks.

Rationale. The Consumer Confidence Index reflects how consumers feel about the present and future economic situation. If you are already in a recession environment, a drop in the Consumer Confidence Index in the most recent month confirms that consumers are not confident about economic conditions and may continue to postpone some purchases of goods and services, resulting in lower corporate earnings and an underperforming stock market. Conversely, if the Index rises in value for at least two successive months, consumers are gaining confidence. Purchases of goods and services will increase, raising corporate earnings and brightening prospects for company stock prices.

INVESTMENT RULE 16

In a recession, news (or anticipation) of a drop in the monthly retail sales report could be viewed as bearish for stocks. News (or anticipation) of (at least) a three-month consecutive rise in the retail sales report could be viewed as bullish for stocks.

Rationale. As a proxy for consumer spending, strong retail sales indicate strong economic activity, pushing corporate earnings, and stock prices, upward. However, historically, the retail sales release can be choppy from month to month, and it might be prudent to take a longer view (e.g., a three-month trend) of the report to get a sense of consumer spending levels. A solid retail sales performance over several months sends a favorable signal to investors and pumps up stock prices. Categories to target are apparel retailers, nondurable household products, and entertainment and leisure.

> ### INVESTMENT RULE 17
>
> Purchase stocks if you observe that the Consumer Confidence Index is rising substantially toward the end of a recession.

Rationale. The Consumer Confidence Index reflects an appraisal of how consumers feel about the present economic situation. Historically, consumers usually gain confidence toward the end of a recession, providing a valuable signal of when the economy is about to enter a recovery period, and sending stock prices upward.

> ### INVESTMENT RULE 18
>
> Purchase stocks, particularly housing-related companies, if you observe that housing starts are rising substantially toward the end of a recession.

Rationale. Housing starts reflect activity in the construction of single-family and multifamily residences. Historically, housing starts rise toward the end of a recession. Target the following categories: home builders, mortgage lending companies, and realtors.

> ### INVESTMENT RULE 19
>
> If the economy is in recession and you observe a consistent rise in durable goods orders during a two- to three-month period, purchase stocks, particularly manufacturing-related companies, but proceed cautiously.

Rationale. Durable goods orders serve as a proxy for estimating businesses' fixed investments. Businesses in the United States must cover expenditures for office buildings or rental space, factories, plant and equipment, computer and communications systems, and various vehicles. A rise in durable goods orders usually signals economic strength, portending favorably for stock prices. However, historically, durable goods orders are choppy from month to month; you need a three- to six-month trend instead. If the trend is identified and indicates increasing strength, purchase stocks, but cautiously.

INVESTMENT RULE 20

In a recovery period, if the National Association of Purchasing Managers (NAPM) Index rises above 50 percent in at least two successive months, place a greater investment emphasis on manufacturing/industrial sector stocks.

Rationale. The NAPM Index reflects the new orders, production, employment, and supplier deliveries of manufacturers. An index reading of 50 percent or greater indicates that the manufacturing sector is expanding. Historically, the NAPM Index usually hits 50 percent or higher toward the end of a recession. Usually, any reading above 50 percent is received favorably by stock investors. Target the following company categories: heavy machinery, factory equipment, transportation equipment, electrical components, and building materials.

INVESTMENT RULE 21

If the economy is in recovery and the Federal Reserve continues its recession-induced accommodative policies by lowering the federal funds rate by at least ¼ of a percentage point, place a greater buying emphasis on the broad-based stock indexes and on interest-sensitive stocks.

Rationale. During a recovery period, a lowered federal funds rate exerts downward pressure on all interest rates, providing a more favorable environment for businesses. The lowered rate is also a signal that the Federal Reserve will continue to pursue accommodative policies until the economy is well on its way to expansion. This climate portends favorable conditions for corporate earnings growth and stock prices, as well as interest-sensitive stocks.

INVESTMENT RULE 22

If the economy is in recovery and the level of the GDP exceeds its prerecession highs, broaden your scope of stock investments.

Rationale. Once the level of the GDP exceeds its prerecession highs, the economy is officially in the early stages of expansion. At this juncture, most sectors of the economy should be participating, or will participate in the near future, in the expansion, providing favorable investment opportunities.

INVESTMENT RULE 23

Throughout an expansion period, from time to time, there are sectors that earn a "favored son" status among investors.

Rationale. Throughout an expansion, there are sectors of the economy that investors are keen on. These sectors earn a "favorite son" status, and they usually outperform other sectors for a certain period of time. For example, as shown in Table 6–6, presented earlier in this chapter, a number of sectors outperformed the S&P 500 Index. From April 1993 to March 1999, the S&P 500 Index grew by 213 percent, but the technology sector grew by a whopping 542.5 percent. The financial, bank, health care, insurance, communication, and industrial sectors grew by 314 percent, 262.6 percent, 252 percent, 245.7 percent, 242.9 percent, and 217.4 percent, respectively, so the technology sector was certainly a "favorite son" during the 1990s expansion. The financial, bank, and health care sectors could also be considered "favorite sons." These sectors get a lot of media attention, and they house some prominent companies that are experiencing historic growth spurts.

INVESTMENT RULE 24

If the economy is expanding and operating close to full employment, and if the nonfarm payroll gains of the monthly Employment Report are viewed as excessive (e.g., 200,000 or more employees), avoid purchasing stocks.

Rationale. If the economy is close to full employment, invest with caution just before the release of the Employment Report. Investors are overly sensitive to the prospects of strong economic growth because robust growth could exert upward pressure on inflation in a full-employment economy. Payroll gains of 200,000 or more employees are consistent with economic growth that exceeds its noninflationary trend and exerts upward pressure on inflation. Because higher inflation (which brings increasing interest rates) can be damaging to corporate earnings and to bond values, it may be wise to temporarily avoid investing in stocks.

INVESTMENT RULE 25

If the economy is expanding and operating close to full capacity, a higher-than-expected Consumer Price Index (CPI) could send stock prices falling, and a lower-than expected CPI could generate increases in stock prices.

Rationale. Stock prices are particularly volatile and sensitive to the CPI report when the economy is operating dangerously close to full employment. In this situation, investors are overly sensitive to the prospects of higher inflation because strong economic growth could be inflationary, which might damage company earnings prospects.

INVESTMENT RULE 26

If the economy is close to full employment and there is a dramatic increase in inflation, as measured by the monthly CPI, seek out inflation-hedge companies (e.g., oil and gas companies and mining companies) and non-interest-sensitive companies.

Rationale. The stock market usually reacts adversely to dramatic increases in interest rates that are linked to inflation concerns. For example, if the yield on a 30-year Treasury bond increases by ¼ of a percentage point (i.e., 25 basis points) during one day, stocks, as measured by the broad market indexes, will most likely fall in value. High interest rates exert downward pressure on profit margins by raising company borrowing costs. Inflation-hedge companies, such as oil and gas companies and mining companies, perform relatively well in a rising rate environment.

INVESTMENT RULE 27

If the economy is operating close to full employment and the capacity utilization rate rises and is approaching 84 percent, avoid investing in stocks immediately following release of the capacity utilization report.

Rationale. In effect, the capacity utilization rate reflects how much more the economy can grow before inflationary pressures begin to build. In recent years, the utilization rate has climbed well into the 83 percent range without setting off inflationary pressures. However, as the rate approaches 84 percent, the labor markets begin to tighten, which creates some upward pressure on wages and prices. Inflation worries are a negative for both stocks and bonds. Target the following company categories: heavy machinery, factory equipment, transportation equipment, electrical components, and building materials.

INVESTMENT RULE 28

If the retail sales report posts strong growth numbers for several consecutive months, invest in consumer-based stocks. If the retail sales report posts weak numbers for several consecutive months, avoid consumer-based companies.

Rationale. As a proxy for consumer spending, strong retail sales indicate strong economic activity, pushing corporate earnings—and stock prices—upward. The retail sales report can be choppy from month to month, so prudence dictates taking a longer view (e.g., a three-month trend) of the report to get a sense of consumer spending levels. A solid retail sales performance over several months sends a favorable signal to investors and pumps up stock prices. Conversely, a weak retail sales performance sends a danger signal to investors and depresses stock prices. The company categories to target are: apparel retailers, nondurable household products, and entertainment and leisure.

INVESTMENT RULE 29

Avoid investing in the broad stock market indexes and become more selective in sector stocks if quarterly GDP growth turns negative for the first time in an expansion.

Rationale. If GDP growth turns negative for the first time, the economy is likely to be experiencing the early stage of a downturn. (Even if the negative GDP growth is a false alarm, there is little downside to postponing a stock investment for a quarter.) Negative quarterly GDP growth usually indicates the beginning of a downturn period. Investors start to bail out of stocks, which depresses stock prices. However, downturn periods last only about 10 months before giving rise to recoveries and bull stock rallies. Thus, investors need to monitor the GDP report and get back into the stock market when GDP growth turns positive again.

INVESTMENT RULE 30

During the late stages of an expansion, avoid investing in the broad stock market indexes and become more selective in sector stocks if you observe the Consumer Confidence Index plunge over a two- to three-month span.

Rationale. The Consumer Confidence Index reflects how consumers feel about the present economic situation. Historically, consumer confidence plunges just before a recession (usually with a three-month lead time).

INVESTMENT RULE 31

During the late stages of an expansion, if the NAPM Index drops below 50 percent, avoid investing in the broad stock indexes—particularly the manufacturing and industrial sectors—immediately following the Index's release.

Rationale. The NAPM Index reflects the new orders, production, employment, and supplier deliveries of manufacturers. An index reading

of less than 50 percent indicates that the manufacturing sector is contracting (44 percent indicates a recession). The NAPM Index usually
drops below 50 percent just before a downturn period. Usually, any
reading below 50 percent is viewed negatively by stock investors. Avoid
the following company categories: heavy machinery, factory equipment, transportation equipment, electrical components, and building
materials.

INVESTMENT RULE 32

During the late stages of an expansion, if you observe that
durable goods orders have fallen precipitously over a two- to
three-month span, avoid investing in the broad stock indexes, particularly the manufacturing sector, immediately
following the report's release.

Rationale.   The durable goods orders report serves as a proxy for estimating businesses' fixed investments, which include expenditures on office buildings, factories, plant and equipment, computer systems, and
vehicles. However, durable goods orders usually turn down just before a
recession, sending stock prices south. Suspend stock purchases in general, and avoid the following company categories: heavy machinery, factory equipment, transportation equipment, electrical components, and
building materials.

INVESTMENT RULE 33

If the economy is in an expansion phase and the Federal Reserve reverses its monetary policy position by lowering
(rather than raising) the federal funds rate by at least ¼ of a
percentage point, purchase stocks immediately after the
policy maneuver, but use caution.

Rationale.   If the economy is in an expansion phase and the Fed lowers
the federal funds rate, after a series of tightening moves that raised the
rate, investors will interpret the Fed's move as a positive signal that the
central bank will help postpone the expansion's transition to recession.

(This is called a soft landing.) Stock prices will probably rise on the news. However, caution is advised because the Fed's rate drop may be too little and too late to keep the economy from entering a recession.

INVESTMENT RULE 34

If there is an unanticipated large increase in the monthly Consumer Price Index (CPI), avoid purchasing stocks immediately after the release of the CPI.

Rationale.   The stock market usually reacts adversely to dramatic increases in the monthly CPI (e.g., a reported annualized inflation rate that is substantially greater than the current rate of inflation). For example, if the current inflation rate is 3 percent and the monthly CPI release indicates an annualized inflation rate of 4 percent, a large number of stocks will most likely fall in value. As stated elsewhere, bouts of inflation damage the economy, business productivity, and corporate profits. Whether the economy is in a recession, a recovery, or an expansion; and whether the current inflation rate is at a historically low 2 percent or a relatively high 10 percent, a high monthly inflation number always raises investors' eyebrows.

INVESTMENT RULE 35

An unexpected widening of the nation's trade deficit provides a modestly bearish signal for equity investors. A narrowing trade deficit provides a modestly bullish signal for investors.

Rationale.   A widening trade deficit report usually gets the attention of investors, regardless of the economic environment. Running a trade deficit is a drag on the GDP because if we import more than we export, we are spending more money on other countries' goods and services than those countries are spending on ours. Thus, if the trade balance report shows that our trade deficit has widened, investors will view this as inhibiting GDP growth and exerting some downward pressure on stock prices. Avoid purchasing stock immediately after the report's release, but use some caution because changes in our trade balance are somewhat choppy throughout the business cycle. Although the deficit trends downward during an expansion, there is no visible, reliable trend, one way or the other, during recessions. If the trade balance report shows that our trade deficit has narrowed, investors will view this as a positive factor for GDP growth because it will exert some upward pressure on stock prices.

INVESTMENT RULE 36

A widening of the federal budget deficit creates a negative environment for investing in stocks, but should not be the dominant factor in stock portfolio decisions.

Rationale. A widening budget deficit negatively impacts the stock market because corporations' borrowing costs rise when interest rates rise, and profit margins are squeezed. Other factors in the economy—such as GDP growth, inflation, and Federal Reserve behavior—usually push the federal budget numbers into a second-tier status for investors.

Market Psychology

INVESTMENT RULE 37

When you believe a bull stock market is winding down, shift your investment emphasis away from growth stocks and toward blue-chip stocks.

Rationale. When it appears that a bull market is winding down (the market may have already experienced a minor correction), shifting your investments away from growth stocks and toward blue-chip stocks is an appropriate strategy. Blue chips are dividend-paying stocks. They represent relatively more stable companies and are less likely to incur large stock price losses in the event that a bull market turns into a bear market.

INVESTMENT RULE 38

A widespread belief among investors—for example, inflation worries—can dominate the future values of stock investments, despite other news to the contrary.

Rationale. Widespread beliefs or predictions regarding the direction of certain economic variables can tend to dominate values of selected financial assets for a period of time. For example, if inflation is running at a relatively tame 3 percent, but investors believe that inflation will reach 5 percent during the next 12 months, this market belief may soon dominate company stock valuations even if current inflation numbers are relatively tame.

INVESTMENT RULE 39

Market rumors can dominate stock price movements and influence short-term investment strategies.

Rationale. Rumors within the investment community can influence stock price movements for a short period of time. For example, a rumor about a large company acquisition could result in up or down stock price movements for the acquirer and the acquired.

INVESTMENT RULE 40

A widespread belief among investors that the Federal Reserve will raise or lower interest rates will tend to dominate the future values of stock investments, despite other news to the contrary.

Rationale. When there is a universal belief that the Federal Reserve will either raise or lower the federal funds rate, the short-term values (everything else remains the same) of most stock investments become captive to the market's anxiety over the Fed's next interest rate move.

Baby Boomers

> ### INVESTMENT RULE 41
>
> Invest in selected stocks or stock groups that are the primary beneficiaries of the long-term spending patterns of the baby boomer population group.

Rationale. The baby boomers now range in age from 38 to 54 years. These are the peak earning and buying years. Home buying, renovations, retirement homes, second homes, country clubs (and golf courses), and automobiles are just some of the sectors of the economy that will be positively impacted by the boomers' spending patterns.

> ### INVESTMENT RULE 42
>
> Invest in health-care sector stocks as a relatively safe, long-term (10 to 20 years), boomer-related investment.

Rationale. Baby boomers will be spending a good deal of their money on health care as they age, so the value of health care companies is expected to rise over time. The stocks of health care companies therefore represent a relatively safe long-term (10–20-year) investment. Health care stocks are described as relatively safe because there will always be a need or demand for health-care-related services as people age.

> ### INVESTMENT RULE 43
>
> Invest in financial services companies as an ongoing boomer-related investment strategy.

Rationale. As boomers enter their peak earning years, they require more financial services, bolstering the prospects of the financial services sector as an equity play.

The Internet

> ### INVESTMENT RULE 44
>
> Target, for equity investments, industries that are projected to be heavily influenced by Internet commerce during the next several years.

Rationale. Investors need to identify the industries that will prosper from Internet commerce, and treat these industries as growth industries. The Internet has already created growth opportunities for many economic sectors, and identifying the industries that will be heavily dominated by Internet commerce will help investors position their portfolios with solid growth stocks. Industries in which E-commerce is projected to rise substantially in market share by 2003 are listed on page 106.

> ### INVESTMENT RULE 45
>
> Select a strong Internet-based company in an industry in which E-commerce is projected to post significant gains over the next few years.

Rationale. Investors need to (1) identify industries in which the buying and selling of products and services is transitioning to E-commerce, and (2) select a financially strong company that promises to be a market leader in the industry's Internet environment. This is a relatively conservative investment strategy because the company chosen is already established, but it reduces the high price volatility that is associated with start-up growth companies.

> ### INVESTMENT RULE 46
>
> If you are seeking a high-growth company for your investment portfolio, select a start-up Internet-based company in an industry that is projected to experience substantial gains in E-commerce.

Rationale. Listed on page 106 are several industries that are projected to experience significant gains in E-commerce transactions. Home electronics, computing, auto, chemicals, and utilities have the highest projections.

Company/Industry-Specific Rules

INVESTMENT RULE 47

Identify the economy's emerging industries, and then invest (for the long term) in the most successful company (based on its financial performance and size) for each identified industry.

Rationale. Emerging industries represent the future for the continued health of the U.S. economy. But not all companies within an emerging industry will flourish over time. More likely, today's top company in the emerging industry will continue to be at or near the top as the industry matures. An example in the late 1990s was the equity play in Internet stocks. The Internet represented one of the greatest emerging industries of the twentieth century. Investors who selected one of the Internet's top companies, America Online, have been rewarded handsomely.

INVESTMENT RULE 48

Generally, high-quality companies that experience one or more stock splits during a reasonable amount of time are relatively more attractive to investors than quality stocks that have not experienced stock splits.

Rationale. Stock splits experienced by high-quality companies signal to investors that there is a strong demand for these companies' stocks and a probability that the stock price will be bolstered in the future. Stock splits also reduce the price of the stock, making the stock available to smaller investors (who can now afford to purchase shares of the company stock for less out-of-pocket money).

INVESTMENT RULE 49

When possible, hold a particular stock investment for at least one year to take advantage of the long-term capital gains provision of the Internal Revenue Code. Long-term capital gains are taxed at a maximum of 28 percent for more than 1 year, but not over 18 months, and a maximum of 20 percent for more than 18 months. Short-term holding periods of 1 year or less are taxed at a maximum tax rate of 39.6 percent.

Rationale. This is pretty straightforward. If you are contemplating selling one of your stocks, the amount of taxes you pay to Uncle Sam is dependent on the length of the holding period. The longer you hold on to a stock investment, the less you will have to pay the government for your capital gains.

INVESTMENT RULE 50

If the economy is experiencing a prolonged expansion, and if you can identify an emerging industry, invest in the initial public offerings (IPOs) that are issued by companies in that industry and are generally recommended by the investment community.

Rationale. Investing in initial public offerings (IPOs) issued by companies in emerging industries proved to be a winning strategy in the 1990s. Although IPOs historically are risky investments because most companies do not have a long performance record, their results during the great 1990s economic expansion were impressive.

INVESTMENT RULE 51

According to the 1990s business cycle, certain sectors—homebuilding, banks, capital goods, transportation, financial, and utilities—usually deteriorate in stock value well before a recession.

Rationale. The homebuilding, banks, and capital goods sectors began to display poor stock performance 11 months in advance of the 1990–1991 recession, and the transportation, financial, and utilities sectors led the recession by 10, 9, and 7 months, respectively. Rising interest rates toward the end of the expansion hurt most of these interest-sensitive sectors. Thus, it would be prudent to avoid and/or sell off these sectors during the late stages of an expansion period.

INVESTMENT RULE 52

According to the most recent (1990s) business cycle, certain sectors lose stock value coincident with an economic downturn: chemicals, energy, health care, industrials, retail stores, technology, insurance, and oil.

Rationale. All of these sectors began to deteriorate coincident with (i.e., within one month of) the 1990–1991 recession. Thus, it would be prudent to avoid and/or sell off these sectors during the early stages of an economic downturn.

INVESTMENT RULE 53

According to the most recent (1990s) business cycle, certain sectors such as banks, chemicals, consumer cyclicals, consumer staples, financial, homebuilders, retail stores, and transportation, outperform other sectors during recovery periods.

Rationale. During the 1991–1992 recovery period, the bank, chemicals, consumer cyclicals, consumer staples, financial, homebuilders, retail stores, and transportation sectors posted double-digit growth as measured by the S&P sector indexes. Among the reasons why these sectors climbed out of their recession woes were: favorable responses to falling interest rates (positively impacting the interest-sensitive bank, consumer cyclicals, financial, and homebuilders sectors), and favorable responses by "necessity sectors" to the early growth stages of the recovery (the positively impacted necessity sectors included consumer staples, chemical, retail stores, and transportation). Thus, a winning strategy would be to target these sectors for investment as the first signs of recovery are surfacing.

INVESTMENT RULE 54

The capital goods, communications, energy, health care, industrials, insurance, and utilities sectors performed relatively poorly during the last recovery (1991–1992), compared with other sectors of the economy.

Rationale. These sectors posted either single-digit or negative growth (as measured by their S&P indexes) during the 1991–1992 recovery period. These sectors are not interest-sensitive and thus did not receive a boost from lower interest rates. Most of these sectors (e.g., capital goods and industrials) usually require other sectors of the economy (such as housing) to recover before they can gain momentum.

INVESTMENT RULE 55

For longer-term investment horizons, in general, favor small-cap companies over large-cap companies, to raise the long-term return of your portfolio.

Rationale. Over the past 70 years, small-cap companies have provided returns that were superior to those of large-cap companies. For example, small-cap companies earned a 12.4 percent average return versus 11.2 percent for large-cap companies.

INVESTMENT RULE 56

For longer-term investment horizons, identify large-cap companies that are globally oriented, and add them to your investment portfolio.

Rationale. Historically, small-cap companies have outperformed large-cap companies. An exception was globally oriented large-cap companies during the 1994–1999 period. Investment strategies need to focus on the ability of large-cap companies to generate profits in today's globalized economy.

INVESTMENT RULE 57

In an economic downturn, in general, favor large-cap companies over small-cap companies.

Rationale. In a recession, large-cap companies outperform small caps because investors have more confidence in the larger, more established companies during bad times. Large caps are also more liquid (i.e., higher volumes of shares are traded), which makes it easier to sell and buy them during times of uncertainty.

INVESTMENT RULE 58

In times of world economic crises, favor investing in the largest and strongest large-cap companies (i.e., blue-chip companies).

Rationale. In financial crisis, investors worldwide look for safe havens for their funds, and U.S. Treasury bonds and U.S. blue-chip equities are two of the most popular investments. Blue-chip companies are the most highly capitalized companies. Investors have the comfort of these stocks' long record of surviving any crisis.

INVESTMENT RULE 59

In general, investments in penny stocks should be targeted during expansions and avoided during recession and recovery periods.

Rationale. Investing in penny stocks during recessions and recoveries is risky. Penny companies are small and undercapitalized, and they may not be able to survive bad economic times. Avoiding these companies during bad times and evaluating them during good times is a sensible investment strategy.

Other Factors

INVESTMENT RULE 60

In general, if a large portion of the United States experiences a long spell of unusually brutal winter weather, housing-related stocks become, temporarily, out of favor.

Rationale. When unusually brutal winter weather affects a large portion of the United States, it is certainly difficult to dig holes in the ground and build houses. The short-term stock value of building and construction companies is likely to fall, and a reduction in their holdings may be an appropriate course of action.

INVESTMENT RULE 61

In general, government-sponsored agencies are a good stock bet and should be part of any diversified stock portfolio.

Rationale. Government-sponsored agencies, such as Fannie Mae and Freddie Mac (the largest purchasers of mortgage loans in the nation), have a built-in advantage over private companies: They have an implicit government guarantee in the event of failure. This guarantee gives these agencies a decided advantage in the credit markets; they can borrow funds at rates lower than those available to their private counterparts. Thus, their profit margins are usually wider than those of comparable private companies. For example, both Fannie Mae and Freddie Mac have consistently registered return on equity (ROE) ratios exceeding 25 percent, far greater than the 10 to 18 percent ROEs of private housing-related companies.

INVESTMENT RULE 62

Buy stocks in anticipation of or immediately after a major company's positive announcement, such as an earnings-per-share number that exceeded analysts' projections. Avoid the purchase of stocks immediately after a company's announcements of negative events such as company layoffs or plant closings.

Rationale. Any major announcement from a publicly traded company—layoffs, strikes, higher-than-expected earnings, and so on—is likely to cause the value of that company to either fall or rise, depending on whether the announcement is negative or positive. A reduction or an increase in equity holdings may be an appropriate course of action.

INVESTMENT RULE 63

If the price/earnings (P/E) ratio of a company is below the S&P 500 Index P/E average and the company's earnings performance is improving, this may be a sound investment. Conversely, if the P/E ratio of a company is greater than the S&P 500 Index P/E average and the company's earnings performance is deteriorating, it may be prudent to avoid investing in this company.

Rationale. The price/earnings (P/E) ratio measures a company's current stock price as a percentage of its earnings per share. Historically, price/earnings ratios were in the 12 to 18 range (that is, 12 to 18 times the earnings per share), but, recently, typical price/earnings ratios have been a bit more than 20 times the earnings per share. Any company with a P/E ratio well above the S&P 500 Index P/E average (about 24, as of this writing) is viewed as expensive. A company with a P/E ratio well below the S&P 500 Index P/E average is viewed as a relatively cheap purchase. For investment purposes, if the P/E ratio of a company is viewed as weak and the company's earnings performance is improving, this may be a sound investment. On the other hand, if the company's P/E ratio is viewed as overstated and the company's earnings performance is deteriorating, it may be time to sell the stock.

7

INVESTING IN BONDS
AND OTHER
FIXED-INCOME SECURITIES

Intentionally walking home-run slugger Mark McGwire with the bases loaded may be considered lunacy by most casual fans, but baseball junkies might actually see it as a safe play. By walking the St. Louis Cardinals' slugger, the opposing team gives up one run to avoid potentially giving up four runs if his bat delivers a grand slam. On the other hand, by pitching to McGwire, the opposing team might get him out and avoid giving up any runs. The choice for the pitcher and his manager is how much risk they are willing to assume. Do they really want to pitch to the game's greatest home-run hitter with the bases loaded?

Investing in bonds and other fixed-income securities provides investors with opportunities to play it safe rather than risking everything in other investment vehicles (e.g., stocks). Generally, bonds offer a relatively secure income stream from interest, making them a safer harbor for investors' money. However, just like walking McGwire was not completely risk-proof (the next batter after McGwire could end up hitting a home run), the bond market could also do damage to the value of your investments from time to time. In fact, the most dramatic bond market collapse in history is still very much etched in investors' memories. In 1994, interest rates rose dramatically in a short period of time, sending bond prices plunging, and wiping out about $1.5 trillion in bond values worldwide.

Bonds and other fixed-income securities are viable investment alternatives to equities. On average, bond returns for most investment periods are lower than equity returns, but so are the risks. There is less price variation in bonds than there is in stocks. Bonds versus stocks are trade-offs investors have to make every day; most investment portfolios are a combination of both. As Table 7–1 reveals, long-term corporate and long-term government bonds registered 6.0 percent and 5.6 percent returns on investment during the 1926–1999 period—far less than the 11.6 percent return registered by both large-company and small-company stock indexes during the same 70-year period. However, during that period, the volatility of returns (i.e., annualized monthly standard deviations—a volatility measure) was substantially less for long-term corporate and long-term government bonds: 6.0 and 7.1 percent, respectively, compared with volatility measures of 20 percent and 30.6 percent for large-company and small-company stock indexes. Compared with stocks, bonds are safer investments but yield lower returns.

Most individual investors are likely to invest in bonds via mutual funds and money market funds, rather than purchasing bonds directly. Bonds usually come in big sizes (e.g., $100,000, $1,000,000, etc.) that are a bit expensive for the average individual investor. However, bonds can be purchased through a broker as easily as purchasing stocks. Whatever investments are selected, bonds and other fixed-income securities play a crucial role in every investor's portfolio. During both short-term and long-term holding periods, bonds offer consistent cash flows that are

Table 7–1 Compound Annual Rates of Return and Volatility of Returns, 1926–1999

	Annual Rates of Return	Volatility of Returns
Large Companies	11.3%	20.1%
Small Companies	12.6	33.6
Long-Term Corp. Bonds	5.6	8.7
Long-Term Govt. Bonds	5.1	9.3
Intermed. Govt. Bonds	5.2	5.8
Treasury Bills	3.8	3.2
Inflation	3.1	4.5

Source: Ibbotson Associates.

widely desired among investors. Simply stated, bonds (or any fixed-income instruments) are essential ingredients in any investor's diversified investment portfolio. By knowing who the players are, understanding the basic concepts of the bond market, and developing a host of rule-of-thumb investment strategies, investors can prepare for investing in bonds and other fixed-income securities.

The Players

Similar to the stock market, a wide variety of information on bond investments is offered on the Internet. Literally hundreds of quality Internet investment sites offer rates, prices, valuations, and commentary on fixed-income securities. The three major players in the bond market are: (1) professional traders, (2) institutional investors, and (3) individual investors. As the bond markets have grown over the years, they have become more sophisticated and intimidating for individual investors. Computerization, complex financial instruments, and derivative products such as futures, swaps, and options make the bond markets difficult for the nonprofessional to follow.

Bond traders usually work for the major Wall Street investment banking companies. They trade—not in the pits of the exchanges, but via computer screens and telephone lines—among the major investment banks and financial institutions around the world. As in equities trading, traders usually buy and sell for their own account, their company's account, and/or a customer's account. Traders can hold a large position (millions and sometimes billions of dollars) in different types of bonds in their own inventory, or purchase a bond for an institution or investor. Any bonds held in inventory are subject to losses and gains, depending on the direction of interest rates. Institutional investors in the bond markets are usually the same investors who inhabit the equities markets: corporations; the federal, state, and local governments; pension funds; and mutual fund managers. There are some individual investors in the bond markets, but they are a rare breed. Bonds and other fixed-income securities are usually purchased in big lots (pieces), and individual investors usually purchase smaller pieces via mutual funds. However, individual bond purchases are available for securities that are sold in smaller pieces: tax-exempt municipal bonds, mortgage-backed securities, selected corporate bonds, and U.S. Treasury bonds, notes, and bills.

A Bond Market Primer

A bond is a long-term form of debt issued by a corporation or a government. Investors in bonds and other fixed-income securities (e.g., U.S. Treasury bills and notes, and commercial bank certificates of deposit) *lend* money to a company or the government. This is in contrast to an investor in stocks, who becomes a very small part-owner of a company. A bond represents a debt of a corporation or government—an IOU it is obliged to repay regardless of whether the corporation makes a profit or the government runs a deficit. A corporation issues bonds because it uses the borrowed money to run its business and earn the profits needed to pay the fixed-interest installments to the bondholders. Governments—local, state, and federal—issue bonds as an alternative to taxes. Issuing bonds is a way of raising money.

There are basically three categories of fixed-income securities (particularly for U.S. Treasuries):

1. *Bonds* come in large denominations, usually ranging from $10,000 to $1 million.

2. *Notes* are usually intermediate-term debt and have a maturity (when the repayment of principal is due) of between 1 and 7 years.

3. *Bills* are usually short-term notes of a year or less in maturity.

Bond Basics

Although bonds and other fixed-income securities seem like complex investments to most nonprofessional investors, they are really quite simple if one takes the time to examine them. For example, if you invest in a $10,000 bond issued, say, by General Electric, you pay a sum equal to the face value of the bond: $10,000. Essentially, you are lending $10,000 to General Electric. You can resell the bond at more (or less) than the face value, depending on the market for bonds. The market value of a bond is determined by the supply and demand for bonds, which, in turn, is heavily influenced by the interest rate the bond pays. In return for the $10,000, the corporation is committed to making two sets of payments to you, the bondholder: (1) interest payments, periodically, until the maturity date, and (2) repayment of the $10,000 face value (or principal) when the date of maturity finally arrives. Effectively, a bond commits the issuer to making payments of interest and principal, and it provides the purchaser with a steady income stream (provided the corporation avoids bankruptcy).

Here is the basic information every investor needs to know about bonds:

1. Face value—the original value of the bond. If you purchase an originally issued bond for $1,000, that is the face value. After issuance, the market price of the bond may change (the price of the bond could go down or up), but the original face value of the bond never changes. It represents the amount of funds payable to the holder at maturity.

2. Coupon rate—the fixed dollar amount of interest the bondholder collects at regular intervals (usually, every 6 months). For example, if the coupon rate on a $1,000 bond is 5 percent, the investor can expect to receive $50 every year until the bond matures. Note that the coupon rate and payment amount stay constant at 5 percent and $50, respectively, even though the value of the bond (i.e., the market price), and interest rates, could fluctuate throughout the holding period.

3. Current yield—initially, a bond investor pays close to the face value of the bond and receives, on a regular basis (e.g., every 6 months), a fixed payment that is determined by the bond's coupon rate (see above). For example, you would pay $1,000 for a bond that has a face value of $1,000 and a coupon rate of 5 percent. The bond's current yield would be 5 percent. However, if interest rates rise to 10 percent after the bond is issued, the value of the bond drops substantially below $1,000. (The actual price would be $700; see the bond price formula presented in the next section.) No investor would pay $1,000 for a bond that yields 5 percent when other bonds are currently offering investors a 10 percent return. Thus, the current yield of the bond market is now 10 percent. To calculate the current yield, divide the coupon rate into the current or actual market price $\frac{\$700}{7\%} = 10\%$.

4. Maturity date—the date when the bond matures and the principal (i.e., the face value of the bond) is paid back to the investor.

Table 7–2 Bond Quality Ratings		
Standard & Poor's	Moody's	Quality
AAA	Aaa	Highest quality
AA	Aa	High quality
A	A	Upper medium grade
BBB	Baa	Medium grade
BB	Ba	Speculative elements
B	B	Speculative
CCC, CC	Caa	Default possible
C	Ca	Default—partial recovery possible
D	C	Default—recovery not likely

5. Yield to maturity—a calculation that combines the current yield and the price paid for a bond. Effectively, it is the real return from the income earned on the bond, plus the capital gain if the bond is held to maturity.

6. Credit rating—the bond's credit (quality) rating. It is crucial to check the rating before investing any money in a security. Bonds are evaluated by credit rating agencies such as Standard & Poor's and Moody's, and assigned a rating. The stronger the company in terms of its financial strength and earnings prospects, the higher the rating (AAA at S&P and Aaa at Moody's are the highest quality). U.S. Treasury bonds, notes, and bills need no rating because they are backed by the full faith and credit of the U.S. Government and are considered the safest of securities. Table 7–2 is a quick guide to the two most widely used bond rating companies: Standard & Poor's and Moody's.

Determining the Bond Price

Because the issuer of a bond promises to make future cash payments to the investor, the pricing of a bond is a direct application of the *present value* formula. The present value is based on the notion that the value of money is influenced when it is received; that is, investors have a time preference for money. A dollar today is worth more than a dollar received at some future date. The farther out in the future that you receive dollars, the less they are worth. Thus, lenders must be paid for the time value of their money. That payment is made in the form of an interest rate. The price of a bond is the present value of the future cash flow (coupon payments and principal amount), discounted by the interest rate that individuals place on the time value of money. The formula for the price of a fixed-coupon bond with n periods to maturity is:

$$PB = \frac{C_1}{(1+i)^1} + \frac{C_2}{(1+i)^2} + ... + \frac{C_n + F_n}{(1+i)^n}$$

where

PB = price of the bond (or the present value of the future cash flows);
C_t = coupon payment in period t;
$t = 1...n$;
F_n = the face value to be paid at maturity;
i = the interest rate or yield to maturity;
n = the number of periods (e.g., years) to maturity.

The formula has five variables: bond price, coupon, face value, interest rate, and term to maturity. If we know four of the variables, the fifth variable can be solved from using the formula. For example, assume we want to purchase a 3-year bond with a face value of $1,000 and a coupon of 7 percent, so that the coupon payments are $70 per period. If we assume coupon payments are made annually and the current market interest rate is 8 percent, the price of the bond, using the above formula, is:

$$PB = \frac{\$70}{(1.08)^1} + \frac{\$70}{(1.08)^2} + \frac{\$1,070}{(1.08)^3}$$

$$= \$64.81 + \$60.03 + \$849.40$$

$$= \$974.24.$$

The pricing of bonds can be simplified by using Table 7–3, which shows the present value of $1 paid at the end of each year for 20 years, for interest rates ranging from 3 percent to 10 percent. To illustrate, at an interest rate of 8 percent, the present value of a dollar not received until 3 years from now is $0.7938. Using Table 7–3, the calculation of the price of

Table 7–3   Present Value of a Dollar

Year	3%	4%	5%	6%	7%	8%	9%	10%
1	.9709	.9615	.9524	.9434	.9346	.9259	.9174	.9091
2	.9426	.9246	.9070	.8900	.8734	.8573	.8417	.8264
3	.9151	.8890	.8638	.8396	.8163	.7938	.7722	.7513
4	.8885	.8548	.8227	.7921	.7629	.7350	.7084	.6830
5	.8626	.8219	.7835	.7473	.7130	.6806	.6499	.6209
6	.8375	.7903	.7462	.7050	.6663	.6302	.5963	.5645
7	.8131	.7599	.7107	.6651	.6227	.5835	.5470	.5132
8	.7894	.7307	.6768	.6274	.5820	.5403	.5019	.4665
9	.7664	.7026	.6446	.5919	.5439	.5002	.4604	.4241
10	.7441	.6756	.6139	.5584	.5083	.4632	.4224	.3855
11	.7224	.6496	.5847	.5268	.4751	.4289	.3875	.3505
12	.7014	.6246	.5568	.4970	.4440	.3971	.3555	.3186
13	.6810	.6006	.5303	.4688	.4150	.3677	.3262	.2897
14	.6611	.5775	.5051	.4423	.3878	.3405	.2992	.2633
15	.6419	.5553	.4810	.4173	.3624	.3152	.2745	.2394
16	.6232	.5339	.4581	.3936	.3387	.2919	.2519	.2176
17	.6050	.5134	.4363	.3714	.3166	.2703	.2311	.1978
18	.5874	.4936	.4155	.3503	.2959	.2502	.2120	.1799
19	.5703	.4746	.3957	.3305	.2765	.2317	.1945	.1635
20	.5537	.4564	.3769	.3118	.2584	.2145	.1784	.1486

the 7 percent coupon bond used in the previous example is (there will be minor differences in the real formula calculations, due to rounding):

$$PB = \$70\,(0.9259) + \$70(0.8573) + \$1{,}070(0.7938)$$
$$= \$64.81 + \$60.01 + \$849.37$$
$$= \$974.19.$$

Types of Fixed-Income Securities

U.S. Treasuries

Perhaps the safest investments in the world are securities backed by the full faith of the United States Government. It is no secret that when things go wrong somewhere in the world—resulting in anything from economic turmoil to war—investors park their money in U.S. securities because the American economy is the largest, strongest, and most stable in the world. Investors label this phenomenon a "flight to quality," and it is almost always foreign money flying across oceans to purchase U.S. Treasury securities.

U.S. Treasuries come in three forms: (1) Treasury bonds, (2) Treasury notes, and (3) Treasury bills. The interest earned from U.S. Treasury securities is exempt from state and local taxes but not federal taxes.

Treasury bonds are sold in denominations ranging from $1,000 to $1 million, and they have maturity terms ranging from 10 years to 30 years. The 30-year Treasury bond, called the "long" bond, is the most widely cited bond quote in the nation.

Treasury notes are federal securities that have terms ranging from 2 to 10 years. They are considered intermediate debt obligations of the U.S. Government. Their popularity grew substantially throughout the 1990s because of their attractive maturity range. Investors who do not want to lock in their funds for a substantial period of time (i.e., 10 or more years), but need a stable cash flow for a period of time, are attracted to notes.

Treasury bills have durations of three months, six months, or one year. The minimum investment in a T-bill is $10,000. T-bills are somewhat unique in that, unlike other fixed-income securities, they don't pay interest at regular intervals. Investors purchase bills at a discount and then receive the face value of the bill (e.g., $10,000) when the bill matures. For example, if you purchase a one-year T-bill for $9,500, you would earn $500 in interest at the end of 12 months. The effective return (interest rate) you would receive would be: $500 divided by $9,500 = 5.26 percent.

Treasury securities can be purchased through the 12 Federal Reserve banks across the nation (see Table 7–4). Treasuries can also be purchased from commercial banks or through a stockbroker. The easiest and most popular way to invest in the U.S. Treasury market is to purchase shares in mutual funds that possess a significant amount of U.S. securities in their portfolios. The government is always issuing new U.S. Treasury securities. Treasury bills are auctioned about every week; Treasury notes are auctioned monthly; Treasury bonds are auctioned about four times per year.

Table 7–4   Federal Reserve Banks

Board of Governors of the Federal Reserve System
20th and C Streets, NW
Washington, DC 20551
(202) 452-3000

Federal Reserve Bank of **Boston**
600 Atlantic Avenue
Boston, MA 02106
(617) 973-3000

Federal Reserve Bank of **New York**
33 Liberty Street
New York, NY 10045
(212) 720-5000

Federal Reserve Bank of **Philadelphia**
Ten Independence Mall
Philadelphia, PA 19106
(215) 574-6000

Federal Reserve Bank of **Cleveland**
1455 East Sixth Street
Cleveland, OH 44114
(216) 579-2000

Federal Reserve Bank of **Richmond**
701 East Byrd Street
Richmond, VA 23219
(804) 697-8000

Federal Reserve Bank of **Atlanta**
104 Marietta Street, NW
Atlanta, GA 30303
(404) 521-8500

Federal Reserve Bank of **Chicago**
230 South LaSalle Street
Chicago, IL 60604
(312) 322-5322

Federal Reserve Bank of **St. Louis**
411 Locust Street
St. Louis, MO 63102
(314) 444-8444

Federal Reserve Bank of **Minneapolis**
90 Hennepin Avenue
P.O. Box 291
Minneapolis, MN 55480-0291
(612) 204-5500

Federal Reserve Bank of **Kansas City**
925 Grand Boulevard
Kansas City, MO 64198
(816) 881-2000

Federal Reserve Bank of **Dallas**
2200 North Pearl Street
Dallas, TX 75201
(214) 922-6000

Federal Reserve Bank of **San Francisco**
101 Market Street
San Francisco, CA 94105
(415) 974-2000

U.S. Savings Bonds

Many of us have invested in U.S. savings bonds whether we wanted to or not. Many newlyweds, especially in the post-World War II years, were off on their own with a small nest egg of these bonds. A savings bond is an attractive present because the giver spends $50, but the face value of the bond reads $100.

Many people bought savings bonds in times of crises, as a way to invest in and support the U.S. Government. But are they a good investment today? They probably were not, when market interest rates were relatively high (e.g., the double-digit interest rates in the 1970s and early 1980s), but they increasingly improved throughout the low-interest-rate environment of the 1990s. The U.S. Treasury Department has made some significant changes, in an effort to make savings bonds more attractive to investors. Interest rates on the popular Series EE savings bonds now fluctuate with the general direction of interest rates. The return on EE bonds held for five years is fixed at 85 percent of the average of six-month Treasury bill yields for the preceding three months. Also, Series EE savings bonds range from $50 to $10,000, and, as always, investors pay only half the face value upon purchase. The time it takes to double the investment (i.e., cash in the bond at maturity) depends on the direction of interest rates. Lower interest rates mean longer terms to maturity; higher interest rates mean shorter terms to maturity.

Similar to U.S. Treasury securities, the interest on savings bonds is exempt from both local and state taxes. And because the bond pays interest and principal at the conclusion of (not during) the term, the bondholder pays no federal taxes until the bond is redeemed at maturity.

Tax-Exempt Municipals

There's a myth that municipal bonds are only for the rich and famous. Depending on your tax situation, investing in "munis" could be a wise strategy. Most municipal bonds are those rare bonds that are exempt from federal taxation. And if you happen to purchase munis in your state of residence, you will probably be exempt from paying local and state taxes as well.

The bulk of municipal bonds are called *public purpose bonds*—bonds that are issued by a town, city, or state for the purpose of borrowing large sums of money to fund the building of schools, roads, bridges, and so on. Typically, the stated yields on municipals are lower than on other bond yields, but their after-tax yield makes them relatively more attractive to investors in high-income tax brackets. To convert the tax-exempt municipal yield to a taxable yield for investment comparisons, divide the tax-exempt yield by 1 minus your tax rate. For example, if you are in the 39 percent tax bracket and are contemplating investing in a tax-exempt municipal bond yielding 5 percent, the tax equivalent bond yield would be $5.00/1 - 0.39 = 8.19$ percent. Remember that if you purchase the municipal bonds of your state of residence, they will be exempt from federal, state, and local taxes. Thus, the tax rate you use in your calculations should reflect the federal rate plus state and local tax rates. It is easy to see why municipal bonds are a popular investment for tax-conscious investors.

Tax-exempt municipal bonds are subject to the risk of default. The credit quality of the bond is only as good as the quality and financial strength of the issuer—usually, a city, county, or state. Similar to corporate bonds, municipals are rated by Moody's or Standard & Poor's. It is very easy to assume that a city's or county's likelihood of defaulting on its payment obligations is zero, but a reality check suggests that cities and counties do fail. Remember Orange County, California? Its bonds were rated Aa by Moody's just days before its financial problems were made public. The county was forced to default on a significant amount of its bonds because of questionable investments in its portfolio.

To invest in municipals, you can either purchase them directly from a stockbroker (usually in $5,000 pieces) or invest in a municipal mutual fund. If you are planning to purchase municipals on your own (via a stockbroker), be careful about the bid/ask quotes. The spread between the bid price (the price at which the broker will buy the bond from you) and the asking price (the price at which the broker will sell the bond to you) is wide. Thus, most investors who purchase municipals have a strategy of holding the bonds until maturity and avoiding the bid/ask process altogether. This strategy fits well with most investors' retirement accounts.

Zero-Coupon Bonds

Zero-coupon bonds are securities that have no coupon payment but deliver a single payment at maturity. The interest earned by the investor is the difference between the price paid at the original purchase time and the amount of funds received at maturity. The most popular zero-coupon bonds are U.S. Treasury bills and U.S. savings bonds.

Investing in zero-coupon bonds is like dining on liver and brussels sprouts—either you like them or hate them; there is no in-between. If you are an investor who wants to receive interest payments on a regular basis, zero-coupon bonds are not for you. And this investment gets even worse: You still have to pay taxes on the interest that you have not even received. On the other hand, zero-coupon bonds are very attractive to investors who want to put out only a small amount of money, but receive a large return many years out.

Zero-coupon bonds usually begin at $1,000 and often have a term of 10, 20, or 30 years. Depending on the interest rate, a 30-year, zero-coupon bond with a face value of $1,000 may cost only $50 at the date of origination. Because they are relatively cheap up-front investments but require tax payments throughout their term, these bonds have become popular investment vehicles for a child's college education account and/or for retirement accounts (e.g., IRAs and Keoghs). In these accounts, the negative impact of paying taxes without receiving interest is minimized because a child is usually exempt from paying taxes (or pays at a low tax rate) or, in the case of retirement investing, the investment is usually in a tax-deferred account.

Ginnie Mae Securities

Ginnie Mae securities provide a way to invest in government-insured mortgage loans. Government National Mortgage Association (Ginnie Mae) securities are relatively attractive bond investments because they are backed by the full faith and credit of the federal government. Basically, qualified mortgage lenders that originate Federal Housing Administration (FHA) and Veterans Administration (VA) loans assign these loans to Ginnie Mae. These loan packages are the basis of securities issued and guaranteed by Ginnie Mae. The Ginnie Mae securities are then sold to investors who market them in minimum denominations of $25,000.

Ginnie Maes are essentially mortgage-backed securities that provide investors with monthly principal (due to amortization of the principal of the mortgage loan) and interest payments. Because these securities are virtually guaranteed by the U.S. Government, there is little risk to the investor. Ginnie Mae securities provide investors with a cash flow of interest plus some principal every month.

There are two primary risks inherent in Ginnie Mae security investments: (1) reinvestment risk and (2) prepayment risk. Reinvestment risk exists because, every month, investors have to reinvest the payment of partial principal in new investments that could yield lower or higher returns, depending on the direction of interest rates. Prepayment risk is present when there is an unusually high number of mortgage refinancings. To illustrate these two risks, consider the following example. Assume an investor owns $100,000 in a 15-year Ginnie Mae security yielding 8 percent. His reinvestment risk is reinvesting the principal he gets back every month. If the Ginnie Mae security were paying interest only, like a bond, the investor would receive about $604 in interest (for an 8 percent coupon) every month, and he would receive his $100,000 investment back at the end of 15 years. But this Ginnie Mae security pays back some portion of the $100,000 principal every month. (Remember, someone is making a monthly mortgage payment in which both interest and principal are being paid.) In the first month, the investor would receive a total of $956, of which $665 is interest and $291 is principal. Thus, he needs to reinvest $291 at the current market interest rate, which could be lower or higher than the original 8 percent. This is his reinvestment risk. With a traditional bond, there is no reinvestment risk on the principal. Investors receive their principal investment back at the bond's maturity. With Ginnie Mae securities, there is reinvestment risk every month.

Prepayment risk just adds to the investment risk. If someone refinances a home mortgage loan, he or she is "prepaying" the loan before maturity. Thus, the investor in a Ginnie Mae will receive even more principal payments if a lot of refinancing occurs in the pool of mortgages on which the Ginnie Mae security is based. In our above example, the Ginnie Mae security would be subject to a great deal of prepayment risk if mortgage rates suddenly fell to 7 percent. Some of the FHA/VA mortgage loans in the pool of mortgages that backs the Ginnie Mae security would be paying off because borrowers are refinancing their mortgages to the lower mortgage rates. As they refinance their loans, the 15-year Ginnie Mae investment term may be shortened considerably, leaving Ginnie Mae securities holders with the problem of reinvesting a large sum of money in the marketplace at a lower interest rate. Thus, investors face both reinvestment risk (investing cash flows at new market-determined interest rates) and prepayment risk (households refinancing their mortgages and, in effect, returning their principal back to the investor).

Fannie Mae/Freddie Mac Securities

Perhaps the most prominent "quasi" government bonds are Fannie Mae and Freddie Mac securities. They are similar to the mortgage-backed Ginnie Mae securities in that they provide investors with monthly principal (due to amortization of the principal of mortgage loans) and interest payments.

Fannie Mae is the Federal National Mortgage Association, the largest company, as measured by assets, in the United States. Freddie Mac, the Federal Home Loan Mortgage Corporation, is smaller than Fannie Mae but is still one of the largest corporations in the United States. Both of these companies are called government-sponsored agencies, which gives an impression that the United States would financially support them in times of need. They were conceived by the federal government, but both companies are publicly traded on the stock exchanges and have private boards of directors. Fannie Mae's and Freddie Mac's primary mission is to purchase mortgage loans originated by mortgage lending companies and then securitize these loans by selling mortgage-backed securities in the financial marketplace.

The attraction for investors is that both Fannie Mae and Freddie Mac guarantee payment of interest and principal to investors, even if a homeowner misses his or her mortgage payments. The key here is that the markets believe that both Fannie Mae and Freddie Mac are as close as a private company can get to being backed by the full faith and credit of the federal government. They both have an implicit guarantee from the U.S. Government of up to $3.5 billion in case of default. For investors, Fannie Mae and Freddie Mac bonds represent relatively safe investments (almost, but not quite, as safe as U.S. Government bonds), but the real kicker is that these bonds have a higher return than Treasury bonds. So, if you are looking for an investment that is almost as safe as U.S. federal debt, but pays higher returns, Fannie Mae and Freddie Mac securities qualify.

Corporate Bonds

Corporations can raise funds either by issuing stock (offering investors a part ownership opportunity) or by borrowing money via a bond issue. Corporate bonds are riskier than U.S. Treasury bonds and other government-guaranteed bonds (e.g., Freddie Mac bonds) because they are backed by the financial strength (or lack thereof) of private corporations rather than the U.S. Government. The financial strength of a company is its ability to pay off its debt even during a worst-case scenario (e.g., a recession). Most corporate bonds are debenture bonds, which means that they are backed by the financial strength of the corporation rather than a real asset (such as the value of a house, in the case of a mortgage-backed security). Corporate bonds can be purchased via a stockbroker. The minimum investment is usually about $1,000.

Standard & Poor's and Moody's rank each corporate issue. The return on even the safest AAA-rated corporate bond is higher than a U.S. Treasury bond because the risk level is higher. In general, the return on corporate bonds rises as the quality rating drops (e.g., from AAA to AA to A to no rating).

Junk Bonds

A special category of corporate bonds possesses an unusual level of risk that attracts investors who wish to take a chance on a potential loss, in return for a higher interest payment. These bonds are called junk bonds because the regular marketplace looks on them as junk, in contrast to the more traditional, safe, high-quality corporate bonds. Junk bonds are high-yielding bonds that are also risky investments. The issuers of these high-yield bonds are usually less traditional, smaller companies that need to offer higher interest rates on their bond offerings to attract investors. The bottom line on junk bonds: In favorable economic environments, be careful and take a flier on them. When economic times turn downward, companies issuing junk bonds may have difficulty surviving the downturn (and may default on their debt obligations), so the rewards earned from junk bonds may not be worth the risks.

A low-interest-rate environment makes high-yield bonds look appealing to many investors. There are a number of junk bond funds, and during the mid-1990s junk bond insurance have been setting records with each passing year.

Certificates of Deposit and Other Short-Term Investments

For investors who need to invest in the short term, there are four basic investment options: (1) Federal Deposit Insurance Corporation (FDIC)-insured savings accounts, (2) FDIC-insured certificates of deposit (CDs), (3) money market accounts, and (4) money market mutual funds.

All of us can deposit our short-term funds in a savings account at a commercial bank or thrift institution. We will receive interest on a regular basis, and there is no term on our investment; we can take our money out of the savings account on demand. The trade-off for this luxury is that savings accounts usually pay interest rates that are far lower than other short-term security yields. Savings accounts are almost risk-free investments; up to $100,000 is insured by the FDIC.

Certificates of deposit (CDs) provide opportunities to commit funds for a relatively short period of time and receive higher rates than savings accounts. Investors can arrange CDs at just about any commercial bank; terms range from three months to five years. The minimum investment may vary from about $250 to $1,000, depending on the financial institution. CDs are FDIC-insured up to $100,000.

Commercial banks and other financial services companies (e.g., investment banks) invest in short-term securities in money market accounts. Banks create a money market account by investing in a diversified portfolio of money market securities, such as CDs, Treasury bills, and commercial paper (issued by corporations). In these money market accounts, the money deposited is payable on demand, but the interest earned is variable. An investor could earn a 5 percent return the first year, but, depending on the type of investments in the account, the return the following year could go up, go down, or stay flat.

Money market mutual funds are essentially money market account-type investment portfolios sold by mutual funds. The host of available money market mutual funds satisfies almost all of the needs and tastes of investors who prefer short-term investing. There are funds that invest only in U.S. Treasuries. Other more diversified funds invest in Treasuries, local government securities, CDs, commercial paper, and so on. Funds are popular investments because they are relatively safe. Their returns are competitive and the money deposited in them is payable on demand. However, an administrative/management fee is charged for participating in these funds.

Bonds and Interest Rates

Several years ago, I attended a seminar on economic policy, in Chicago. One speaker, a prominent business leader, gave his views on why and how the U.S. Government manages to screw corporate business at every turn. A statement he made during the question-and-answer session after his speech has stuck with me ever since. Someone in the audience asked him for his outlook on interest rates. He paused, thought for a moment, and then looked the questioner straight in his face and said, very matter-of-factly, "Interest rates are going to fluctuate, they are either going to fluc up, or fluc down." The audience burst into laughter. I chuckled, but his response kept nagging at me the rest of the day. He was an enormously successful corporate executive, yet he was helpless in knowing which direction interest rates, one of the economy's most crucial variables, were headed.

Investing in bonds and other fixed-income securities is a bet on the direction of interest rates. There are two ways of earning money on a bond investment: (1) collecting interest payments and (2) price appreciation (i.e., the difference between what you paid for the bond and the price at which the bond is sold) a.k.a. capital gains. There is an inverse relationship between the direction of interest rates and the price of a bond. If interest rates go up, bond prices fall; if interest rates go down, bond prices increase.

If you have a long-term investment horizon, you need not worry too much about the direction of interest rates. Just hold on to your bond investment until maturity. However, if your horizon is shorter, the value of your bond investment will fluctuate with changes in interest rates and/or a downgrade on the financial condition of the bond issuer (which raises the likelihood of default).

Suppose you purchased an IBM bond with a 10-year term and a face value of $1,000, yielding 8 percent. Initially, your expected return on this investment is an 8 percent annual return (i.e., $80) for 10 years. And if you hold on to this bond, you will receive an 8 percent return (called the coupon rate) every year for the remainder of the term. However, if market interest rates rise by 2 full percentage points, and newly issued 10-year IBM bonds are now yielding 10 percent, you are no longer happy with your investment. You are now holding on to a bond that is yielding less than current bond yields of similar quality. If you try to sell your IBM bond, you will not get the $1,000 price that you originally paid. The price of the bond will go down, to reflect current market rates on IBM bonds. Thus, the price will fall to $800 and you will incur a $200 capital loss on your investment (your purchase price was $1,000). The lesson to be learned here is: Pay attention to the direction of interest rates when managing a bond portfolio. The value of your investments is extremely sensitive to interest-rate changes.

A side benefit of investing in interest-bearing securities is that they generally provide an opportunity to take advantage of compounding interest payments (e.g., CDs and bond funds). Compounding assumes that the interest earned on a security is reinvested at the end of each year for the remainder of the investment's term. Thus, you can accumulate a substantial amount of funds in a relatively short period of time. For example, suppose you invest $1,000 at 6 percent interest, and the interest is compounded annually. It would take you approximately 12 years to double your money.

Look at any compound interest table and you will be able to calculate how your money builds over time for a stated interest rate. In fact, a simple rule, the "rule of 70," tells you how long it will take for you to double your money, given a particular interest rate. Just take the interest rate and divide it into 70. In the example above, we would divide 6 percent into 70. The result, 11.6 years, is how long it would take to double your money in a security yielding 6 percent, compounding interest annually. The greater the interest rate, the less time it will take to double your money. At 8 percent interest, it would take $70/8 = 8.75$ years to double your money.

Compounding interest demonstrates the importance of selecting the highest-yielding security for the given amount of risk that you are willing to take on. The lesson learned here is that it pays to shop around for interest-bearing investments. By investing in an 8 percent versus a 6 percent security (as illustrated above), you would have doubled your money in about three years less time!

Bonds and Terms to Maturity

In normal economic times, the bond yield curve is usually positively sloped, which means that long-term bond yields usually are higher than short-term bond yields. Investors have a built-in bias to purchase longer-term securities in order to earn higher interest. However, for a given rise in interest rates, long-term bond prices will drop by a greater amount than short-term bond prices because the price of a bond reflects the present value of the future cash flows (i.e., what the future cash flows are worth in today's money). Present value is determined by interest rates and by the length of the term to maturity. The greater the term to maturity, the more influence it has on the bond price. Thus, although longer-term bonds usually generate higher annual interest earnings, they are also subjected to wider variations in their prices. The implications for investing in the bond market are that investors tend to favor longer-term bonds for longer-term investment horizons (the wider gyrations in prices do not mean as much in the longer run), but they lean toward shorter-term bonds for shorter-term investment horizons.

Bonds and the Federal Reserve

Bond investors and the Federal Reserve are like Siamese twins. One cannot make a move without the other knowing about it. The Federal Reserve's greatest power is in the control it has over the direction of interest rates (i.e., the federal funds rate) via *open market operations* [the purchase (or sale) of government securities by the Federal Reserve on the open market]. The Fed can increase and decrease the nation's money supply by buying and selling U.S. government securities on the open market. By increasing or decreasing the supply of money, the Fed is essentially influencing the direction of interest rates (particularly the federal funds rate) and of bond prices. Most professional bond investors keep a very careful eye on the Federal Reserve, monitoring its behavior on a daily basis. It is not uncommon for most bonds and other fixed-income securities to experience significant changes in values, responding to an announcement of a change in Federal Reserve policy with regard to the federal funds rate.

To develop bond investment strategies, investors need to be able to evaluate current as well as future Fed behavior. Sometimes the market leads the Fed, sometimes the Fed is out front. Usually, when rates go up, the market leads the Fed because risk averse investors develop a nervous twitch about inflationary pressures and bid bond prices down (and interest rates up). When interest rates go down, the Fed leads the market, easing the central bank's worries about stimulating the economy.

Investment Rules for Bonds

The value of bonds and other fixed-income securities depends on the phase of the business cycle and the relative levels of inflation and interest rates. Interest rates usually drop during downturns and rise during expansions. The result is a favorable bond price performance when interest rates drop, and a not-so-favorable bond price performance when interest rates rise.

You can and should invest in bonds in every economic environment—in good times and in bad times; during recession, recovery, and expansion—because they provide stable cash flows regardless of their movements in value. Recession is perhaps the most likely environment for capturing the benefits of a stable cash flow (derived from bonds' coupon payments) that earns substantial capital gains. A recession is usually characterized by falling interest rates (i.e., rising bond values). Investors therefore receive a steady flow of coupon payments. During the early stages of a recession, interest rates are at cyclically high levels. (Rates rise during the final stages of expansion.) This means that investors can bolster their expected future cash flows by purchasing bonds that offer high coupon payments. Thus, during a recession, investors have the possibility of receiving high coupon payments and earning substantial capital gains on their bond investments.

Investors must keep a watchful eye on the creditworthiness of the bonds' issuers during a recession. Downturns are usually associated with weakening corporate earnings and a surprisingly high number of business failures, which make it difficult to satisfy company debt obligations. One way around this is to focus investments on high-quality issuers—the federal government (viewed as riskless), quasi-government agencies (e.g., Fannie Mae and Freddie Mac), and AAA corporate bonds. The issuers of these debt obligations are more likely to survive the hardships of recession.

A recovery period creates some interesting opportunities for investing in bonds. Interest rates are usually falling during recoveries, and the Federal Reserve tends to be accommodative by exerting downward pressure on rates. Furthermore, investors are usually bullish on stock investments because expected corporate earnings are on the rise during a renewal of economic activity. For bonds, this means that companies are better able to meet their debt obligations, so the credit quality of bond issuance improves.

The challenge for bond investors is to anticipate changes in interest rate direction during expansions. Expansions are usually associated with a strong job market, gains in corporate earnings, and rising consumer confidence. For bond investments, the key is to identify when interest rates turn up. Interest rate direction is somewhat unpredictable during expansions. Rates may drop, stay relatively flat, or rise.

If the bond markets go into a tailspin, don't panic and dump some of your bond investments. Think the situation through first. Interest rates are volatile, and they are subject, at times, to extreme swings. Pay attention to the economic indicators. They will give you a sense of whether the change in interest rates is really permanent. (Some of the investment rules that follow were developed for this type of situation.)

By putting together everything we've learned about bonds, plus the basic principles for investing in both bad and good times (Chapter 5), we have developed investment rules for bonds and other fixed-income securities. The top ten list of "Grow-Rich" rules is highly recommended for investors. These rules are general in nature and easy for investors to digest and follow. For investors seeking to drill deeper and expand their options, a list of "More Grow-Rich Rules for Bonds" is given at the end of the chapter. These rules tend to be more specific and require a bit more monitoring by investors.

The Top Ten Grow-Rich Rules for Bonds

INVESTMENT RULE 1

If the economy is in a recession and the GDP growth is negative, bond investments, in general, will generate greater returns than stock investments.

Rationale. Negative quarterly GDP growth usually indicates the beginning of a downturn period, prompts investors to bail out of stocks, and depresses stock prices. Fortunately, downturn periods also are opportunities for bond investments. Historically, interest rates turn down during recessions but eventually turn upward by the end of a recovery period. Bonds are therefore relatively attractive investments throughout the downturn, as long as you plan to hold them until the recovery period.

> ## INVESTMENT RULE 2
>
> During the early stages of a downturn, investing in high-quality bonds is likely to generate cyclically high cash flows as well as price appreciation.

Rationale. During the early stages of a recession, interest rates are usually at cyclically high levels. The rising rates during the expansion have not yet made the transition to the recession. The cyclically high interest rates suggest that investors can purchase bonds offering high coupon payments. And because interest rates usually fall during recessions, a bond purchased at the beginning of a recession and held throughout the recession's duration could also earn substantial capital gains. Purchase only high-quality bonds—government, quasi-government (e.g., Fannie Mae), and AAA corporate bonds—because the profit performance of most companies during recessions is strained, as a result of reduced demand for their goods and/or services. During a recession, some companies are more likely to default on their debt obligations.

> ## INVESTMENT RULE 3
>
> Place greater investment emphasis on longer-term bonds than on shorter-term bonds during a recession.

Rationale. During a recession, interest rates are usually falling. Longer-term bonds will therefore provide greater price appreciation than shorter-term bonds. It is just mathematics: If interest rates are falling, the price appreciation on a long-term bond will exceed the price appreciation on a short-term bond.

> ## INVESTMENT RULE 4
>
> During a recession, look for the Federal Reserve to follow an accommodative monetary policy (i.e., exerting downward pressure on interest rates) that will enhance the attractiveness of bond investments.

Rationale. The Federal Reserve is usually accommodative during a recession. It brings interest rates downward in an effort to spur economic activity. Falling interest rates provide a favorable environment for bond investments.

INVESTMENT RULE 5

If the economy is in recovery, begin moving some of your bond investments away from government bonds and toward nongovernment bonds that are paying higher interest rates.

Rationale. Recovery presents an opportunity for investors to selectively invest in higher-yielding corporate bonds. Corporate earnings begin to grow, which raises the quality of debt issuance. AAA and AA corporate bonds become solid investments when the economy is well into recovery.

INVESTMENT RULE 6

In an expansion that is experiencing periods of sustained and rising inflation, take advantage of high interest rates by investing in shorter-term bonds (fixed-income securities).

Rationale. Prolonged bouts of inflation are harmful to both bond and equity values. The best strategy is to take advantage of rising interest rates by investing in short-term securities. In this way, you will realize relatively high returns and regain your full principal in a relatively short time period (e.g., one year). You can then reinvest the funds in another short-term security that yields an even higher interest rate. (Rates will be rising.) By avoiding longer-term securities, you are minimizing your capital losses on the value of the bonds (caused by the rise in rates). Also, by staying short, you are minimizing the likelihood of bond defaults, which are more likely in a high-inflation environment because profit margins are narrowing.

> ## INVESTMENT RULE 7
>
> In an expanding economy associated with falling inflation and interest rates, invest in longer-term bonds.

Rationale. If you have identified a falling interest rate and an inflation environment, invest in long-term bonds as soon as you can. Locking into today's high interest rates will add to your wealth tomorrow, when rates continue to drop. This is a no-brainer investment. By investing in long-term bonds, you are essentially locking in a relatively high return investment, which can only rise in value as interest rates fall.

> ## INVESTMENT RULE 8
>
> If the economy is entering the final stages of an expansion and the Federal Reserve is showing signs of accommodation, place a greater investment emphasis on bonds versus stocks, but select only high-quality instruments.

Rationale. A maturing expansion suggests that the economy is beginning to weaken and interest rates will soon turn downward, particularly if the Fed pursues an accommodative monetary policy. This is when you should step up your bond investments relative to stocks. However, if the economy enters a recession period, bond default rates will rise, so it would be prudent to invest in only high-quality bonds (i.e., governments and quasi-governments).

> ## INVESTMENT RULE 9
>
> Whenever the Federal Reserve reverses policy direction and either (a) cuts or (b) raises the federal funds rate by at least ¼ of a percentage point, respond by placing either (a) a greater or (b) a lesser emphasis on bond investing. If the Fed cuts the rate, favor longer-term over shorter-term bonds. If it raises the rate, reduce your bond holdings and shorten the maturity of your bond portfolio.

Rationale. Whenever the Federal Reserve reverses its policy direction, it is very big news to investors. Bond values, in particular, react quickly to any Fed policy change. Lowering the federal funds rate (i.e., increasing the money supply) is a decision of a more accommodative Federal Reserve, and it bodes well for further rate reductions in the future. Placing greater emphasis on your bond portfolio and lengthening the terms to maturity should improve your investment performance. Conversely, raising the federal funds rate (i.e., decreasing the money supply) is a decision of a less accommodative Federal Reserve, and further rate hikes are likely in the future. Over time, bond values are expected to deteriorate, so investors should place less emphasis on bond investments and shorten the terms of their investments.

INVESTMENT RULE 10

In a fully employed economy that is experiencing inflationary pressures, a Federal Reserve interest rate hike (of at least ¼ of a percentage point) could calm investors' jitters and create a favorable bond investment environment, at least in the near term.

Rationale. If the economy is operating near full employment and inflationary pressures are building, bond investors will exhibit anxiety about future Federal Reserve policy actions. Usually, when rates go up, the bond market leads the Fed because risk-averse bond investors develop a nervous twitch about inflationary pressures, and they bid bond prices down (and interest rates up). By raising interest rates, the Fed may, in fact, calm investors' jitters about inflationary pressures. Bond investors need to be very careful in this type of investment environment. Although, in general, raising interest rates lowers future bond values, in this particular market setting, raising rates may lower inflationary expectations, which would have the offsetting effect of raising bond values.

More Grow-Rich Rules for Bonds

The additional investment rules for bonds form a lengthy list. Some of these rules require monitoring of Internet investment sites on a monthly basis; others require only some common sense. Investors should scan the following rules and identify those that might be implemented with minimal investment burden. To make them easier to follow, some rules are categorized as Indicators, Market Psychology, and Other Factors.

INVESTMENT RULE 11

If the economy has been in recession and the quarterly GDP growth turns positive for the first time, you may want to make your maturity range on bond investments slightly shorter, in anticipation of a possible upturn in interest rates.

Rationale.   When the quarterly GDP growth turns positive for the first time after a recession, it is signaling that the economy has made a transition from downturn to recovery, which usually means a rise in corporate profits, stock prices, and, eventually, interest rates. Although interest rates may be flat for some time and may not rise until well into the expansion period, it may be prudent to shorten the average maturity of your bond portfolio in anticipation of a future rate rise.

INVESTMENT RULE 12

As the economy transitions from recovery to expansion, you may want to shorten your maturity range on bond investments, in anticipation of an eventual upturn in interest rates.

Rationale.   The final stages of recovery represent an opportune time to shorten your maturity terms on new bond investments. Historically, the direction of interest rates has been uncertain. Unless the economy is approaching capacity, interest rates could stay relatively flat for some time. The possibilities of rate direction pose an element of uncertainty for investors. Shortening your maturity range on future bond purchases may be a prudent course of action.

Indicators

INVESTMENT RULE 13

If the economy is operating close to capacity and the quarterly release of the GDP registers a robust growth rate of 3.5 percent or greater, avoid purchasing bonds (or sell your existing bonds).

Rationale. Robust GDP growth is a sign of a healthy, growing economy. If it is close to full capacity, inflationary pressures are expected to build, placing downward pressure on bond prices.

INVESTMENT RULE 14

Purchase bonds, particularly longer-term instruments, when you observe that housing starts growth has turned negative toward the end of an expansion period.

Rationale. Housing starts reflect the construction activity of single-family and multifamily residential homes. However, housing starts usually turn down just before a recession, sending stock prices south and bond prices north. At this point, you should immediately begin to favor bond investments over stock investments. Emphasize long-term bonds over short-term bonds, to take advantage of future capital gains on the long-term securities as interest rates spiral downward throughout the recession.

INVESTMENT RULE 15

Purchase bonds, particularly longer-term instruments, over stocks, when you observe that durable goods orders growth has turned negative toward the end of an expansion period.

Rationale.   The durable goods orders report serves as a proxy for estimating business fixed investments (the investment expenditures of U.S. businesses: spending on office buildings, factories, plants and equipment, computer systems, and trucks). However, durable goods orders usually turn down just before a recession; stock prices then drop, and bond prices increase. You should begin to favor bond investments over stock investments. Emphasize long-term bonds over short-term bonds, to take advantage of future capital gains on the long-term securities as interest rates spiral downward throughout the recession.

INVESTMENT RULE 16

A higher-than-expected rise in the monthly Consumer Price Index (CPI) could send bond prices falling. A lower-than-expected increase or a drop in the CPI could generate increases in bond prices.

Rationale.   The bond market usually reacts adversely to dramatic increases in the monthly CPI (e.g., a reported annualized inflation rate that is substantially greater than the current rate of inflation), and it reacts favorably to better-than expected inflation news. For example, if the current inflation rate is 3 percent and the monthly CPI release indicates an annualized inflation rate of 4 percent, there will most likely be an upward tick in interest rates, perhaps as much as ¼ of a percentage point. If you were planning on investing in a fixed-income security, it would be prudent (and probably profitable) to postpone the purchase until the markets have had sufficient time to adjust to the negative news. Most likely, bond prices will fall, and you will end up purchasing the security at a lower price. Conversely, falling inflation rates are always viewed favorably by investors in the bond market. A dramatic drop in the CPI is probably unexpected good news that could generate a more favorable bond investment environment. Getting in early, when news like this is revealed, is a good investment strategy.

INVESTMENT RULE 17

If the economy is operating close to full employment, a higher-than-expected nonfarm payroll number could send bond prices reeling. A lower-than expected nonfarm payroll number could generate increases in bond prices.

Rationale. If the economy is close to full employment, proceed cautiously with your bond investing just before the release of the Employment Report. A higher-than-expected nonfarm payroll number (usually, more than 200,000 employees) generally means robust GDP growth. If the economy is close to full capacity, inflationary pressures are expected to build, placing downward pressure on bond prices. In addition, after a strong Employment Report, investors may believe that the Federal Reserve is one step closer to tightening monetary policy by raising short-term interest rates. A lower-than-expected nonfarm payroll number (usually, less than 100,000 employees) generally means weakening GDP growth in an economy operating close to full capacity. The resulting downward pressure on inflation usually exerts upward pressure on bond prices. After a weaker-than-expected Employment Report, investors may believe that the Federal Reserve will postpone any thought of tightening monetary policy by raising interest rates.

INVESTMENT RULE 18

If the economy is operating close to capacity, unexpected news in either direction for the monthly retail sales report or the Consumer Confidence Index could move bond prices either up or down.

Rationale. A weak retail sales figure indicates slowing economic activity, which is usually a blessing to bond market investors when the economy is operating dangerously close to full capacity. However, if retail sales numbers are stronger than expected, investors may believe that inflationary pressure will build and will apply downward pressure on bond prices. The Consumer Confidence Index reflects how consumers feel about the present economic situation. If consumer confidence plunges when the economy is operating close to capacity, investors will be jubilant and send bond prices upward. Conversely, if consumer confidence dramatically rises, investors may fear inflationary pressures that will send interest rates upward (bond prices will then fall).

INVESTMENT RULE 19

If the economy is operating close to full employment and the capacity utilization rate rises and is approaching 84 percent, avoid investing in bonds immediately following the report's release.

Rationale. A higher-than-expected capacity utilization number, particularly when the economy is operating close to full employment, could send strong inflationary signals, placing downward pressure on bond prices. (Interest rates would then rise.) In effect, the capacity utilization rate reflects how much more the economy can grow before inflationary pressures begin to build. In recent years, the utilization rate has climbed well into the 83 percent range without setting off inflationary pressures. However, as the rate approaches 84 percent, the labor markets begin to tighten, creating some upward pressure on wages and prices. In addition, with capacity utilization approaching alarming numbers (about 83 to 84 percent), investors may believe that the Federal Reserve is one step closer to tightening monetary policy by raising short-term interest rates.

INVESTMENT RULE 20

If the economy is operating close to full employment and the NAPM Index is higher than expected and well above 50 percent, avoid investing in bonds immediately following the Index's release.

Rationale. The NAPM Index reflects the new orders, production, employment, and supplier deliveries of manufacturers. An index reading of greater than 50 percent indicates that the manufacturing sector is expanding. A higher-than-expected NAPM number, particularly when the economy is operating close to full employment, could send strong inflationary signals, placing downward pressure on bond prices. (Interest rates would rise.) In addition, with the manufacturing sector continuing to expand in an almost fully employed economy, investors may believe that the Federal Reserve is one step closer to tightening monetary policy by raising short-term interest rates.

INVESTMENT RULE 21

Favor bonds over stocks, but with some caution, if the economy is operating close to full employment and the trade deficit report reveals an unexpected widening of the deficit.

Rationale. Running a trade deficit is a drag on the GDP because if U.S. imports exceed exports, we are spending more money on other nations' goods and services than those nations are spending on our goods and services. Thus, if the trade balance report shows that our trade deficit has widened, investors will view this increase as inhibiting GDP growth, exerting some downward pressure on stock prices, and placing upward pressure on bond prices. In an economy operating close to full employment, investors and the Federal Reserve are very sensitive to inflationary pressures, and a widening trade deficit is viewed as giving an overheating economy some relief.

INVESTMENT RULE 22

Unanticipated gains or losses in the growth estimates of the major economic releases will move bond prices (in either direction) by more than anticipated gains or losses.

Rationale. Whenever an economic report contains unanticipated news, market psychology comes into play. Generally, unanticipated news creates an element of uncertainty for investors; bond prices move more than they do in response to anticipated news. For example, the value of

30-year Treasury bonds may drop considerably on the unexpected news that nonfarm payrolls gained 300,000 employees during the previous month (in a fully employed economy) rather than the expected (i.e., the market consensus) 150,000 gain. For each major economic release, knowing the market's prior projection of the content helps you to know whether the release's information satisfies, disappoints, or exceeds the market's expectations.

INVESTMENT RULE 23

A widening of the federal budget deficit creates a negative environment for bond investments, but should not be the dominant factor in bond portfolio decisions.

Rationale. A widening budget deficit negatively impacts the bond market because government borrowings crowd private borrowings and apply upward pressure on interest rates. Other factors in the economy, such as GDP growth, inflation, and Federal Reserve behavior, usually push the federal budget numbers into a second-tier status for investors.

Market Psychology

INVESTMENT RULE 24

A widespread focus among investors—for example, inflation worries—can dominate the future values of bond investments, despite other news to the contrary.

Rationale. Widespread beliefs regarding certain economic variables can tend to dominate values of selected financial assets for a period of time. For example, if inflation is running at a tame 3 percent pace, but investors believe that inflation will accelerate to a 5 percent pace during the next 12 months, they will incorporate this perception into their pricing of bonds and will demand higher interest rates on their loanable funds.

INVESTMENT RULE 25

Market rumors can dominate bond price movements, influencing short-term investment strategies.

Rationale. Rumors within the investment community can influence bond price movements for a short period of time. For example, if a speech presented by a member of the Federal Reserve's Federal Open Market Committee (FOMC) contained inferences that the Fed was contemplating an interest rate hike, a deterioration of bond prices in the near term could result.

INVESTMENT RULE 26

A widespread belief among investors that the Federal Reserve will raise or lower interest rates will tend to dominate the future values of bond investments, despite other news to the contrary.

Rationale. When there is a universal belief that the Federal Reserve will either raise or lower the federal funds rate, the short-term values (everything else remaining the same) of most bond investments become captive to the market's Fed worries.

INVESTMENT RULE 27

If a crisis somewhere in the world has caused uncertainty and you are seeking a safe haven for your investment funds, purchase U.S. Treasury bonds, notes, or bills.

Rationale. Perhaps the safest investment in the world is securities backed by the full faith of the U.S. Government. It is no secret that when things go wrong somewhere in the world, investors park their money in

U.S. Treasury securities. Increased demand for these securities will eventually apply downward pressure to Treasury yields and upward pressure on prices. The strategy for savvy investors is to purchase Treasury securities at the beginning of a crisis situation. They will almost guarantee realized capital gains by the end of the crisis.

Other Factors

INVESTMENT RULE 28

If you are seeking relatively safe investment vehicles that generate greater monthly cash flows than traditional bonds, invest in mortgage-backed securities such as Ginnie Maes, Fannie Maes, and Freddie Macs. They provide investors with monthly principal and interest payments.

Rationale. Mortgage-backed securities provide investors with monthly principal (due to amortization of the mortgage loan) and interest payments. These securities represent excellent investment vehicles for investors who can handle the monthly cash flows, which are part principal and part interest. Investors in these securities need to have some other need for the returned principal every month, or they must assume the risk of reinvesting the principal at market rates. Ginnie Maes, Fannie Maes, and Freddie Macs all have some form of explicit or implicit government guarantees. These investments are among the safest securities available in the financial marketplace. In addition, because of their cash flow and safety features, these instruments usually have relatively attractive yields.

INVESTMENT RULE 29

Take advantage of higher-yielding corporate securities (relative to Treasury securities) during recovery and expansion periods. Purchase investment-grade (BBB and above) corporate securities during expansions, but only high-quality AAA corporate securities during recovery periods.

Rationale. Generally, corporate bonds are riskier than U.S. Treasury bonds, but they also generate higher returns. Take advantage of the good times (when corporate defaults are less likely), and invest a good portion of your bond funds in corporate securities. During expansion periods, the best of times, you can gain extra return if you go down to BBB-rated securities. However, during recovery periods, the jury may still be out as to the financial performance of some companies, and your investments should be limited to AAA-rated securities only.

INVESTMENT RULE 30

If you have some speculative funds available in your bond portfolio, invest, carefully, in high-yielding junk bonds during favorable low-interest-rate economic expansions.

Rationale. If you have some funds for which you are willing to take a chance on a potential loss in return for a higher interest payment, invest in junk bonds. Companies that issue junk bonds are usually less traditional, smaller companies that need to offer higher interest rates to attract investors. However, know the risks that the company issuing the junk bond is assuming.

INVESTMENT RULE 31

For investing in the short term, look into FDIC-insured/government-backed investment vehicles such as commercial bank certificates of deposit, money market accounts, and money market mutual funds backed by a pool of government-insured/guaranteed short-term securities.

Rationale. Certificates of deposit (CDs) provide investors with opportunities to commit funds for a relatively short period of time and receive higher rates than savings accounts. Money market accounts and money market mutual funds are essentially run by money managers who invest in short-term securities for you.

INVESTMENT RULE 32

You can determine how long it will take you to double your money in an investment vehicle that offers compound interest by following the "Rule of 70." Simply divide the security's stated interest rate by 70.

Rationale. The Rule of 70 provides investors with an easy calculation of how long it will take to double their money. The alternatives are: Look up this information on a compound interest table, or use a financial calculator.

INVESTMENT RULE 33

If you observe an inverted yield curve (i.e., short-term interest rates are higher, on average, than long-term interest rates), place a greater emphasis on purchasing shorter-term securities, to take advantage of their higher returns.

Rationale. Although inverted yield curves are rare, short-term interest rates do rise above long-term interest rates—usually, when expectations of higher inflation for the near term are high, and expectations for inflation over the long haul are somewhat lower. If and when the inversion occurs, a sensible investment strategy would be to shore up your bond portfolio with shorter-term securities, to take advantage of the higher returns offered on the shorter end of the yield curve.

INVESTMENT RULE 34

When you believe a bull stock market is winding down, shift some of your investment funds toward bonds.

Rationale. When it appears that a bull market is winding down (maybe the market has already experienced a minor correction), shifting your investments away from stocks and toward bonds is a prudent and usually successful investment strategy. As investors begin to believe that the bull stock market is winding down, they will begin to park a substantial portion of their portfolio funds in fixed-income securities, exerting upward pressure on bond prices.

INVESTMENT RULE 35

When possible, hold a particular bond investment for at least one year, to take advantage of the long-term capital gains provision of the Internal Revenue Code, which taxes long-term capital gains at a maximum of 28 percent for more than one year but not over 18 months, and at a maximum of 20 percent for more than 18 months. Short-term holding periods of one year or less are taxed at a maximum tax rate of 39.6 percent.

Rationale. This is pretty straightforward. If you are contemplating selling one of your bond investments, the amount of taxes you pay to Uncle Sam will depend on the length of the holding period. The longer you hold on to a stock investment, the less you will have to pay the government for your capital gains.

INVESTMENT RULE 36

To convert a tax-exempt municipal yield to a taxable yield for investment comparisons, divide the tax-exempt yield by 1 minus your marginal tax rate.

Rationale. This simplest of calculations should be made if you are looking at after-tax yields on all of your bond investments.

INVESTMENT RULE 37

If you are seeking a long-term investment of a relatively small amount of funds for a child's college education and/or for a retirement account, and you are willing to forgo receiving interest payments, invest in zero-coupon bonds.

Rationale. Zero-coupon bonds are attractive to investors who can invest only a small amount of money but want to receive a large return many years later. Depending on the interest rate, a 30-year zero-coupon bond with a face value of $1,000 may cost you only $50 at the date of issuance. These bonds have become popular investment vehicles for children's college education accounts and/or retirement accounts (e.g., IRAs and Keoghs). In these accounts, the negative impact of paying taxes without receiving interest is minimized because a child is usually exempt from paying taxes (or pays a low tax rate).

8

INVESTING IN
REAL ESTATE

" I used to drive a fourteen-wheeler, carrying orange crates from Florida to New Jersey, earning $9 an hour. I would come home, dead tired, and not have enough energy to spend quality time with my pregnant wife and four kids, ages 3, 5, 7, and 10. One night, the stars must have been aligned because I was changing channels on my TV when I stumbled upon the one and only Dick Gotyou in an infomercial on how to buy homes with no money down, and my life has never been the same. Today, I own 25 rental homes and have a net worth close to $2 million! And I only work 10 hours per week! Dick Gotyou is a Godsend."

Does this sound familiar? Putting infomercials (and the *How to Make a Million Dollars in Real Estate* books that accompany them) and exaggerations aside, it is true that real estate is the Mark McGwire of investments for many people. Real estate has provided opportunities for many investors to hit the big home run.

Returns on Real Estate Investing

You can make money in real estate, but it has become increasingly difficult to hit the home run in recent years. The real estate market essentially collapsed in the late 1980s and early 1990s. Property prices plummeted, and investors were caught with their financial pants down.

Overbuilding and an increasing dependence on favorable real estate tax laws were the primary reasons for the debacle. Many investors learned a valuable lesson.

In recent years, the real estate market picked itself up, and it is now back on the road to recovery. Historically, the overall return–risk rewards on real estate investments compare favorably to both bonds and stocks, and real estate is a viable investment alternative. The annual total return for commercial real estate properties averaged 8.72 percent during the 1978–1999 period, compared with 15.3 percent for large and small company stocks, and 12.2 percent for long-term Treasury bonds. However, these returns also reflect the market collapse in the late 1980s and early 1990s. As shown in Table 8–1, the return on Real Estate Investment Trusts (REITs) tax-advantage trusts investing primarily in real estate averaged 16.76 percent during the 1978–1997 period. Surprisingly, the risks of investing in commercial properties are less than the risks of investing in the stock market and bond market. The variation of returns for real estate (i.e., the standard deviation) was only 8.72 percent during the 1978–1999 period, compared with a variation of about 18 percent for stocks and 12.5 percent for long-term bonds. The variation of returns for REITs compared favorably as well, averaging a standard deviation of returns of 13.09 percent. But perhaps the most attractive feature of real estate investments is that they have a low correlation with stocks and bonds and provide diversification benefits in an overall investment portfolio.

In summary, real estate investments have proven, over the years, to be worthy additions to anyone's investment portfolio. The attractiveness of real estate as an investment comes from several directions:

1. The total returns from real estate investments (including REITs) are comparable to the returns associated with stocks and bonds, particularly if we include the variation of those returns (i.e., the risks).

2. Because the real estate business has a low correlation with the equity and bond markets, it offers substantial diversification benefits to an investment portfolio.

3. Over the long term, because its value is highly correlated with inflation, real estate provides an inflation hedge to an investment portfolio.

Table 8–1   Return Characteristics:
REITs vs. Commercial Properties
(1978–1997)

	REITs	Commercial Properties
1978	10.34%	16.11%
1979	35.86	20.46
1980	24.37	18.07
1981	6.00	16.63
1982	21.60	9.44
1983	30.64	13.32
1984	20.93	13.04
1985	19.10	10.10
1986	19.16	6.63
1987	−3.64	5.49
1988	13.49	7.04
1989	8.84	6.21
1990	−15.35	1.47
1991	35.70	−6.07
1992	14.59	−4.36
1993	19.65	0.56
1994	3.17	6.85
1995	15.27	8.83
1996	35.25	11.00
1997	20.26	13.63
1998	−17.50	16.26
1999	−4.62	8.02*
Average	16.76%	8.72%
Standard deviation	13.09	7.07

*Through third quarter. REIT returns are from the NAREIT Index. Commercial property returns are based on the NCREIF Index.
Source: The Roulac Group, Inc.

The Players

Homeownership aside, the players in the real estate investment marketplace are not numerous. A limited number of people invest in home/apartment rental properties. Professional investors, including commercial banks, insurance companies, and pension funds, invest in all types of commercial properties.

A Real Estate Primer

Directly investing in real estate is not trivial. A wide variety of properties are for sale, and the curve for learning how to invest in them is steep. Investors need to learn how to acquire and manage a property. Anyone who has purchased a home has experienced "the closing." There are literally hundreds of papers to sign and endless liability paragraphs to read (which no one does because it would take too long). A closing is an intimidating process.

Purchasing rental and/or commercial properties is even more intimidating. Investors need to understand how to evaluate the true worth of a property, and they must have the financial acumen to calculate the projected cash flows of the investment. Many investors take a short cut and invest in real estate via real estate mutual funds and REITs. Our focus here will be on directly investing in a rental home or indirectly buying all types of commercial real estate through mutual funds, REITs, and limited partnerships.

Real Estate Mechanics

Directly investing in real estate (i.e., a rental home) is somewhat different from investing in the stock or bond markets. Investors need to do some homework—study the proposed property and understand the predicted cash flows from the investment. The ultimate goal is to earn (1) a competitive return from the annual cash flows of the property and (2) large capital gains upon the sale of the property. The combination of the cash flows and the long-term capital gain will determine the rate of return earned on the investment property.

As an individual investor, you may invest directly in a rental home. You are then officially considered a landlord, which means that you have to maintain the upkeep of the home and play the part of a "Mr. Fix It" if something like a dishwasher breaks. If you are not the repairman type, you will need a card file of various other Mr. Fix Its, or you may decide to hire a professional management service, which would arrange for these types of activities.

The purchase of a property involves making a down payment and borrowing the remaining funds from a mortgage lending company or a bank. The more you leverage (i.e., the lower your down payment), the higher the potential returns on your investment. The ability to leverage is what separates real estate investments from traditional stock and bond investments. If you had $10,000 to invest, most people would avoid margin accounts and purchase only $10,000 worth of stocks or bonds. But the same $10,000 could be a down payment (assuming a 10 percent down payment is required) on a $100,000 rental home. Thus, in real estate, your $10,000 would control a $100,000 investment.

It is important to note that most people avoid using margin accounts because there is a good deal of risk in purchasing stocks on margin. After a stock purchase, if the company that issued the stock experiences financial difficulties and its stock price plummets, investors on margin stand to lose a great deal of money. Highly leveraged stock transactions are not for everyone. However, a highly leveraged real estate transaction differs from a stock margin transaction in two important ways:

1. Real estate prices usually do not fluctuate widely (with the exception of the late 1980s' real estate collapse); there is some downward stickiness. In fact, real estate prices for residential homes have averaged about 4 to 5 percent inflation in price during the past several years.

2. In a worst-case scenario of a price collapse, investors can fall back on the value of their collateral (i.e., the real estate itself) to minimize their potential losses. Investors involved in stock margin transactions have no such luxury. They must pay off their borrowed funds immediately after the stock sale.

The financial benefits from leveraging are clear. If the price of the rental home and the price of a stock investment both rose by 5 percent after one year, $5,000 (.05 × $100,000) would be earned on the home investment, but only $500 (.05 × $10,000) on the stock investment.

An important consideration when directly investing in real estate is: Can the property carry the cash flows? The annual income from rents (or lease payments) on the property has to cover the mortgage payments and other expenses (e.g., home maintenance). However, there are also certain tax advantages. An amount representing the depreciation of the property can be deducted from the income earned each year from the property investment. Any improvements made to the property are also deductible. For these reasons, real estate investing is sometimes considered a special type of tax shelter for investors. Never complete a "direct purchase" transaction without the advice of an accountant.

If you are indirectly investing in real estate, via mutual funds and REITs, you can apply most of the principles that are involved in the purchase of stocks and bonds. You can purchase shares of a mutual fund or REIT from a broker or directly online on the Internet. The key is to know when to make the real estate investment. Understanding how to directly invest in real estate will help you make intelligent decisions on indirect investments in real estate as well.

The Internet offers a wealth of information for real estate investors. Literally hundreds of quality real estate sites offer data, market analyses, and investment advice for a variety of real estate ventures, ranging from buying your own home to investing in office buildings, shopping centers, and rental properties. Among the more popular real estate sites are those offered by Grubb & Ellis, yahoo real estate, the International Council of Shopping Centers, the Mortgage Bankers Association, and AOL Real Estate. A number of universities across the nation have Real Estate Centers that offer Web links to their data on analyses of the markets. NYU's Jack Brause Real Estate Library (nyu.edu/library/rei/brcom) and the University of Cincinnati's Real Estate Center (cba.uc.edu/getreal) are among the leaders.

Real Estate Terms

Whether you are directly or indirectly investing in real estate, some terms and characteristics are common to each approach. For direct investments, your success in negotiating the purchase price will be somewhat dependent on an intimate knowledge of these terms. For indirect investments (e.g., mutual funds and REITs), familiarity with these terms is crucial, particularly if you are reviewing a prospectus for a limited partnership and/or REIT.

absorption rate: The annual rate at which new space in commercial properties is being occupied.

amortization: The repayment of debt in installments of principal and interest over a period of time. Because of the amortization schedule, monthly payments on a 15-year mortgage include higher principal payments than monthly payments on a 30-year mortgage.

appraisal: An estimate of the value of a property. Appraisals are done as a matter of practice during the underwriting of a mortgage loan. The lender usually requires an appraisal because the property serves as the collateral for the mortgage loan. The estimate is usually based on the property's location, comparable property values, and other market factors.

assessed value: The value attributed to a property by the assessor, for property-tax purposes.

balloon payment: A final (often larger) payment at the end of a partially amortized loan.

capitalization rate: The rate of discount that converts income to capital value.

comparables (comps): A term used to refer to current area rents, competitive rental properties, and area properties that have been recently sold. They are assumed to be comparable in size, location, condition, and so on.

depreciation: A decrease in the value of a property over time. For example, an owner of a rental property can depreciate the property's loss in value as it ages. The depreciation amount can be deducted from the income earned from the property each year.

gross possible income: If a property is 100 percent occupied and the owner receives market rent, the total is the gross possible income.

lessee: The tenant.

lessor: The landlord.

leverage: The use of credit to enhance one's speculative capacity. Leverage is the key ingredient in any real estate investment. The monetary advantages of buying property are dependent, to a large extent, on how much leverage is in a transaction. Most investors can borrow up to 80 percent of the cost of a property, which means they give 20 percent of the cost as a down payment. In some instances, close to 100 percent of the cost of the property can be borrowed.

net operating income: The effective gross income less net operating expenses. For valuing commercial real estate properties, investors will look at the net operating income of the income-producing property.

passive income: Income from activities designated as passive by the Tax Reform Act of 1986 (e.g., rental income).

prepaid interest: Advance payment of interest on a loan.

vacancy rate: A measure of the rate of occupancy for a commercial property. For example, if the vacancy rate is 6 percent for an apartment building, the building's units are 94 percent occupied, or 6 percent vacant. When contemplating investing in rental property, it is important to know the vacancy rates in comparable rental properties in the neighboring area.

Types of Real Estate Investments

What are real estate investments? The home you live in; the office building you work in; the shopping center where you buy clothes, food, and furniture; the beach house where you spend part of your summer vacation; and all the land around you. Aside from the house you live in, the majority of real estate investments—rental homes, apartments, office buildings, shopping centers, hotels, and industrial parks—can be classified as income property.

rental homes: A rental home is a home purchased as an investment. The owner performs as a landlord and earns rental income.

apartments: Multifamily units that represent acceptable direct and indirect investments for a real estate portfolio.

commercial real estate properties: Among the host of properties classified as commercial real estate properties are: shopping centers, hotels, industrial parks, warehouses, and shopping malls.

raw land: Unused land that is not a site of a residential or commercial structure.

Indirect Real Estate Investments

As mentioned above, a direct investment in real estate via purchase of rental properties may be too cumbersome. Three primary investments are available to investors as alternatives that permit them to participate in the real estate markets without getting their hands dirty: (1)Real Estate Investment Trusts (REITs), (2) limited partnerships, and (3) real estate mutual funds.

Real Estate Investment Trusts

Real Estate Investment Trusts (REITs) were established by Congress in 1960 to provide a vehicle for companies focused on owning and operating commercial real estate property. (Some REITs are comprised of mortgage loans as well.) The primary objective, in establishing REITs, was to enable small investors to make investments in large-scale, income-producing real estate. The idea was to "pool" funds from average investors so that the REIT vehicle could purchase commercial properties that were otherwise unavailable to individuals. Unfortunately, REITs played a limited role in the real estate markets for the first 30 years of their existence. REITs had a difficult time attracting capital because investors preferred to purchase commercial real estate as tax shelters. (Interest and depreciation could be deducted against their income.) But when the 1986 Tax Reform Act severely limited commercial real estate investments as tax shelters, interest in REITs gained momentum. Between 1978 and 1998, equity REITs had a total annual return of 14.35 percent, exceeding the 8.72 percent return of direct property investments. The number of publicly traded REITs tripled during that 20-year period.

REITs are attractive for their tax advantages as well as their pooling advantages. A REIT may deduct from its corporate tax bill the dividends paid to shareholders, as long as the trust distributes at least 95 percent of its earnings every year. REITs are well on their way to supplanting pension funds as the primary funding source in the real estate equity markets. Investments in these trusts are similar to investments in mutual funds. Shareholders simply select the REIT that focuses on their investment target. REITs specialize in all kinds of properties: regional shopping malls, warehouses, office buildings, or a mix of all real estate property types.

REITs offer investors three attractive features: (1) liquidity, (2) security, and (3) a competitive return on investment. REITs give individual investors access to the commercial real estate business, and they provide liquidity to the market and permit investors to buy and sell shares of a diversified real estate portfolio. Individuals looking for a steady cash flow (REITs pay large dividend percentages) and involvement in the real estate marketplace will find REITs attractive.

Limited Partnerships

Limited partnerships consist of individual investors (partners) and a general partner. The purpose of the partnership is to invest in real estate properties. The individual partners are classified as limited partners because their liability is limited to their initial investment. The general partner(s) usually manages the portfolio of properties and earns management fees while also sharing in the cash flows and capital appreciation of the properties. In recent years, the popularity of limited partnerships has markedly diminished. Many of the earlier tax advantages have been stripped away during the past decade, so there is little incentive to form partnerships.

However, there are companies that offer limited partnerships in commercial real estate ventures. These companies usually specialize in acquisitions, mergers, and development of commercial real estate. For investors who prefer to limit their participation in the direct purchase of properties such as apartment buildings, hotels, office properties, and shopping centers, limited partnerships remain an attractive option. The general partner will usually perform the following tasks in the partnership: create the new limited liability company; acquire properties; conduct due diligence on new acquisitions; manage the debt and equity placement; provide asset management services and eventual disposal of the properties.

Real Estate Mutual Funds

Today, a host of real estate mutual funds is being offered to the investment community. Investors can find real estate mutual funds that are heavily weighted toward commercial properties, rental units, and/or apartments, or a mix of all three real estate types. Companies offering real estate funds range from AIM Advisor Real Estate Funds to the Van Kampen Real Estate Funds.

A typical real estate mutual fund will provide the following information for potential investors:

- A profile of the fund: the percentage of funds invested in income-producing real estate assets.
- The targeted property types and/or REITs.
- The fund manager's biography.
- Fund performance: year to date, 1 month, 3 months, 6 months, 1 year, and life.
- Historical performance.
- Fees, loads, and expenses.
- Price history.
- Distribution schedule: dividends and capital gains.
- Holdings: domestic and foreign asset allocation.
- Major market sectors.
- Purchase minimums.
- How to order a prospectus.

Real Estate and the Economy

Like most investments, the value of real estate is dependent on the swings of the economic pendulum. Real estate investors need to be sensitive to movement in the three primary measures of economic activity: GDP, inflation, and interest rates. The impact of GDP growth on the value of real estate investments is straightforward. A healthy and growing economy creates a favorable environment for most income-producing real estate investments. In a healthy and growing economy, people have jobs and can pay their rent; they are buying at shopping centers, filling up office buildings, and keeping industrial parks and warehouses busy filling orders. Conversely, an economic downturn could prove costly to income-producing properties. Commercial tenants might be forced out of business or unable to meet their lease obligations in office buildings, retail shopping centers, and so on. In addition, families may face difficult times in a recession. If they experience job losses and/or reduced wages, it will be difficult for them to pay their rents to landlords.

The impact of inflation and interest rates on the value of real estate investments is not as straightforward as the impact of GDP, but it is just as influential. Rampant inflation usually means higher costs for building a home, which puts upward pressure on the prices of new homes. As these prices rise, so (eventually) do the prices of existing homes. Thus, for investors, higher inflation usually means greater capital appreciation. Higher inflation also means higher interest rates, and for investors who have already locked in their borrowing costs with long-term fixed-rate mortgages, rising interest rates could generate substantial benefits. The true cost of mortgage borrowing usually goes down when interest rates go up for fixed-rate borrowers. For example, if you are locked into a 7 percent, 30-year, fixed-rate mortgage loan, and mortgage rates rise to 9 percent, you are now paying below-market borrowing costs. For investors contemplating real estate investments, rising interest rates mean that the costs of borrowing are rising. In some locations where rent increases are not keeping pace with inflation, rising borrowing costs may make a real estate investment prohibitive because the projected revenues (i.e., rents) may not be enough to offset the borrowing costs plus other expenses. The 30-year fixed-rate mortgage is the primary interest-rate indicator for residential real estate. For commercial mortgages, 5-, 7-, and 10-year Treasury yields are key indicators because these loans are usually priced off the Treasury yield curve.

The value of real estate is also influenced by monetary and fiscal policy. The Federal Reserve influences the direction of interest rates. The federal government's tax policies influence real estate values via changing depreciation rules, tax rates, and favored tax status for real estate properties.

Investors need to recognize that the commercial real estate sector sometimes marches to its own drummer. Commercial real estate has its own cycles, which are heavily influenced by the general ups and downs of the economy. Commercial real estate is in a down cycle when there is an overabundance of properties (i.e., overbuilding). This was the case in the early 1990s. When commercial real estate is in a recession, rental rates drop, vacancies rise, and values plummet. If investors take a long-term view of commercial real estate investing, a good time to buy properties is when the industry is in recession, and a good time to sell properties is when the industry is approaching a peak in expansion, as represented by low vacancies and rising rental rates.

Real Estate and Taxes

Anyone who has invested in real estate knows that the tax rules are changed as frequently as the diapers on a six-month-old baby. The current era is no exception. Before investing in real estate, *review the tax consequences with your accountant*. A cursory glance at the tax consequences of real estate investing is given here, but there are no guarantees that the tax rules will be the same when you are ready to pull the trigger and invest in real estate.

Under the current tax laws, owners of real estate investments are subject to a two-tiered tax rate:

1. Investors will pay 20 percent on any gain between the purchase price and selling price.

2. Any depreciation deductions will be taxed at a 25 percent rate (this is called the recapture rate).

To illustrate, suppose you purchased a $200,000 rental home last year, sold the home for $220,000 this year, and are claiming $20,000 in depreciation deductions during the time you owned the home. The depreciation deductions would total $5,000 (25 percent of $20,000), and the capital gains tax would total $4,000, for a total tax bill of $9,000.

The current 20 percent capital gains rate on stocks and bonds appears to be a bit more attractive than the 20–25 percent tax rate mix on rental real estate. But you need to remember that the difference in tax rates between real estate and stocks/bonds should not be the overriding factor. For some investors, owning a physical asset that is totally under their control is more attractive than indirectly owning a company via equities. And, investors have much greater leverage with real estate. A rental property can be purchased with a relatively small down payment. But perhaps the most attractive feature of a rental property investment is that the mortgage loan is essentially being paid off by the cash flows (i.e., rent) from the property, while the property is appreciating in value.

Investors also benefit from the ability to depreciate their asset (i.e., the rental property). In the example above, the investor claimed $20,000 per year in depreciation deductions. If the investor were in the 28 percent tax bracket, the depreciation would translate into $5,600 (28 percent of $20,000) in reduced taxes. However, as pointed out earlier, when the property is sold, the investor will be forced to pay 25 percent of the depreciation deductions. So, the investor in this example earned $600.

Investment Rules for Real Estate

As an investor, your objective is to achieve a competitive return on your real estate investments. For direct real estate investments (i.e., investing in rental property), the combination of the cash flows and the long-term capital gain will determine the rate of return you will earn. For indirect real estate investments (e.g., mutual funds and REITs), your objective should be to achieve a return that far exceeds that of inflation. And if the real estate markets go into a tailspin, *do not* dump some of your rental property investments without thinking through the possibilities. The key to investing in real estate is to focus on the long-term capital gains from the eventual sale of the property or properties. Property values may go up or down, depending on the state of the economy and the direction of interest rates and inflation. If you have a longer-run view and the cash flow from your property covers your mortgage costs plus expenses, or if your REIT continues to pay hefty dividends, don't change course for the sake of change.

Like stocks and bonds, real estate investments are dependent on the phase of the business cycle and the relative levels of inflation and interest rates. Real estate values usually rise in expansions and are more sluggish during recessions. Real estate values are also heavily influenced by the direction of inflation and interest rates. But changes in real estate values do not march to the same drummer as changes in stocks and bonds. Real estate values are not as sensitive to fluctuations in economic activity as stock and bond values are. It would be unwise to buy and sell investment properties in response to a monthly economic report. Even if you have invested in a REIT or a real estate mutual fund, be patient and keep an investment eye on longer-term real estate trends. Don't do anything capricious.

Specifically, real estate, like other sectors of the economy, is vulnerable to an economic downturn. A recession could bring hardship to commercial tenants, who may be forced out of business or have difficulty meeting their lease obligations. The value of commercial real estate would then be depressed. Recession also means that consumers are cutting back on shopping, which dampens business profits. That sequence has negative implications for income-producing properties, particularly retail shopping centers and office buildings. With the stock market out of favor during a recession, investors will look for competitive returns, and real estate may be a good place to park some funds. A recession may present an opportunity to selectively purchase real estate properties at relatively low prices in anticipation of good times ahead.

A recovery and expansion usually bode well for real estate investing. The good times are usually associated with a strong job market, gains in corporate earnings, and rising consumer confidence. Office, industrial, and warehouse properties all perform well during upturns. Similarly, robust consumer spending lifts all boats for retail shopping properties and hotels. And finally, job growth and wage gains provide a favorable backdrop for apartment properties.

The following investment rules are based on identifying trends in real estate values rather than market-timing investments. By putting everything we've learned about real estate investing together with the basic principles for investing in both bad and good times (Chapter 5), we can create an excellent backdrop for developing investment rules for real estate. A top ten list of "Grow-Rich Rules" for real estate investing is augmented by "More Grow-Rich Rules for Real Estate" at the end of this chapter.

The Top Ten Grow-Rich Rules for Real Estate

INVESTMENT RULE 1

In general, an expanding economy that is experiencing sustained periods of high inflation creates a favorable investment environment for rental properties and other real estate properties and/or investments.

Rationale. Rising inflation usually means that the costs of building a home are rising, which increases the prices of new homes. When the prices of new homes rise, so do (eventually) the prices of existing homes. Thus, for investors, higher inflation usually means greater capital appreciation. When the economy is expanding, higher inflation usually means higher prices for residential and commercial real estate properties.

INVESTMENT RULE 2

During the late stages of an expansion, place a greater emphasis on commercial real estate investments than on stocks and bonds.

Rationale. Historically, real estate has been one of the best assets to hold during the late stages of an expansion. In a robust economy, income-producing property performs well because rising incomes give investors the financial wherewithal and confidence to take mortgages and place higher bids on properties. Rising corporate profits permit corporations to expand their real estate activities, increasing the demand for commercial property. Increased purchasing of REITs and real estate mutual funds could be a good alternative when the stock market indicates that it may be due for a correction and investors are anticipating a recession.

INVESTMENT RULE 3

If the economy is experiencing an expansion, all types of real estate investments are generally in favor, unless there is overbuilding in a specific market.

Rationale. A healthy and growing economy creates a favorable environment for most income-producing real estate investments. In a growing economy, people have jobs and can pay their rent. In a healthy economy, people are buying at shopping centers and workers are filling up office buildings and keeping industrial parks and warehouses busy filling orders. All of these developments are favorable for the value of commercial and residential properties.

INVESTMENT RULE 4

Assuming you have a long-term investment horizon, the environment and timing for investing in commercial real estate are favorable if the commercial real estate sector is experiencing its own "recession" during an expansion period, as evidenced by falling rental rates and rising vacancies.

Rationale. Commercial real estate has its own cycles, which are heavily influenced by the general ups and downs of the economy. Basically, commercial real estate is in a down cycle when there is an overabundance of properties (i.e., overbuilding). This was the case in the early 1990s. When commercial real estate is in a recession, rental rates are dropping, vacancies are rising, and values are plummeting. If investors take a long-term view of commercial real estate investing, a good time to buy properties is when the industry is in recession. Investors can bottom-fish, and history tells them that property values will eventually rise.

INVESTMENT RULE 5

If the economy is in the early stages of a downturn, selective investing in commercial real estate via mutual funds, REITs, and/or rental properties may be a viable alternative to out-of-favor stocks.

Rationale. When the stock market is out of favor, investors looking for competitive returns may find them in commercial real estate. One of the benefits of commercial real estate is that its performance is not highly correlated with the stock market. Commercial real estate values are dependent on such market factors as overbuilding and interest rates, which may be independent of whether the economy is mired in recession. Thus, investing in commercial real estate may be a viable alternative for reducing holdings in the stock market. A careful selection of REITs, mutual funds, and/or rental properties may help diversify your portfolio holdings.

INVESTMENT RULE 6

If the economy is in a downturn and consumer spending is slowing down, avoid retail properties, particularly shopping centers.

Rationale.   Consumer spending slows appreciably during a recession, potentially reducing consumer traffic at shopping malls. Retail property owners may be faced with the prospects of replacing tenants that are experiencing financial difficulties.

INVESTMENT RULE 7

A recession may not be a good time to directly purchase rental home properties. Families (renters) may be facing hard times ahead.

Rationale.   Purchasing your first rental home during a recession may be bad timing. Recessions are usually associated with job losses, divorces, bankruptcies, and so on. Tenants find it more difficult to meet their monthly rent obligations.

INVESTMENT RULE 8

A recession, particularly if inflationary pressures have subsided, may be an opportune time to bottom-fish for commercial real estate properties.

Rationale.   You cannot market-time commercial real estate investments. The purchase of a commercial property is a long-term investment. Taking advantage of bad times and picking off quality properties at bargain prices is a solid strategy. Look for properties rented by stable tenants that can generate a steady cash flow during both bad and good times.

INVESTMENT RULE 9

Postpone direct real estate investments (in rental property) if interest rates are rising and market rents are lagging inflation.

Rationale. Rising interest rates mean that the costs of borrowing are rising. In locations where rent increases are not keeping pace with inflation, rising borrowing costs may make a real estate investment prohibitive. The projected revenues (i.e., rents) may not be enough to offset the borrowing costs plus other expenses.

INVESTMENT RULE 10

Place a greater emphasis on real estate investments if interest rates are falling and properties are retaining their value.

Rationale. A decline in interest rates means that the costs of borrowing are falling. In locations where properties are retaining value, direct real estate investments (in rental properties) usually offer favorable performance characteristics.

More Grow-Rich Rules for Real Estate

INVESTMENT RULE 11

If the Federal Reserve cuts (or raises) the federal funds rate by at least ¼ of a percentage point, it may be a good time to purchase (or sell) REITs or real estate mutual funds, which are interest-sensitive investments.

Rationale. A decision to lower the federal funds rate originates from an accommodative Federal Reserve (it is increasing the money supply). Lower interest rates are always viewed favorably by real estate investors.

Because lower rates reduce the costs of borrowing to cover real estate purchases, they help REITS and real estate mutual funds. In addition, a more accommodative Fed eventually spurs a pickup in economic activity, providing a more favorable backdrop for the real estate markets. Conversely, a raise in the federal funds rate indicates that a less accommodative Federal Reserve is reducing the money supply. Investors usually view higher interest rates as a negative development in the markets. Higher interest rates raise the cost of borrowing for real estate purchases. REITs and real estate mutual fund performance are harmed. In addition, a less accommodative Fed portends an eventually slowing of economic activity, which also poses a threat to real estate values.

INVESTMENT RULE 12

Invest in specific real estate categories that are the primary beneficiaries of the long-term spending patterns of the baby boomer population group.

Rationale. The aging baby boomers are now in the 35–44 and 45–54 age groups; these are their peak earning and buying years. Selected categories in the real estate sector, such as retirement homes, second homes, trade-up homes, and vacation homes, are among the real estate investments that will be positively impacted by the boomer spending patterns.

INVESTMENT RULE 13

Invest in health-care-related real estate properties as a relatively safe, long-term (10- to 20-year), boomer-related investment.

Rationale. Baby boomers will be spending heavily on health care as they age. Health-care-sector real estate projects (developments) are relatively safe long-term (10- to 20-year) investments because there will always be a need (i.e., demand) for health-care-related services as people age.

INVESTMENT RULE 14

In general, if you are contemplating directly investing in real estate, look for a residential rather than a commercial property.

Rationale.   The learning curve for investing in residential rental properties is much flatter than the learning curve for investing in commercial real estate. Acquiring a residential property is virtually identical to purchasing your own home (which many of us have already done), with the exception of learning how to be a landlord. In contrast, if you acquire commercial properties, you will need to learn the art of valuing commercial real estate, projecting cash flow, calculating an internal rate of return, and so on. Office buildings, shopping centers, warehouses, and industrial parks are only some of the commercial properties you might encounter.

INVESTMENT RULE 15

If you are investing in a residential rental property, place a greater emphasis on three-bedroom, two-bath homes.

Rationale.   This is a no-brainer investment play. Three-bedroom, two-bath homes are safer investments because, in most communities, there is a relatively high demand for this size of home, so prices stay firm. In addition, these homes attract relatively small families, which tend to be more stable renters.

INVESTMENT RULE 16

If possible, invest in the cheapest or worst house in the most expensive and best neighborhood.

Rationale.   By investing in a home in poor condition in a neighborhood in which the other homes are in good or excellent condition, you are acquiring a home with enormous upside potential for future value. Some minor work, such as a partial remodeling of the kitchen or wallpapering or painting some rooms, may create immediate value in your investment.

INVESTMENT RULE 17

Emphasize location, convenient transportation, schools, and shopping when selecting a property.

Rationale. As any real estate agent will tell you—location, location, location. However, it is equally important to emphasize how accessible the property is to good transportation (e.g., buses, trains, highways, an airport), a good school system, and a wide variety of shopping outlets. These neighborhood factors are essential in attracting relatively young families—your primary target as renters.

INVESTMENT RULE 18

Before financing a property through a financial institution, ask the seller of the property if he or she is willing to offer some financing.

Rationale. If you find a house you would like to buy and you have not yet shopped for a mortgage, ask the seller of the property if he or she is willing to offer some financing. Depending on how anxious the owner is to sell, favorable seller financing terms may be an option.

INVESTMENT RULE 19

Take advantage of the tax benefits (i.e., mortgage interest, depreciation, and property tax deductions) of a real estate investment by purchasing your (retired) parents' home and leasing it back to them.

Rationale. If your parents are near or at retirement, it may be wise to purchase their home and lease it back to them. You can then take advantage of the usual tax deductions (i.e., mortgage interest, property taxes, and depreciation), which will benefit you more than your elderly parents because you will be in your high-tax-bracket years.

INVESTMENT RULE 20

When selecting a REIT investment, pay more attention to the underlying property(ies) than to the current yield.

Rationale. A Real Estate Investment Trust (REIT) is a financial entity that permits investors to pool their funds for real estate investment. REITs are relatively attractive because they offer certain tax pooling advantages. The current yield on REITs can be somewhat misleading; before making any real estate investment, become familiar and comfortable with the underlying property(ies). When you study the prospectus, focus on the value of the property, especially its ability to generate cash flows.

INVESTMENT RULE 21

When possible, hold a real estate investment for at least 18 months so that you can take advantage of the long-term capital gains provision of the Internal Revenue Code. Long-term capital gains are taxed at a maximum of 25 percent for a holding period of more than 18 months. Short-term holding periods of 18 months or less are taxed at a maximum tax rate of 39.6 percent.

Rationale. This is pretty straightforward. If you are contemplating selling one of your real estate investments, the amount of taxes you pay to Uncle Sam will depend on the length of your ownership (holding period). The longer you hold on to an investment, the less you will have to pay the government for your capital gains.

INVESTMENT RULE 22

If you are looking to diversify your investment portfolio, which is now comprised of stocks and bonds, REITs provide a diversified investment alternative.

Rationale. Historically, investment returns on real estate march in a different parade than equity and bond returns. REITs are excellent diversifying investments to add to a stock/bond portfolio.

INVESTMENT RULE 23

Investors may want to avoid investing heavily in REITs during a low and stable inflation period.

Rationale. Returns on REITs depend on the cash flows from real estate owned, as well as the buying and selling of properties (capital gains). Large capital gains on real estate are not likely to be earned in a low and stable inflation environment.

9

INVESTING IN
OPTIONS AND FUTURES

Purchase a dozen eggs and the chances are that one of the eggs will be broken. Put a dozen people in a room and the chances are that one of those people will be a daredevil. A daredevil is not necessarily a bad egg, but in any group of people, there is always someone willing to take a risk or try something new.

There is a little daredevil in all of us—a yearning to ride the Cyclone, the Anaconda, or whatever the largest and scariest roller coaster in town is called. Some people have an urge to jump out of airplanes (hopefully, with parachutes) just for the "kick" of it. In financial situations, some people have a desire to gamble with their money. There are two easy ways to satisfy this urge: (1) go to a gambling casino, or (2) enter the world of high-risk investing in options and futures.

This chapter is for people who just can't break their gambling habit. About 9 out of 10 nonprofessional investors lose money in the options/futures investment game, yet some can't seem to walk away from it. Investors in options and futures take a flier on commodities (e.g., copper, oranges, etc.), stocks, and interest rates. The attraction is leverage. Investing in options and futures offers investors an enormous amount of leverage. Substantial gains can be generated, but so can exceptional losses. The key to options/futures investing is market timing; some less risky uses of options contracts can also assist investors with their portfolio strategies. So sit back, put on your harness, and buckle your seat belt. You're about to take a ride through the wonderful world of options and futures.

Terms and Definitions

buying long (options):   An agreement to purchase a contract in the future at a specific price.

call option: The holder has the option to buy the underlying security.

covered option: An option written against an opposite position in the stock market.

futures contract: A commitment to buy or sell a specific commodity or financial instrument on a designated settlement date at a predetermined price.

intrinsic value: The difference between the strike price of an option and the price of a stock is the option's intrinsic value.

long position (futures contract):   The purchase of a number of futures contracts at a fixed purchase price.

long put (options):   An agreement to sell a specific security at a specified striking price within a given time.

margin (futures):   A deposit on a future commitment to buy or sell a futures contract.

naked option: An option written without having any opposite position. The option writer is exposed to maximum risk.

put option: The holder has the option to sell the underlying security.

short call (options):   A means of providing protection against unknown future borrowing costs by generating income.

short position (futures contract):   The seller of a futures contract agrees to sell the underlying commodity to the buyer on the expiration date and at the fixed sales price.

straddle: A combination trade in which the investor purchases a put and a call on the same stock. Both carry the same exercise price and mature on the same date.

strike price (options):   The price at which a contract must be bought or sold at a stated time.

The Players

There used to be good players and poor players (in more ways than one) in the world of options and futures investing. The good players were and still are the professionals—commodities brokers, mutual fund/pension managers, and financial institutions. The poor players were and always will be the daredevils who want to test their skills by playing the options/futures game. But today there is another category of players—individuals who have learned to conservatively use options and futures to their advantage. They invest in these instruments without taking on too much risk. They also have learned what many institutional investors have known for some time now—investing in futures and options is an effective way of hedging some of the risks (i.e., interest rate risk and price risk) inherent in stock and bond investments. We will spend most of this chapter focusing on these hedging strategies.

How to Invest in Options and Futures

The futures market today can thank the farmers of yesteryear for its existence. In the late 1800s, farmers and buyers of wheat began to commit to future exchanges of grain for cash. These futures exchanges grew out of the farmers' need to "sell" their crops before they were even harvested. For example, a farmer would agree during the winter to deliver 10,000 bushels of wheat to a dealer by the end of June, for a set price. This helped both the farmer and the dealer; the farmer was assured his price, and the dealer knew his costs for the grain in advance. In most instances, the farmer and the dealer exchanged a contract to outline their futures transaction. It was not long before "speculators" came into the picture and began trading (buying and selling) these futures contracts. Hence, the beginning of the futures market.

Investing in the futures/options markets has been made easier and more accessible to investors with the advent of the Internet investment sites. Most sites that offer information on stocks and bonds in the cash market also provide information on futures and options. All of the major futures/options exchanges offer Web links with a long and varied menu of market data, product descriptions, and market analyses. The leading exchanges are: the Chicago Mercantile Exchange, the Chicago Board of Trade, the Chicago Board Options Exchange, the Coffee, Sugar, and Cocoa Exchange, the Kansas City Board of Trade, the London International Financial Futures and Options Exchange, and the New York Mercantile Exchange. These sites—and others, including bloomberg.com, thestreet.com, and most of the investment banking companies (e.g., Morgan Stanley)—offer information and commentary on futures and options traded in agriculture, metals, energy, "softs" (cocoa, sugar, and so on), and financial instruments (bonds and other securities). Essentially, investors can receive news, charts, research, and quotes on all of the above.

Why does playing in the options and futures markets usually result in large gains as well as large losses? Because of leverage. With options and futures, the investor puts up a relatively small amount of money to control a larger sum of money. To better understand the advantages of leverage in the options and futures world, let's walk through how both futures and options investing works.

Futures Investing

A futures contract is a commitment to buy or sell a specific commodity or financial instrument on a designated settlement date at a predetermined price. It is important to emphasize that no real purchase is involved. There is only a contractual commitment to purchase at a later date—if not offset before the contract matures.

Most futures contracts are transacted on exchange trading floors. The traders stand in pits and yell, scream, and hand-signal futures trades on behalf of their clients. The most popular futures exchange is the Chicago Board of Trade, which has large trading pits for U.S. Treasury securities and for agricultural products such as corn and soybeans. There are also futures contracts for such commodities as sugar, orange juice, cocoa, coffee, gold, and heating oil.

When investing in futures contracts, it is important to remember that they expire in a relatively short period of time. Institutional investors and financial services companies primarily use futures contracts for hedging price fluctuations of the underlying commodities or financial instruments, rather than for speculating on the value of the actual underlying commodity.

Here is how the futures arrangement works. The buyer of the futures contract takes a long position and purchases the futures contract at a fixed price. He or she has then entered into an agreement to buy the underlying commodity (e.g., wheat) from a seller at the expiration of the contract. The seller of the futures contract is said to be taking a short position. He or she agrees to sell the underlying commodity to the buyer, at the fixed sales price, when the contract expires. As time elapses, the value of this futures contract fluctuates, depending on market conditions.

It is important to understand that delivery of a futures contract almost never takes place. Both the buyer and the seller get out of the contract before it expires. The buyer, who has a long position, will take an offsetting short position; and the seller, who has a short position, will take an offsetting long position.

Entering the futures market provides investors with an opportunity to invest in their expectations of future prices of the underlying commodity, stock, or financial instrument. For example, investors could invest in stock indexes, such as the S&P 500 Index, every day. But there is also a futures contract on the S&P 500 Index. The futures price of this index reflects not only the current cash prices of the listed companies, but also the expectations of future prices and general economic factors that will influence the value of the S&P 500 Index several months in the future.

Perhaps the most useful application of futures investing involves hedging a specific cash investment or portfolio of investments. Usually, institutions or financial services companies are in the business of hedging their cash positions against the interest rates or price risks of the underlying securities. For example, suppose a commercial bank is holding a portfolio comprised of Treasury securities. If interest rates go up, the value of the bank's securities portfolio falls. For protection against the interest-rate risk, the bank can hedge its position (i.e., interest-rate risk exposure) by selling (taking a short position) enough Treasury futures contracts to cover the expected loss in value of the portfolio if interest rates rise. Because the price of the underlying Treasury securities and the price of the Treasury futures contracts historically move in tandem, the futures position will profit enough to offset the cash Treasury portfolio losses.

For speculators, futures investing has two basic advantages over other investments:

1. Investors can earn a higher return on their investment in the futures market because the investments are more leveraged, and

futures prices tend, on average, to change more quickly than stock prices or real estate. Generally, investors can invest about 15 percent as margin, yet these funds control the full value of the underlying contract as it moves up and down. The investor almost never has to put up the remaining 85 percent because delivery of a contract rarely takes place.

2. Commissions on futures transactions are relatively small compared to stock transactions.

One final point to consider when contemplating investing in futures contracts: Futures prices fluctuate and are more volatile than stock prices. When you purchase equity in a company, it is likely that the company has an earnings history, and its stock price will not be subject to wide swings on a regular basis. On the other hand, most of the commodities and financial instruments that are behind most futures contracts are subject to wide variations in value throughout the year, and their futures price frequently changes in value throughout a trading day. However, investing in the futures market poses challenges. You would lose before you begin if you tried to compete with the institutional investors that professionally trade futures contracts, using both fundamental and technical (i.e., charting) analysis. However, some general movements in the economy might indicate the future direction of an underlying commodity and/or financial instrument. When you are comfortable with your forecast and have a desire to leverage your investment, futures investing may prove beneficial. After a primer on the options market, we will lay out some investment rules to take advantage of the leveraging benefits of futures investing.

Options Investing

Options are like utility infielders in baseball: they give you flexibility and can play most positions on the diamond (first base, second base, third base, or shortstop) as needed. Or better yet, options are like having Batman's utility belt wrapped around your waist. By reaching into your utility belt, you can select the right option and avoid getting into trouble by tailoring your investment position to your own situation and risk level.

An option is a contract between two parties. It grants one the right (but not the obligation) to purchase or sell shares of the underlying stock (security) at a specified price on or before a given date. Once the date has passed, the option expires and ceases to exist. It is important to note that the seller of an option is obligated to sell the shares to the buyer of the option, at the specified price, upon the buyer's request.

The price of an option is known as the *premium*—the amount a buyer pays to insure against an adverse change in the price of a stock or bond. In the stock market, both call and put options are sold. Each is designed to manage the risk of fluctuating security prices and interest rates. The premium represents the maximum amount of risk a buyer assumes when purchasing an option. Unlike an open futures position, an open option position has limited downside risk; a buyer can lose no more than the amount paid for the premium. A call option gives the holder the option to buy the underlying security; a put option gives the holder the option to sell the underlying security. The price at which the option holder has the right to purchase or sell the underlying security is the strike price. Options can be exercised at any time up to the exercise date.

The strike price of an option, relative to the current underlying security price, determines its intrinsic value. For example, if a call option had a strike price of $96 and the underlying share price was $98, the call would have an intrinsic value of $2 ($98–$96). This option is termed *in the money* because you could exercise the option and purchase (long) the underlying company shares at $96, and then offset (sell) the position at $98 for a profit. If, on the other hand, the company share price was $95, the option would be *out of the money* and probably would not be exercised because the buyer could purchase the underlying company shares at a lower price in the stock market. If the stock was priced at $96, the option is *at the money* and has no intrinsic value.

On other side of the options market are the sellers or option writers. They take potentially unlimited risk if the option is exercised. Not to be mistaken for the latest from Calvin Klein fashions, the three types of written options are termed *dressed, covered,* and *naked.* A dressed option is an option written against an opposite position in the stock market; for example, one might dress a short stock position by writing a put against it. A covered option is an option written against a long position in the stock market; for example, an owner of IBM stock covers his or her position by writing a call option on it. A naked option exposes an option writer to the most risk because it is written without having any opposite position. For some investors, the primary motivation in writing options is the fee income generated from the premium charged.

A popular options strategy is the straddle, which combines a put and call option on a given stock. In this combination trade, the investor purchases, on the same stock, a put and a call that carry the same exercise price and mature on the same date. For example, if a stock is selling at $10 per share and the investor wants to hedge against a price move, up or down, he or she will purchase both a call option with a strike price of $11 and a put option with an $11 strike price. Each option costs the investor $1. Profits will be made if either the call or the put increases in value by more than $2. If the stock price significantly rises in value, so will the call option. Similarly, if the stock price significantly falls in value, the put option will rise in value. Only if the stock price stays within a tight range does the investor lose money. And the investor has limited downside risk—he or she can lose only the amount paid for the total of the call and put options: $2.

In summary, investing in options (purchasing calls and puts) can provide investors with flexibility, leverage, and limited risk for the buyer. Furthermore, to investors holding stock portfolios, stock options give these advantages:

1. They can protect their stock or portfolio of stocks against a drop in price.

2. They can add income to their stock portfolio.

3. They can benefit from either an increase or a decrease in a stock's price without actually purchasing or selling the stock.

4. They can take advantage of a large swing in stock price (up or down) without knowing the direction in which prices will move. All of these strategies assume that the investors are comfortable with options trading. Compared to the regulated buying and selling of stocks and bonds, both options and futures investments are complex transactions.

Portfolio Insurance (Stock Index Trading)

In the real world of stock investing, individual investors are up against "elephants." Elephants are the professional investors (major banks, Wall Street investment banks, mutual fund managers, and so on) who are actively involved in *program trading*—computer-assisted market trading that makes continuous stock trades in portfolios as the relative prices between two or more securities change. One of the more popular programs is called *portfolio insurance,* and although an individual investor could not be expected to compete head-on with an elephant, he or she can apply the principles of portfolio insurance to his or her own investment strategies.

Portfolio insurance uses the futures market as insurance against general stock price declines. An investor could sell (take a short position on) S&P 500 Index futures contracts that expire on the date the investor plans to sell his or her stock holdings. If the stock market drops in value (as measured by the S&P 500 Index), the loss in value would be offset by a gain on the S&P 500 futures index. If the stock market rises in value, the investor will lose money on his or her futures position in the S&P 500 Index, but this loss will be offset by the gains in the stock portfolio. Whether the stock market goes up or down, the investor loses nothing but the initial cost of purchasing a futures contract. This is the cost of portfolio insurance.

Options, Futures, and the Economy

The relationships between the options/futures markets and the economy are really no different from the relationships between their underlying markets—the stock, bond, and commodities markets—and the economy. The values of futures contracts or options contracts will move almost in tandem with the underlying cash markets (i.e., the stock, bond, and commodities markets). The difference is that the investment is in a view of the future. But investments in the stock, bond, and commodities markets are really investments in the future as well. For example, when you purchase shares of stock, you do so because you have an expectation of what the future earnings will be for that particular company. Similarly, when you invest in the options/futures markets, you are merely reflecting your beliefs in the cash market. All the fundamentals that apply to the cash market—expectations of GDP growth and the direction of inflation and interest rates—apply to the options/futures market.

Investment Rules for Options and Futures

Our approach for developing investment rules for the options and futures markets will be very different from our development of investment strategies for the stock, bond, and real estate markets. Options and futures are simply a speculative play; they are tools that investors may use in improving investment portfolio performance. There is no magic in employing these instruments during recessions, recoveries, or expansions. Investors are already making decisions on how to invest in stocks, bonds, and real estate, depending on whether the environment is characterized as bad or good. Strategies for using options and futures are: (1) gamble (or speculate) or (2) use the instruments to supplement and/or complement the returns earned on current stock and bond holdings, or to reduce risk on those holdings. If you are speculating, market timing becomes important. If you are attempting to complement your portfolio's returns and risks, executions become important.

Two categories of investment rules are given here: The Top Ten Rules for Futures Investing and The Top Ten Rules for Options Investing. Most, if not all of these rules, could be employed during both bad and good times.

The Top Ten Rules for Futures Investing

INVESTMENT RULE 1

As a general rule, invest in the futures market only if you are comfortable with the inherent risks.

Rationale. This rule may seem very obvious, but it must be drilled home to nonprofessional investors. Investing in the futures market exposes individual investors to enormous risks because of the complexities of the market and the amount of leverage that investors are granted. About 9 out of 10 nonprofessional investors lose money when they invest in the futures market. The key to futures investing is market timing, which, combined with the leveraging privilege, could generate substantial gains or (more frequently) exceptional losses.

INVESTMENT RULE 2

If you are bullish on the direction of stocks and are looking for a highly leveraged investment to bet on a future market rise, take a long position (purchase) in S&P 500 Index futures contracts.

Rationale. Rather than invest in the S&P 500 Index directly in the stock market, bullish investors have the opportunity to invest in futures contracts on the S&P 500 Index. The futures prices of this index reflects not only the current cash prices of the listed companies, but also the expectations of future prices and general economic factors that are expected to influence the value of the S&P 500 Index several months into the future. And, investors can be highly leveraged by investing about 15 percent as margin, while controlling the full value of the underlying contract as it (they hope) moves upward.

INVESTMENT RULE 3

If you are bullish on the direction of bond prices (you believe interest rates will drop) and are looking for a highly leveraged investment to bet on a future bond price rise, take a long position (purchase) in futures contracts on 10-year U.S. Treasury bonds.

Rationale. Rather than invest directly in U.S. Treasury bonds, investors who believe that interest rates will drop in the near future (i.e., bond prices will rise) have the opportunity to invest in futures contracts on U.S. Treasury bonds. The futures price of these bonds reflect not only their current cash prices, but also the expectations of future prices and general economic factors that will influence the direction of interest rates several months into the future. Investors can be highly leveraged by investing about 15 percent as margin, while controlling the full value of the underlying contract as it (they hope) moves upward.

INVESTMENT RULE 4

If you currently own a number of stocks that you wish to hold, but believe the stock market will turn down in the near term, you can protect (hedge) against a stock price drop by selling enough S&P 500 Index futures contracts to cover the expected loss in your stock portfolio.

Rationale. One of the more useful applications of futures investing is hedging a specific cash investment or portfolio of investments. Investors who turn bearish but do not want to sell their equity holdings can turn to the futures market for assistance. They can effectively hedge their cash positions and protect against a stock price drop by selling enough S&P 500 Index futures contracts to cover the expected loss in their stock portfolio.

INVESTMENT RULE 5

If you currently are invested in bonds and do not want to sell your holdings, but you believe that interest rates will rise in the near term, you can protect (hedge) against an interest rate rise (i.e., a drop in bond prices) by selling enough Treasury bond futures contracts to cover the expected loss in your bond portfolio.

Rationale. One of the more useful applications of futures investing is hedging a specific cash investment or portfolio of investments. Investors who believe interest rates will rise in the near term but do not want to sell their bond holdings can turn to the futures market for assistance. They can effectively hedge their cash positions and protect against a bond price drop by selling enough Treasury bond futures contracts to cover the expected loss in their bond portfolio.

INVESTMENT RULE 6

You can use the futures market as insurance against general stock price declines (this is called portfolio insurance) by selling S&P 500 Index futures contracts that expire on the date you plan to sell your stock holdings.

Rationale. Essentially, portfolio insurance is using the futures market as insurance against general stock price declines. An investor could sell (take a short position) S&P 500 Index futures contracts that expire on the date that the investor plans to sell his or her stock holdings. If the stock market drops in value (as measured by the S&P 500 Index), the loss in value would be offset by a gain on the S&P futures contract. Of course, if the stock market rises in value, the investor will lose money on his or her futures position in the S&P 500 Index, but this loss will be offset by the gains in the stock portfolio. Whether the stock market goes up or down, the investor loses nothing but the initial cost of purchasing a futures contract. This is the cost of portfolio insurance.

INVESTMENT RULE 7

If you anticipate a higher-than-expected increase in the monthly consumer price index (CPI), take a short position in Treasury bond futures contracts in advance of the CPI release, to earn speculative profits and/or to protect against an expected loss in your current bond holdings. Conversely, if you anticipate a lower-than-expected drop in the monthly CPI, take a long position in Treasury bond futures contracts in advance of the CPI release, to earn speculative profits.

Rationale. The bond market usually reacts adversely to higher-than-expected increases in the monthly CPI. For example, if the current inflation rate is 3 percent and the monthly CPI release indicates an annualized inflation rate of 4 percent, there will most likely be an upward tick in interest rates, which could be as much as ¼ of a percentage point. Taking a short position (selling contracts) in Treasury bond futures contracts will likely generate substantial profits when the CPI news breaks. Conversely, falling inflation rates are always viewed favorably by investors in the bond market, and there will most likely be a downward tick in interest rates. Taking a long position (buying contracts) in Treasury bond futures contracts will likely generate substantial profits when the CPI news breaks.

INVESTMENT RULE 8

If the economy is operating close to full employment and you anticipate a higher-than-expected nonfarm payroll number, take a short position in Treasury bond futures contracts in advance of the release, to earn speculative profits and/or to protect the value of your current bond holdings. Conversely, if the economy is operating close to full employment and you anticipate a lower-than-expected nonfarm payroll number, take a long position in Treasury bond futures contracts in advance of the release, to earn speculative profits.

Rationale. If the economy is close to full employment, a higher-than-expected nonfarm payroll number (usually greater than 200,000 employees) generally means robust GDP growth and building inflationary pressures, which will exert downward pressure on bond prices. Taking a short position in Treasury bond futures will likely generate substantial profits. And if the economy is close to full employment, a lower-than-expected nonfarm payroll number (usually less than 100,000 employees) generally means weakening GDP growth and easing inflationary pressures, which will exert upward pressure on bond prices. Taking a long position in Treasury bond futures will likely generate substantial profits.

INVESTMENT RULE 9

If you anticipate a Federal Reserve interest rate hike and believe that it is the first in a series of tightening moves, take a short position in Treasury bond futures contracts in advance of the Fed announcement, to earn speculative profits and/or protect the value of your current bond portfolio. If you anticipate a Federal Reserve interest rate cut and believe that it is the first in a series of accommodative moves, take a long position in Treasury bond futures contracts in advance of the Fed announcement, to earn speculative profits.

Rationale. Raising the federal funds rate (i.e., decreasing the money supply) is the action of a less accommodative Federal Reserve. Further rate hikes are likely in the future. Over time, bond values are expected to deteriorate, prompting investors to place less emphasis on bond investments and to shorten the terms of their investments. Taking a short position in Treasury bond futures will likely result in profits. Lowering the federal funds rate (i.e., increasing the money supply) is the action of a more accommodative Federal Reserve. Further rate reductions are possible in the future. By placing greater emphasis on your bond portfolio and lengthening the terms to maturity, you should improve your investment performance. Taking a long position in Treasury bond futures will likely result in substantial price gains.

INVESTMENT RULE 10

If a crisis somewhere in the world has caused uncertainty and U.S. Treasury bonds become a safe haven for foreign funds, take a long position in Treasury bond futures, to earn speculative profits.

Rationale.   Increased demand for U.S. Treasury securities will eventually apply downward pressure to Treasury yields and upward pressure on prices. The strategy for savvy futures investors is to purchase Treasury futures contracts at the beginning of a crisis situation. This almost guarantees realized gains by the end of the crisis.

The Top Ten Rules for Options Investing

INVESTMENT RULE 1

If you are bullish on the direction of a particular stock and/or the general direction of the stock market, and you want to participate in the company's and/or market's rise but with limited downside risk, purchase the appropriate call options.

Rationale.   Investing in call options offers investors an opportunity to participate in a rise in prices, but with limited downside risk. The investor purchases a call option on (1) a particular company, to bet on the company, or (2) the S&P 500 Index, to bet on the entire market. An open option position has limited downside risk; a buyer can lose no more than the amount paid for the premium. Rather than invest in a particular company and/or in the S&P 500 Index directly in the stock market, bullish investors have the opportunity to invest a smaller amount of funds but to participate in the same gains if the company and/or S&P 500 Index rises in value.

> ### INVESTMENT RULE 2
>
> If you are bullish on the direction of bond prices (you believe interest rates will drop and want to participate in the market's rise but with limited downside risk), purchase call options on 30-year Treasury bonds.

Rationale. Rather than invest directly in U.S. Treasury bonds, investors who believe that interest rates will drop in the near future (i.e., bond prices will rise) have the opportunity to purchase call options on 30-year Treasury bonds. An open option position has limited downside risk; a buyer can lose no more than the amount paid for the premium, but he or she can also participate in the same gains as the underlying bond investment.

> ### INVESTMENT RULE 3
>
> If you are bearish on the stock market and want to protect your current portfolio of stocks against a drop in value, purchase put options on the S&P 500 Index.

Rationale. If you purchase a put option on the S&P 500 Index and the stock market drops in value, the profits you will earn on the option contract will partially or fully offset the loss in value on your stock portfolio.

> ### INVESTMENT RULE 4
>
> To earn fee income, write a covered call option against a long position in the stock market.

Rationale. Writing a covered call option against an underlying stock earns an investor fee income generated from the premium charged. If the price of the underlying stock goes down, the investor earns the full fee income on the written call option. However, if the stock price goes up, the purchaser of the call option may exercise the option. In this case, the investor already owns the underlying stock and can use those proceeds to pay off the option buyer.

INVESTMENT RULE 5

If stock market prices are volatile (as measured by the S&P 500 Index) and you want to make money on the stock market's volatility, invest in a S&P 500 Index options straddle.

Rationale. A popular investment strategy designed to take advantage of the stock market's volatility is the option straddle on the S&P 500 Index. In a straddle, an investor combines a put and a call option on the same stock, with both carrying the same exercise price and maturing on the same date. For example, if the S&P 500 Index is selling at $10 per share and the investor wants to hedge against a price move, up or down, he or she will purchase a call option with a strike price of $11 and a put option with a strike price of $11. Each option costs the investor $1. Profits will be made if either the call or the put increases in value by more than $2. Only if the stock price stays within a tight range does the investor lose money. The investor has limited downside risk. He or she can lose only the amount paid for the total of the call and put options: $2.

INVESTMENT RULE 6

If you want to invest in a particular company but do not want to commit to a substantial investment in its stock, you can invest a relatively small amount of money in a call option on that particular company and still participate in any future stock price gains the company experiences.

Rationale. A call option gives the holder the option to buy the underlying security. The price paid for this option is relatively small and is called the premium. A buyer can lose no more than the amount paid for the premium. On the other hand, if the underlying security goes up in value, so will the value of the premium. The investor then will participate in the rise in the company's stock price by selling the option at the higher premium.

INVESTMENT RULE 7

If you believe that the stock price of a particular company will fall in the near future, you can take advantage of the price drop by investing in a put option of the underlying company.

Rationale.   A put option gives the holder the option to sell the underlying company stock. The price at which the option holder has the right to sell the underlying company stock is the strike price. Suppose you own a put option for 100 shares of stock with a strike price of $20 per share, and the company stock price falls to $15 per share. Your put option gives you the right to sell 100 shares of the company stock at $20 per share. You can then buy 100 shares at the current $15 price and pocket the $5-per-share difference.

INVESTMENT RULE 8

If you are bullish on a particular stock and want to control a larger number of shares than your current funds can buy, purchase out-of-the-money call options.

Rationale.   The strike price of an option relative to the current underlying security price determines its intrinsic value. If a call option had a strike price of $96 and the underlying share price was $95, the option would be out of the money. Because this option could not be exercised until the underlying share price rose to at least $96, the premium (the price paid) for this out-of-the-money option should be relatively small. Many out-of-the-money options are priced at about $\frac{1}{8}$ to $\frac{3}{4}$ of a dollar. For just a small investment, you can control a large number of shares of stock at these low prices. The trade-off is that the underlying share price must rise by a relatively large amount before your out-of-the-money option is in the money (i.e., worth something).

> ## INVESTMENT RULE 9
>
> If the economy is operating close to capacity and you anticipate a Federal Reserve interest rate hike, purchase put options on the S&P 500 Index to take advantage of the anticipated drop in equity values as a result of the Fed's action.

Rationale. Raising the federal funds rate (i.e., decreasing the money supply) is the action of a less accommodative Federal Reserve. Further rate hikes are likely in the future. Over time, stock values can be expected to deteriorate, prompting investors to place less emphasis on stock investments. Purchasing put options on the broad stock market indexes is a way of cashing in on the stock market's anticipated tumble.

> ## INVESTMENT RULE 10
>
> If a crisis somewhere in the world causes uncertainty and U.S. Treasury bonds become a safe haven for foreign funds, purchase call options on 30-year Treasury bonds.

Rationale. Increased demand for U.S. Treasury securities will eventually apply downward pressure to Treasury yields and upward pressure on prices. The strategy for savvy options investors is to purchase call options on 30-year Treasury bonds at the beginning of a crisis situation. This almost guarantees realized gains by the end of the crisis.

10

INTERNATIONAL INVESTING

As we begin the twenty-first century, it is increasingly clear that the U.S. economy has become the central focal point of a globalized marketplace. America's economy is by far the largest in the world, but it is increasingly dependent on the international trading of its goods and services as well as the exchange rate of the U.S. dollar versus other currencies around the world.

The globalization of the world's economies has strongly influenced investment practices. The era when only well-to-do and institutional investors placed their money in countries other than the United States has ended. Globalization does not discriminate, and the PC/Internet revolution knows no borders. Through the Internet, information about other nations' economies and about foreign stock and bond markets is easily within reach. Today, investing in the European or Japanese equity and bond markets is almost as easy and as accessible as investing in the comparable U.S. markets.

To invest successfully in foreign markets, you must know more than what is happening in the U.S. financial markets. The values of foreign investments are influenced, to a large degree, by economic activity in the home country, not the United States. You must understand and monitor the economic growth prospects as well as the direction of inflation and interest rates for the countries in which you plan to commit a meaningful amount of investment funds.

Most of the Internet investment sites offer economic and investment coverage of all of the major nations in the developed world. Sites such as AOL International, Financial Times, The Economist, and Money Magazine provide a wealth of international information for investors. For example, The Economist site gives useful insight into current political and economic concerns in its Economic Indicator section—a source for economic data (e.g., GDP growth), national outlooks, forecasts, political structures, and key political players in a long list of countries. By clicking into some of the Wall Street investment banking company sites, such as Salomon Smith Barney, investors receive investment analyses and recommendations on foreign companies' stocks and bonds in all the major countries in the developed world.

International investing offers a wide range of opportunities that can add value to your portfolio. However, keep in mind that foreign economies might be in a different phase of the business cycle. When the U.S. economy is expanding, another country's economy may be contracting, or vice versa. The fiscal and monetary policies of other nations may also be strikingly different from those of America and those of other nations in the same geographic region. On the positive side, nations with economies that march to a different drummer may benefit your portfolio's overall performance by adding diversity.

The political situations in some foreign countries may be risky or even openly unstable. An economic system is only as strong as the political timber that supports it. In a span of just 20 years, the world witnessed the crumbling of communism in the Soviet Union (Russia) and Eastern Europe, the unification of Germany, Great Britain's transfer of Hong Kong to China, and Europe's attempt to unify its economies by using a single currency. Some experts have compared the process of unifying Europe's economies via a single currency to trying to make an omelet without breaking any eggs. Eventually, however, the effort is expected to be successful.

Terms and Characteristics

Although it is not necessary for most individual investors (who will depend on outside expertise) to be conversant on all of the international investment jargon, a more-than-surface understanding of the major terms and concepts will make you a more intelligent international investor.

country risk: Country risk arises whenever countries interfere with international transactions in their currencies. Some common interferences by governments are: restrictions on foreign investments by residents; limitation of the flow of capital from abroad; and regulation of the local exchange markets. Interferences almost always affect the movement of exchange rates, so they can be disruptive for currency traders. Banks, investment banks, brokers, and mutual fund managers deal with country risk by employing a staff that analyzes country risk exposure for each country with which these organizations deal (commit investments). The social, economic, and political stability of each country usually is an important factor in an assessment. The amount of currency exposure to any one nation is based on the recommendations of these country risk reports.

exchange rate: The price of one currency in terms of another. Generally, for each transaction, there is a bid (buying) rate and an offer (selling) rate. Banks and/or brokers generate income from the bid–offer spread rather than by charging a commission for each transaction.

foreign exchange markets: Foreign exchange markets arise primarily because transactions in international trade involve the currencies of different countries. For example, if a U.S. firm exports to Germany goods that must be paid for in dollars, the German importers must sell German marks to purchase U.S. dollars in the foreign exchange market.

foreign exchange transaction: A purchase or sale of one country's currency against another's.

forward transaction: A contract to purchase foreign currency when the value dates are more than two days (in the future). The forward price (rate) is fixed at the time the transaction is agreed. The currency is paid for only when the contract matures. The primary reason for buying and selling foreign currency forward is to accommodate international transactions that are not consummated in a short time. Months elapse between the time a U.S. importer of stereo systems places an order in Japan and the time the stereos are delivered. The U.S. importer has committed to pay a certain amount of yen *upon delivery.* In the meantime, the value of the yen relative to the dollar may change, for myriad reasons, and the dollar cost of the merchandise may be affected. If the importer wishes to insure against this exchange risk, he or she will enter into a forward transaction, thereby guaranteeing the current exchange rate.

spot transaction: A foreign exchange transaction that takes place in the present. The majority of foreign exchange transactions are conducted in spot.

The Benefits of International Investing

Why go international when the U.S. offers some of the greatest investment opportunities in the world? Here are two convincing reasons:

1. *Promising investment opportunities.* Substantial investment opportunities are available outside of the United States. With 96 percent of the world's population living outside U.S. borders and producing about 75 percent of the world's goods and services and almost 55 percent of the world's equity market capitalization, the opportunities outside the United States cannot be denied. Some of the largest and best companies are foreign-based, for example, Nestlé (Great Britain) and Toyota (Japan). By investing abroad, U.S. investors gain opportunities to participate in exciting and promising trends, such as the rebuilding of Eastern Europe and the expanding markets in Taiwan, Singapore, and other emerging Asian nations.

2. *Diversification.* The addition of foreign investments, particularly foreign stocks, to a portfolio reduces the investment risk because the values of U.S. investments seldom move in sync with the values of foreign investments. For instance, if the U.S. economy is experiencing an expansion, other nations' economies, somewhere in the world, may be stalled in recession. An expanding U.S. economy bodes well for stock prices, but a foreign economy in a downturn depresses stock prices abroad. Even more important, U.S. investors can lean heavily on investments in expanding foreign economies when the U.S. economy is in recession. Generally speaking, international markets experience business cycles different from those of the U.S. markets.

Perhaps the simplest way to invest overseas is to purchase international mutual funds. A wide variety are currently available to U.S. investors:

- Balanced international funds that purchase equities and bonds overseas.

- Equity international funds that are well diversified among companies all over the world.

- International equity funds that invest only in established economies in Europe (e.g., United Kingdom, Germany, and France) and the Pacific Rim nations (e.g., Japan, Hong Kong, and Australia).

- Funds that invest in companies residing in the emerging nations (e.g., Argentina, Brazil, and Indonesia).

- Single-country funds that limit their investments to companies residing in one country (e.g., Japan).

- Global mutual funds that invest in both U.S. and foreign stocks.

There are substantial "growth plays" in the emerging and/or developing nations. For example, during the past five years, China's economy has grown astronomically, compared with the more established industrialized nations of the world. Observing a nation make the transition from an infant economy to a leading industrial economy can be somewhat overwhelming, but participating in that "growth play" via investments can bring huge rewards.

If you are focused on investing in foreign bonds, your attention should be on interest rate spreads between U.S. securities and other nations' securities. If the spread is wide enough (to compensate for the exchange risk, political risk, and so on), purchasing foreign bonds may prove fruitful. The most popular investments are foreign government bonds, which have lower inherent risks than foreign company bonds. Again, for individual investors, investing in the international bond markets is usually accomplished by buying shares in a mutual fund that invests in the international bond markets—a strategy that I highly recommend. However, it is possible to invest directly in foreign companies trading on other nations' stock exchanges. Table 10–1 lists some of the leading stock exchanges around the world.

Investment Performance

A primary reason for expanding your investment horizons globally is the potential for greater returns and diversification. The factors that influence movements in the stock prices of foreign companies are the same factors that influence stock price movements of domestic companies. The value of all companies, worldwide, is influenced by the prospects for

Table 10–1   Some Leading Stock Exchanges Around the World

New York Stock Exchange	Brussels Exchange
American Stock Exchange	Stockholm Exchange
Toronto Exchange	Sydney Exchange
London Exchange	Singapore Exchange
Frankfurt Exchange	Hong Kong Exchange
Zurich Exchange	Taipei Exchange
Paris Exchange	Tokyo Exchange

corporate earnings, the health of the economy, the level and direction of interest rates and of inflation, the nation's monetary and fiscal policies, and the companies' underlying financial condition.

The U.S. equity markets do not outperform the rest of the world's equity markets year in and year out. In fact, every year, some foreign equity market(s) leads the performance statistics. The key to successful international investing is to be well diversified. You will then be invested in an equity market that will outperform the U.S. market in any given year or over the long term. Although the risks of investing in smaller economies around the world may be high, the potential for larger returns may be

Table 10–2   Average Annual Stock Market Returns
(12/31/87 to 12/31/99)

Nation	Stock Market Return
Sweden	22.28%
Hong Kong	20.04
United States	19.73
Netherlands	19.03
France	17.26
Germany	16.07
United Kingdom	14.14
Japan	2.13

Source: Morgan Stanley Capital Indexes; S&P 500 Index for U.S. stocks.

higher, too. Table 10–2 compares some of the smaller nations' stock market performance relative to the U.S. stock market during a recent ten-year period. The returns show that the U.S. stock market is not the only game in town.

Investors need to select their international stocks carefully, on a year-by-year basis. Table 10–3 shows a wide dispersion of annual stock returns for each nation's stock market. Overseas markets are driven by forces different from those that affect the U.S markets. For example, you could have earned a remarkable 99.7 percent return in Japan's stock market in 1986, and lost 36 percent in 1990. Similarly, you could have earned a 47.1 percent return in the German stock market in 1989, but lost 8.9 percent the very next year. The lesson here is that you must know the economic prospects for any nations being considered for investments. In 1996, Japan's economy was headed south after experiencing both economic growth and financial markets problems within the prior four-year period. The United Kingdom's economy was in far better shape.

If you are not inclined to invest funds in specific countries because of the time constraints (i.e., not enough time to monitor other nations'

Table 10–3   Returns for U.S. and Largest Non-U.S. Stock Markets

	Japan	United Kingdom	Germany	France	United States (S&P 500)
1999	61.8%	12.5%	20.5%	29.7%	22.4%
1998	5.2	17. 8	29.9	42.1	30.7
1997	−23.5	22.6	25.0	12.9	39.1
1996	−15.4	27.4	14.1	21.8	23.3
1995	0.9	21.3	17.0	14.8	37.5
1994	21.6	−1.6	5.1	−4.7	1.3
1993	25.7	24.4	36.3	21.6	10.0
1992	−21.3	−3.6	−9.7	3.4	7.7
1991	9.1	16.0	8.8	18.5	30.5
1990	−36.0	10.3	−8.9	−13.6	−3.2
1989	1.8	21.8	47.1	36.8	31.4

Source: Morgan Stanley Capital Indexes.

economies) or the added investment risks for each country, consider investing in a mutual fund that maintains an overall portfolio of foreign stocks. Among the world's equity markets, the EAFE (Europe, Australia, Asia, and the Far East), a leading benchmark of foreign stocks, provides an excellent comparison of the performance of the world's stocks versus the U.S. equity markets. Table 10–4 shows that, over a ten-year period, the S&P 500 Index outperformed the EAFE Index seven times. However, to give your investment portfolio greater diversity, a relatively small percentage of your funds should be committed to international markets, and a mutual fund that reflects the EAFE would be an appropriate investment strategy. Fund families such as Fidelity and Prudential offer many broad international funds as well as index funds for the EAFE and other countries' stock markets. As a general guideline, your international fund investments should be no more than 20 percent of your total investment portfolio. That ratio gives you the diversification benefits of international investing without taking on disproportionate risks.

The international bond markets offer some viable options to the U.S. securities market. The key is to focus on the spreads between U.S. security

Table 10–4 Annual Returns: EAFE vs. S&P 500 (1988–1997)		
Year	EAFE	S&P 500
1999	25.27%	21.04%
1998	18.23	28.58
1997	2.10	33.40
1996	6.36	22.96
1995	11.55	37.95
1994	8.06	1.32
1993	32.94	10.08
1992	−11.85	7.62
1991	12.50	30.47
1990	−23.20	−3.10
1989	10.80	31.69
1988	28.59	16.61

Source: The Vanguard Marketing Corporation.

yields and foreign bond yields. After adjusting for the currency and political risks for a specific country, there are times when the spread is wide enough (the foreign bond yield is greater than the U.S. comparable yield) to entice U.S. investors to buy into the international bond markets.

Table 10–5 compares returns on international bond funds versus comparable U.S. bond returns. During the decade shown, there were times when investing in foreign bonds generated favorable returns, and times when it did not. For example, the 30-year (bellwether) U.S. Treasury Bond averaged 8.58 percent for the year 1987, while the Japanese government bond averaged 4.51 percent and the German government bond averaged 6.35 percent. Even after adjusting for currency risk (neither country has much political risk), the 2.23 percent U.S./Germany interest rate spread would have produced greater returns than the 4.08 percent U.S./Japan interest rate spread. Another way of stating this is: The 6.35 percent German interest rate was more attractive than the 4.51 percent Japanese interest rate, and investors were rewarded accordingly. It is tempting to invest only

Table 10–5   International Bond Returns vs. U.S. Bond Returns

				U.S./Japan	U.S./Germany
	United States	Japan	Germany	Spread	Spread
1987	8.58	4.51	6.35	4.08	2.23
1988	8.96	4.67	6.57	4.29	2.39
1989	8.45	5.24	6.98	3.21	1.47
1990	8.61	7.36	8.66	1.25	−0.05
1991	8.14	6.41	8.43	1.73	−0.29
1992	7.67	5.25	7.78	2.41	−0.11
1993	6.60	4.20	6.47	2.40	0.13
1994	7.37	4.18	6.81	3.19	0.56
1995	6.88	3.41	6.84	3.47	0.04
1996	6.70	3.03	6.23	3.67	0.47
1997	6.61	2.20	5.67	4.41	0.94
1998	5.58	1.34	4.59	4.24	0.99
1999	5.87	1.73	4.49	4.14	1.38

Long-Term Government Bellwether Bond Yields

Source: Federal Reserve Board.

in U.S. government bonds, especially since their yields are almost always higher than the Japanese and German government bonds. In many similar matchups, U.S. government bonds offer better performance than foreign bonds. But other factors are involved. Investors in U.S. bonds get interest payments in U.S. dollars. If there is a serious inflation, the dollars they get back are not worth as much as when they lent the money. If inflation is low in Japan and Germany, the interest paid in yen or deutsche marks may offer competitive returns. Foreign bonds sometimes do offer higher nominal rates. For example, from 1990 to 1992, German government bonds paid higher interest rates than U.S. government bonds.

International Transaction Costs

Aside from the added risks of international investing, higher transaction costs are usually associated with investing in foreign markets. International mutual funds (which I recommend) charge a higher rate for each transaction. According to the Vanguard Corporation, the expense ratio of the average international stock fund is 1.67 percent, compared to 1.45 percent for the average U.S. stock fund. In addition, many international funds assess sales charges (or loads) on purchases and redemptions. The reason for these cost differentials is obvious: It is simply more costly to transact business overseas. Fees—brokerage costs, exchange fees, and custodial fees—and taxes combine to raise the cost of foreign investments.

The Players

The three major players in the international investment markets are: professional traders, institutional investors, and individual investors. The big difference is that the international investment arena includes all traders, institutions, and individuals around the world. From the vantage point of U.S. investors, the international investment markets have grown substantially during the past decade, and they are now linked by computer screens, satellite dishes, and telephone lines. Sophisticated instruments have been designed to reduce risk as well as add flexibility to international investing.

As with the other markets, traders can hold large positions in international equities, bonds, and currencies. Professional traders and institutional investors have distinct advantages in the international investing arena. Information is king in this marketplace, and the best way individual investors can participate successfully is by purchasing mutual funds and letting the professionals do the work. Relatively sophisticated investment strategies are involved, and only the professionals have the time, energy, and resources to utilize them effectively. Individual investors should at least follow the big mutual fund managers' lead. Probably the best international investment strategy is to invest in the major international mutual funds focused on equities, bonds, and currencies.

A Primer for International Investing

International investing is not for the timid. Committing your funds to foreign equities, bonds, and currencies is like walking into a party and not knowing any of the other guests. The following primer will make some introductions.

The Mechanics of International Investing

There is no global stock exchange for international investing, but information about the various national and regional markets—many of which are quite sophisticated—is available to international investors every business day, through computer networks and satellite communications. For individual investors, the mechanics of actually buying and selling foreign stocks, bonds, and currencies are almost identical to those for buying and selling domestic stocks and bonds. The same Wall Street investment banks (e.g., Merrill Lynch) or discount brokers (e.g., Charles Schwab & Co.) or mutual funds (e.g., Fidelity) that U.S. investors use for their domestic transactions are also used for their international transactions.

Markets for International Investing

The United States has, by far, the largest and most sophisticated economy in the world. When they invest in other nations' economies via stock and bond offerings, many investors who are accustomed to the comforts of steady and reliable America are entering uncharted waters. The various economies in the world range from the well-established industrialized economies (e.g., Japan, England, and France) to the emerging economies (e.g., China, Korea, and Taiwan) and then to the fragile economies (Russia). Table 10–6 offers some broad categories of the economies that are available to investors. These categories are not all-inclusive; the countries

Table 10–6 Types of Economies Available to International Investors

Well-Established Economies (Dependable Economies with a Consistent History)
United States
Japan
Germany
Canada
Great Britain
France
Australia

Established Economies (Dependable Economies But with Some Volatility)
Italy
Sweden
New Zealand
Argentina
Brazil (borderline emerging)
Chile (borderline emerging)
Mexico (borderline emerging)

Emerging Economies (Showing Signs of Becoming Established)
China
Latin America
Eastern Europe
Asia (India, Indonesia, Malaysia, Pakistan, the Philippines, South Korea, Taiwan, Thailand)

Fragile (Speculative) Economies (Economic Infrastructure Is Not in Place)
Russia
Other former Soviet Union nations
Selected nations in Africa

that are listed are just some of the more popular investment choices among international investors.

The Risks of International Investing

Certain risks inherent in international investing distinguish it from domestic investing. Four risks to an investor involved in international transactions are worth noting: (1) currency risk, (2) market risk, (3) liquidity risk, and (4) political risk.

1. *Currency risk.* The primary concern in international investing is the currency risk in the foreign exchange market. Although the foreign exchange market is highly competitive and provides traders and investors with current information at all times, its organization is unlike the stock market or futures exchanges. There is no central marketplace or exchange floor where price quotations are posted almost instantaneously for all currencies. The foreign exchange market consists of the foreign exchange departments of large multinational banks, and a number of specialized traders located throughout the world. The foreign exchange dealers in each bank may specialize in one currency or several. By telephone, they continuously communicate with other dealers regarding exchange prices and quantity information. Trades are usually consummated by dealers' word-of-mouth commitments. It is useful to think of this market as a network of telephone links, video screens, and trust.

Investing in an overseas company or a foreign country's bonds involves exchanging U.S. dollars for that nation's currency so that the shares of stock, or the bonds, can be purchased in that country's currency. The problem is that the exchange rate between the U.S. currency and foreign currencies is not fixed. It varies.

To illustrate, let's say you want to purchase 100 shares of Toyota stock. Assume, for simplicity, that at the current $/yen ($1 can be exchanged for 100 yen) exchange rate, $1,000 could purchase 100 shares of Toyota. If the exchange rate moves to favor the dollar ($1 can be exchanged for 150 yen), the same $1,000 can now purchase 150 shares. The U.S. investor benefits from the exchange rate move. Conversely, if the exchange rate moves in an unfavorable direction for the dollar ($1 can be exchanged for 50 yen), the same $1,000 can now purchase only 50 shares. Because investors either win or lose with a change in the exchange rate, risk-averse investors usually look for nations in which the exchange rate with the U.S. dollar is fairly stable and shows little movement. This takes the exchange rate out of the investment equation. When the currency values are stable, investors can focus all of their attention on the value of the investment.

Individual investors who enlist investment banks, brokers, or mutual funds never have to deal with the intricacies of currency exchange risk. These firms have professional traders who deal with exchange risk through sophisticated hedging and currency swap strategies. For an independent individual investor, the transaction will get done, but, make no mistake, the costs of investing in a country that has a volatile currency will eventually surface as a lower return on the investment.

2. *Market risk.* Changes in the values of foreign investments (particularly stocks) are frequently more volatile than movements in domestic stock values. As noted earlier, most of the world's equity markets are smaller and not as liquid as the U.S. markets, and they are supported by far less stable economies, so wild fluctuations in values can and do occur. Investors must deal with this market risk when they commit funds to foreign stock purchases.

3. *Liquidity risk.* Because most of the world's economies are weaker and smaller than the U.S. economy, foreign stock markets are less liquid. Liquidity is the ability to buy and sell a particular foreign stock. Liquidity problems occur outside the U.S. boundaries because foreign stock markets typically have lower daily trading volume vis à vis the U.S. equity markets. Investors need to be careful not to purchase a stock that may eventually be difficult to sell.

4. *Political risk.* The values of international investments are very much tied to changes in the political winds of a particular country. Political events pose substantial risks to the returns on foreign investments, and political changes can take on many forms: a new government leadership, a coup, revisions in economic policy (e.g., currency controls), adoption of adverse trade policies, and changes in taxation.

Factors Influencing International Investment Values

The principal factors that influence the value of international investments (i.e., bonds and stocks) include the three primary economic indicators—GDP, inflation, and interest rates—plus the currency exchange rate. As in the U.S. markets, other factors—government policy, demographic trends, market psychology, and the financial health and prospects of the underlying companies—exert important pressures on foreign bond and stock values. And the risks inherent to foreign investments—currency risk, market risk, liquidity risk, and political risk—all exert some influence over the values and returns on investment of foreign assets.

All countries around the globe experience good times and bad times. Every nation's economy goes through business cycles, and the direction and levels of GDP, inflation, and interest rates in a particular country largely determine the values of its financial assets. In most established countries, there are secondary indicators (similar to our monthly economic releases) that help investors to anticipate movements in the primary indicators. Government releases on the employment situation, consumer spending, and so on, are typical secondary indicators.

Unfortunately, nonprofessional investors have neither the time nor the abilities to effectively monitor specific monthly or quarterly economic reports for specific countries. Monitoring monthly economic reports in the United States is time-consuming, and additional monthly reports from a number of other countries would become too burdensome for most nonprofessional investors. However, at the very least, investors should paint the economic and business climate of a country or region of the world that they have targeted for investing. By monitoring the direction and levels of a country's GDP, inflation, interest rates, and exchange rates, investors gain information needed to make intelligent international investment decisions. (This information is particularly helpful when deciding which international mutual funds to purchase.)

Gross Domestic Product (GDP)

Knowledge of the economic growth prospects of a country is crucial in making any investment decision. The most recent GDP quarterly (or annual) growth rates for each nation are readily available from a variety of information sources (just type *economic data* into any Internet search engine). Services such as Consensus Economics, Inc. offer international newsletters that provide quarterly or annual forecasts of GDP growth by country. By monitoring GDP growth rates, investors can tell whether the country in question is experiencing bad times (recession) or good times (recovery or expansion).

Inflation

Inflation is a universal problem; it resides in every country in the world. Perhaps the most visible and damaging example was the hyperinflation that inflicted post-World War I Germany. From August 1922 to November 1923, inflation averaged 322 percent per month! Prices at the end of the hyperinflation period were almost 10 billion times the original level. Goods and services got to be so expensive that people carried their money in wheelbarrows when shopping at stores. There are even stories about how people left their wheelbarrows filled with money (i.e., German marks) outside of stores, and robbers would steal the wheelbarrows and leave the money. Investors need to monitor both the current and the expected inflation for any countries they have targeted for international investments. Inflation measures in many countries around the world are somewhat inaccurate, but they still provide valuable information about the future values of financial assets. Inflation indicators (e.g., CPI) are offered by the governments of most of the developed countries, and inflation forecasts are available from the same sources that offer GDP growth forecasts.

Interest Rates

Information about foreign interest rates is easily obtainable from most developed countries around the world. The best rates to monitor are a country's government bond yields. By calculating the spread between the U.S. Treasury bond rate and a foreign country's government bond rate, the comparative levels of U.S./foreign interest rates can be measured. Current government bond yields, as well as forecasts, are available from the same sources that offer GDP growth and inflation forecasts.

Exchange Rates

Movements in exchange rates directly influence the value of international investments. To consummate a purchase, American dollars must be converted into the local currency of the targeted international investment at a market-determined exchange rate. Because exchange rates are always moving in response to changing market conditions, the value of the U.S. dollar vis à vis other currencies is constantly increasing or decreasing the value of international investments, regardless of an investment's price (e.g., stock price). Exchange rates for the major currencies of the world are regularly available from any stockbroker and/or discount broker service, via telephone or Internet. Investors can also obtain exchange rate information on the Internet by typing *currency* or *exchange rates* into any search engine.

Table 10–7 is an example of the international forecasts that are available monthly to investors (offered by Consensus Economics, Inc.). Included are annual projections for GDP, inflation, the three-month

Table 10–7 Consensus of Economic Forecasts
(Year 2000; in Percentage Terms)

Country	GDP Growth	Inflation	Interest Rate	Exchange Rate
United States	**2.7**	**2.4**	**5.0**	**1.11**
Australia	3.2	3.2	5.1	0.697
Canada	2.6	1.7	4.6	1.432
China	7.3	1.4	n.a.	8.408
France	2.7	1.1	2.9	1.11
Germany	2.5	1.4	3.1	1.11
Hong Kong	2.1	0.5	6.0	7.787
Italy	2.2	1.7	3.1	1.11
Japan	–0.2	–0.1	0.2	121.1
Mexico	3.6	12.6	n.a.	10.97
Netherlands	2.4	2.1	2.9	n.a.
Russia	–0.6	33.9	n.a.	32.52
South Korea	4.9	3.0	n.a.	1113.
Spain	3.4	2.2	3.1	1.11
Switzerland	1.9	1.0	1.6	1.777
Taiwan	5.5	1.9	n.a.	32.36
United Kingdom	2.3	2.3	5.2	1.587

n.a. = not available
Source: Concensus Economics, London, England.

government interest rate (when available), and the country's exchange rate for the U.S. dollar (when available). (Most European countries' exchange rates have now been replaced with the European Euro exchange rate, forecast as 1.110 in 2000.)

Rules for International Investing

The following international investment rules assume that your choices include investing in foreign stock, bond, or currency markets. Your investment goals should be to earn competitive returns on your international holdings while also providing diversification benefits to your overall investment portfolio. (Some international equity and bond investments will experience different investment return patterns than their U.S. counterparts.)

Most international investments for U.S. investors are made via international mutual funds, but direct investments in international stocks, bonds, and currencies are consistent with the rules developed below. The value of international financial assets is dependent on movements in national economies, interest rates, and inflation, as well as on specific noneconomic factors such as individual company performance.

Investors who note that a country or region of the world is experiencing recession will most likely observe negative GDP growth, falling interest rates, negative market psychology, and an accommodative central bank. In this environment, some general rules will assist investors in pursuing successful international stock, bond, and currency investment strategies.

Investors who identify countries in a recovery period may become hopeful that these countries will build momentum and realize an expansion. Recovery is a period in which many companies and industry sectors shed the weaknesses exposed during an earlier recession and grow profits and earnings per share. GDP growth is also positive and climbing, and interest rates and inflation are most probably flat or falling. When a recovery turns into an expansion, foreign company earnings growth prospects turn bright, GDP is expanding, and market psychology is positive.

Putting everything we've learned about the international markets alongside the basic principles for investing in both bad and good economic times (Chapter 5), we create an excellent backdrop for developing rules for international investing. A top ten list of "Grow-Rich" rules recommended for international investors is supplemented by "More Grow-Rich Rules for International Investing."

The Top Ten Grow-Rich Rules for International Investing

INVESTMENT RULE 1

If a particular country's economy is expanding and is experiencing prolonged periods of low inflation and low interest rates, invest more in foreign stocks than in foreign bonds.

Rationale. Expansions with a favorable backdrop of relatively low inflation and low interest rates are breeding grounds for prolonged "bull runs" in the stock market, whether domestic or foreign. During expansions, the economy is running on all cylinders, and most industries are the beneficiaries of solid demand for their products and services. Low interest rates usually are associated with relatively low company borrowing costs and widening profit margins. In this environment, company profits rise, suggesting that most company stock prices will exhibit a favorable performance. As soon as this type of market environment is identified, go heavily into stocks.

INVESTMENT RULE 2

To limit your risk in international investing, select countries with favorable GDP growth prospects and a stable exchange rate with the U.S. dollar.

Rationale. Risk-averse investors usually look for nations with solid growth prospects and fairly stable exchange rates with the U.S. dollar. This takes the exchange rate out of the investment equation, and investors can focus all of their attention on the value of the investment—not on currency values.

INVESTMENT RULE 3

If a foreign economy or particular region of the world is experiencing recession, avoid investing in foreign stocks until a recovery period is identified.

Rationale.   A foreign economy in recession (you will observe GDP reports registering negative growth) portends unfavorably for foreign stock investments. Keep your money on the sidelines until a recovery period can be identified (usually when you observe forecasts of positive GDP growth). You are a stranger in a strange land, and a recession is no time to take chances on foreign equity plays.

INVESTMENT RULE 4

If a foreign economy or particular region of the world is experiencing recession, investing in foreign government bonds will, in general, generate greater returns than foreign stock investments.

Rationale.   Recessions (i.e., observable negative GDP growth) usually prompt investors to bail out of stocks, thereby depressing foreign stock prices. Fortunately, downturn periods also are opportunities for foreign bond investments. Historically, interest rates turn down during recessions and eventually turn upward by the end of a recovery period. This sequence makes bonds relatively attractive investments throughout the downturn, as long as you plan to hold the investment until the recovery period. However, purchase only government-backed bonds. The profit performance of most foreign companies during recessions is strained because of a reduced demand for goods and/or services. Some companies are likely to default on their debt obligations during a recession, so government bonds are a safer bet.

INVESTMENT RULE 5

If a particular country's economy is in recovery, begin moving some of your foreign bond investments away from government bonds and toward nongovernment foreign bonds that are paying higher interest rates.

Rationale. Recovery presents an opportunity for investors to selectively invest in higher-yielding corporate bonds. Corporate earnings begin to grow during a recovery, raising the quality of debt issuance. AAA and AA corporate bonds become solid investments when the economy is well into recovery. However, great care must be exercised in selecting foreign company bonds. Moving a portion of your international portfolio holdings into an international mutual fund specializing in foreign corporate funds represents a sensible investment strategy.

INVESTMENT RULE 6

If a particular country's economy has entered an expansion period and there is some upward pressure on both inflation and interest rates, favor shorter-term foreign bonds over longer-term foreign bonds.

Rationale. Expansions (i.e., GDP growth is positive) are usually associated with some building of inflationary pressures and, thus, rising interest rates. Bonds with longer-term maturities will experience greater price declines than those with shorter terms. If you need to invest in bonds, shorten up your maturity preferences.

INVESTMENT RULE 7

If the U.S. economy is in an expansion and U.S. interest rates are rising relative to Country A's interest rates, go short in Country A's currency versus U.S. dollars.

Rationale. Rising U.S. interest rates usually mean greater demand for U.S. dollars. Foreign investors are more inclined to purchase U.S. securities, which lower the value of Country A's currency relative to the U.S. dollar.

INVESTMENT RULE 8

Avoid investing in countries or regions of the world that are perceived to have significant political risk. From time to time, governments interfere with the competitive production of goods and services, and the result is increased volatility of equity prices.

Rationale. Political risk poses a situation that is beyond the control of investors. A nation that is subject to great political risk is likely to interfere with the competitive marketplace by placing downward pressure on company profit margins. Investors should avoid committing funds into a country that is subject to wide swings of political instability.

INVESTMENT RULE 9

If there is a major crisis somewhere in the world (e.g., the Asian economic crisis of 1998), dump foreign bonds in favor of U.S. Treasury bonds. Foreign investors turn to U.S. securities as a safe haven for crisis-related investments.

Rationale. The U.S. economy is the largest and the U.S. military is the most powerful in the world, so international investors always commit their funds to the U.S. markets in times of crisis. U.S Treasury bonds represent perhaps the most popular safe haven among foreign investors. Thus, in times of crisis, the value of U.S. bonds rises relative to the value of foreign bonds.

INVESTMENT RULE 10

If the foreign/U.S. bond interest rate spread is wide enough to adjust for the perceived political and currency exchange risks of a particular country, invest in that country's bonds.

Rationale. Professional investors running mutual funds, financial institutions, and pension funds are always looking at the interest rate spreads between U.S. securities and other nations' securities. If the foreign/U.S. spread is wide enough to compensate for the exchange risk, political risk, and so on, these professional investors will purchase foreign bonds.

More Grow-Rich Rules for International Investing

INVESTMENT RULE 11

If a particular country is experiencing recession and you identify that its central bank is pursuing an accommodative monetary policy (i.e., exerting downward pressure on interest rates) to help stimulate the economy, favor foreign government bond investments over foreign equity investments.

Rationale. A country's central bank is usually accommodative during recession; interest rates will be brought downward in an effort to spur economic activity. Falling interest rates provide a favorable environment for government bond investments.

INVESTMENT RULE 12

During a recession, place a greater investment emphasis on longer-term foreign bonds rather than shorter-term foreign bonds.

Rationale. Investments in longer-term bonds provide greater price appreciation than shorter-term bonds during a recession, because interest rates are usually falling. It is just mathematics: If interest rates are falling, the price appreciation on a long-term bond will exceed the price appreciation on a short-term bond.

INVESTMENT RULE 13

If the U.S. economy is in recession and U.S. interest rates are falling relative to Country A's interest rates, go long in Country A's currency versus U.S. dollars.

Rationale.   Investing in other countries' currencies requires that you understand how the value of the U.S. dollar changes, relative to other currencies. Falling U.S. interest rates usually mean less demand for U.S. dollars because foreign investors are less attracted to U.S. securities. The value of Country A's currency increases relative to the U.S. dollar.

INVESTMENT RULE 14

If a foreign economy is in the early stages of recovery, favor foreign stock investments over foreign bond investments, but do not bail out of bonds.

Rationale.   As a country's economy is lifted out of recession, interest rates are likely to climb, exerting downward pressure on bond prices over the near term. As company profits begin to pick up, stock prices increase. Take advantage of the final stages of a recession or the early stage of a recovery by purchasing high-quality stock companies (e.g., blue chips) rather than high-quality bonds. However, during the recovery period and the early stages of expansion, bond prices might stabilize, making bonds a relatively safe investment, particularly if you need regular cash flows in your portfolio.

INVESTMENT RULE 15

If you observe that either the International Monetary Fund or the World Bank has rewarded a struggling country with a substantial long-term loan, investing in that country's foreign assets (bonds and/or equities) may represent a solid investment strategy.

Rationale. Loans granted by the International Monetary Fund and/or the World Bank to a struggling economy usually indicate that this economy has been evaluated very carefully and the loans will help it get back on its feet. (This is not always the case. Russia recently defaulted on its loans.) Most loans from these lenders are associated with some type of austerity program. The debtor nation must buckle down and get its financial and economic house in order. Debtor countries' financial assets may display some retreat in value in the near term, but are usually good investments in the longer term.

INVESTMENT RULE 16

Avoid investing in countries with significant "country risk." From time to time, some countries interfere with international transactions in their currencies. The movement of exchange rates and the value of investments can be adversely affected.

Rationale. Country risk arises whenever countries interfere with international transactions in their currencies. Some common interferences are: government restrictions on foreign investments by residents, limitations on the flow of capital from abroad, and regulation of the local exchange markets. Interferences almost always affect the movement of exchange rates and can be disruptive for currency traders.

INVESTMENT RULE 17

If U.S. interest rates fall abruptly relative to foreign interest rates, there may be investment opportunities in foreign bonds that could improve bond portfolio returns.

Rationale. As U.S. interest rates drop, the foreign/U.S. bond rate spread improves, making foreign bonds relatively more attractive than before U.S. interest rates moved downward. A dramatic drop in U.S. interest rates should serve as a reminder for international investors to investigate investing in international bonds.

11

INVESTING FOR
RETIREMENT

In adults of all ages, the thought of retirement strikes a nervous chord. Can we grow our wealth to a high enough level, so that we can earn the right to retire and still live happily ever after in our golden years? According to a recent Massachusetts Mutual Life Insurance Company survey, Americans are not off to a running start for accumulating retirement savings. Consider the following tidbits:

- Less than one-half of American households have put aside money specifically for retirement.

- Nearly 8 out of 10 American households will have less than half of the income they will require to retire *comfortably.*

- The average American spends 18 years in retirement—up from 10 years, less than a century ago.

- Nearly one-third of those who are eligible to participate in a defined contribution plan do not take advantage of this saving opportunity.

- Eleven percent of Americans retire with a net worth of zero, and only 2 percent of Americans retire with a net worth of over $500,000.

- In 1990, adults age 55 and older made up 21 percent of the U.S. population. In 2020, they will account for 50 percent of the U.S. population.

Americans can do a better job of preparing for retirement. A host of retirement vehicles and financial products are available to assist individuals in satisfying their retirement needs. On the Internet, there is no dearth of information on retirement investing. Type in *retirement* on any major search engine, and you will retrieve literally hundreds of sites offering retirement advice and analysis. Among the most resourceful sites are those linked to the large mutual funds, such as Fidelity, or to companies that are highly active in managing 401(k) plans for employees, such as Mass Mutual. These sites will help you track your retirement portfolio and will provide retirement strategies that take into account your current portfolio performance and your number of years to retirement. In addition, America Online and Money Magazine are among a host of other investment sites that offer useful tips (e.g., money.com presents five steps to a great retirement).

It is important to understand that investment strategies geared for retirement are very different from investment strategies focused on growing rich quickly. Retirement investing emphasizes income and the preservation of principal, and this emphasis is sometimes in conflict with some of the risk-taking and market-timing strategies for growing rich. Keep in mind that following the right retirement investment strategies during your early work years also help you grow rich.

Growing a nest egg (i.e., wealth) is the primary mission of retirement investing. Many of us begin with the knowledge that we will receive Social Security payments and, maybe, pension benefits at retirement age, but they will provide a minimum cash flow that will only partially offset the income lost from not working anymore. Social Security is a good start, but the payments are not nearly enough to permit a comfortable life during retirement.

How much do we need to grow our retirement wealth? For many years, most of us thought that $1 million was a nice round number. Although $1 million sounds like a lot of money, unfortunately, for many of us, it will not be enough. Remember: We do not need $1 million today, We need it 20 to 30 years from now. An 8 percent annual return on $1 million today earns you about $80,000 per year. But what will $80,000 per year be worth 20 years from now, assuming that the United States will average about 3 percent inflation per year? How about a paltry $30,000? And after taxes, your net income could be about $25,000. A million dollars today doesn't get you too far when you need the money 20 years from now. To make matters even worse, the cash flow from $1 million looks even smaller, the longer you live. Most traditional retirement plans factor in a 20-year life span after retirement, but a large number of retirees are living well beyond 20 years. If you have a $1 million pot of gold and you are fortunate to live a long life, just a few gold nuggets will be left for your children.

Most households are likely to have misguided retirement goals that rely too heavily on an underestimated retirement-wealth target level and on government-promised Social Security payments. This chapter is focused on helping you build a complete set of *realistic* retirement goals, and on rules for investing for retirement. Determining your retirement wealth target, understanding the power of compounding, taking advantage of tax-deferred investing, learning the benefits of rebalancing your retirement portfolio, and reviewing some of the retirement investment products available in today's marketplace are important ways to prepare for the important challenge of investing for retirement.

Primer on Retirement Investing

Determining Your Retirement Wealth Target

A basic rule of thumb in planning for retirement is that you'll need about 70 to 80 percent of your preretirement gross income to maintain your standard of living when you stop working. For example, suppose you have been earning $100,000 per year for the past 10 years and you are planning to retire next year.

Your retirement savings should be able to generate an annual income stream that is equivalent to about 70 to 80 percent to your current income. To realize that level of annual cash flow, you would need about a $1 million retirement portfolio today.

Your retirement wealth target would have to be much higher than $1 million if you are not planning to retire for another 20 years. A $70,000 to $80,000 cash flow will not be worth that much in real dollars 20 years from now. If you assume a 3 percent inflation rate every year for the next 20 years (the actual inflation rate could be higher or lower), $80,000 will be worth only $25,000 in real dollars 20 years from now.

To determine your retirement wealth target level, you need to project the present value of a stream of cash-flow payments *n* years into the future. Sound complicated? Retirement planning software packages can run the numbers for you. Just type *retirement* on any online search engine, and literally hundreds of retirement planning sites, from fidelity.com to sageonline.com, will appear. Most of these sites will ask you to fill in the following information:

- Current age.
- Age when you expect to retire.
- Number of years you expect to live.
- Current annual income.
- Percent of salary you will need for retirement.
- Expected annual Social Security benefit.
- Projected annual pension income.
- Other expected annual retirement income.
- Current value of your 401(k) or 403(b) plan.
- Current total value of any IRAs, SEPs, and Keoghs.
- Current total value of all other retirement savings.
- The future annual rate of inflation.
- The future annual return on your retirement investments.

When you have gathered all of the above information, you will be able to determine your retirement wealth target: the amount of wealth that you have to accumulate by the time you retire. You will be able to live off the income generated from this portfolio and still leave your whole portfolio to your children when you die.

The steps for building your retirement wealth portfolio are:

1. Decide the percentage of your preretirement income that you will need, to maintain your standard of living. (I recommend using 70 percent.)

2. Start saving! The greatest mistake many people make is: They don't take retirement seriously until their backs are against the wall. Allocate a certain percentage of your after-tax income to your retirement portfolio. For every year that you postpone starting or adding to your retirement portfolio, you will have to put in a bigger share of your income in the future. For example, if you are 30

years old and are beginning a retirement plan, you have about 35 years until retirement. Assuming that, to live comfortably, you will need 70 percent of your current gross salary per year, you would probably have to allocate about 10 percent of your salary per year for the next 35 years. However, if you begin your retirement planning at age 40, you have to allocate 21 percent of your income per year. Table 11–1 matches the starting retirement planning ages with their corresponding allocation percentages.

3. Call the Social Security Administration at 1-800-772-1213 and ask for a free Personal Earnings and Benefit Estimate Statement (PEBES). Social Security pays average retirees about 40 percent of their preretirement earnings. However, the percentage will be significantly less if you earn over $100,000 during your work years.

4. Sign up for your employer's retirement [i.e., 401(k)] plan, and participate in any employer contribution arrangement (covered later in this chapter).

5. Set up an Individual Retirement Account (IRA), Simplified Employee Pension (SEP) plan, or other retirement account (covered in a later section).

6. Estimate the annual benefits you might receive from your employer's pension fund (if available) upon retirement from the company.

7. If you own a home, determine the projected equity from the home at the time of your retirement.

Table 11–1   Percentages of Current Savings Needed to Achieve 70 Percent of Gross Salary During Retirement

Starting Age	Percentage to Save
30	10%
40	21
50	48
55	84

From Sage Online, Inc.

8. Identify a family of mutual funds and/or stocks that are geared toward long-term retirement investing.

9. *Manage* your retirement wealth portfolio. Set investment goals and rebalance the portfolio when necessary. (Rebalancing is covered in a later section.) Keep a long-term perspective, and stay heavily invested in stocks.

Compounding and Your Retirement Portfolio

Compounding, the growth of an investment's principal and reinvested gains, is the retirement investor's greatest ally. Depending on the investment vehicle, compounding takes different shapes and sizes. For stocks, compounding usually means investing the dividends paid from the stock to purchase additional shares. For bonds, compounding means reinvesting the interest payments to buy more bonds. You can also compound mutual funds by reinvesting the dividend, interest, and/or capital gains distributions in additional mutual fund units. The earlier you begin a retirement plan using compounding, the more your retirement portfolio will grow.

To illustrate the power of compounding, imagine that you are investing $10,000 in a fixed-income mutual fund that will earn an 8 percent return during the next 30 years. During the first year, you earn $800, so your total investment grows to $10,800. During the second year, that $800 will earn $64 (assuming you reinvest the funds at an 8 percent interest rate). An additional $64 may not seem like much, but the benefits of compounding become significant over a long period of time. The second year, your 8 percent interest on $10,864 would generate $869.12. Compounding is like a snowball rolling down a hill; it picks up snow and becomes increasingly bigger as it makes its way to the bottom of the hill. The initial $10,000 investment, earning an 8 percent return for 30 years and compounded annually, would yield $100,626.57, or a 906 percent return on your money!

The growth of your retirement portfolio depends heavily on your length of time to retirement and the available rate of return on your investment. Table 11–2 indicates the future value of a $10,000 investment for 10 years, 15 years, 20 years, and 30 years, with an 8 percent return. Table 11–3 projects the future value for a 30-year retirement period, when the interest earned varies from a low of 5 percent to a high of 10 percent. The investment horizon and the return on investment are critical to the success of a retirement plan. When investments lose money (generating a negative

Table 11–2   Future Value of $10,000
(8% Return)

Years to Retirement	Future Value
10 years	$ 21,589.25
15	31,721.69
20	46,609.57
30	100,626.57

return due to a recession or bankruptcy), compounding no longer applies. Fortunately, most retirement investments earn positive returns. If you start taking your retirement objectives seriously at an early age, you will reap the benefits from compounding.

Tax-Deferred Investing

Here is one fact you should never forget: The U.S. Government subsidizes retirement investing via tax-deferred vehicles. This subsidy provides a great advantage for individuals investing to build a retirement portfolio, compared with individuals investing to build an investment portfolio. Every employed individual needs to take advantage of this subsidy. As we will learn below, investing in tax-deferred vehicles generates substantial returns over traditional investment vehicles.

Table 11–3   Future Value of $10,000 for 30 Years
(At Various Rates of Return)

Annual Interest Rate	Future Value
5%	$ 43,219.42
6	57,434.91
7	76,122.55
8	100,626.57
9	132.676.78
10	174,494.02

Tax-deferred plans are tailor-made for employed persons and the self-employed. Here is a brief overview of some of the best tax-deferred plans for your retirement.

401(k) Plans

A 401(k) plan borrows its name from Section 401(k) of the Internal Revenue Code of 1981, which established this retirement plan. The federal government intended the 401(k) plan to be a retirement savings plan that is funded by employee contributions and (sometimes) matching contributions from the employer. Contributions are made pretax, and any earned interest, dividends, and/or capital gains are also recognized as tax-free earnings.

The advantages of a 401(k) plan are obvious, and they outweigh the disadvantages. Because the employee's contribution is made pretax, the amount of income tax paid to the government each year is reduced. In addition, most employers make contributions to the employee plan at no cost to the employee. Furthermore, the interest, dividends, and capital gains earned from both the employer's and the employee's contributions are not taxed until withdrawal. Thus, the power of compounding is quite dramatic. And finally, employees usually have some flexibility as to where and how they can invest the 401(k) contributions. Employers' 401(k) plans usually offer a family of mutual funds that employees may select from. Typically, mutual fund options include a money market fund, a bond fund, an equity fund, and a balanced fund (a mix of bonds and stocks). On the negative side, it is costly to retrieve your 401(k) retirement savings before age 59½, and 401(k) plans are not insured by the U.S. Government, even though employer pension funds are insured by the Pension Benefit Guaranty Corporation.

An employee may make an annual pretax contribution of $10,500 to a 401(k) plan, and the employer can match any percentage of the employee's contribution. Typical match percentages are about 50 percent of the employee's contribution. Thus, if an individual contributes $10,000 and the employer matches 50 percent of that contribution, the employee effectively is saving $15,000 per year in his or her 401(k) plan. And the bonus is that the entire $15,000 is growing and compounding at a tax-free rate. It is also important to note that individuals who contribute to 401(k) plans may also contribute to other tax-deferred plans (e.g., IRAs). The IRS does limit the combined total amount of deferred income an individual can save in 401(k), IRA, or pension plans to about $30,000 (subject to changes each tax year) or about 25 percent of annual compensation.

It should come as no surprise that, for most Americans, the accumulated savings from a 401(k) plan has become the largest asset in individual retirement portfolios. Almost 30 million employees have now saved more than $1 trillion in 401(k) plans, and the average balance per employee is approximately $40,000. However, most Americans are not making the most of their 401(k) plans. According to a joint study by the Employee Benefits Research Institute and the Investment Company Institute, the average 401(k) portfolio holds only 44 percent of its assets in stocks, and 30.6 percent of participants held no stock funds at all. In a typical 401(k) portfolio, one of the largest investments was in shares of the employer's company (likely to be one of the riskiest assets in the portfolio). Given that 401(k) plans are usually long-term plans that accumulate 20 to 30 years of investing until retirement, it is unfortunate that many of these plans are underfunded with regard to stocks. No other investment with a horizon of 20 years or longer outperforms stocks.

How can you get the most out of your 401(k) retirement plan? Through the power of compounding and with generous matching contributions from your employer, you can easily earn the highest rates of return in your retirement portfolio by investing the maximum allowable amount in your 401(k) plan. For example, let's say you earn $100,000 per year and contribute 10 percent of your salary ($10,500 is the maximum permitted by the IRS) to your 401(k) plan. Your employer's 50 percent matching contribution adds another $5,000 per annum. You earn a 10 percent return on your 401(k) portfolio. You are in the combined federal/state tax bracket of 31 percent, so, by putting away $10,000 in your plan, you save $3,100 in taxes. That reduces the real contribution to your 401(k) plan to just $6,900. At the same time, your company is putting $5,000 into your retirement plan. You now have effectively $15,000 in your 401(k) plan, earning 10 percent and compounding tax-free. By the end of the first year, your initial $6,900 investment has grown (via the power of monthly tax-free compounding) to $15,706.96, for a 128 percent return! The lesson: If you are financially able, invest to the maximum in your 401(k) plan.

It is also important to select an asset mix. Over 20 or more years, the allocation of your retirement funds into bonds versus stocks will have enormous impact on the eventual size of your retirement portfolio. Stocks held for 20 or more years have always outperformed bonds, so it makes sense to permit stocks to dominate your retirement portfolio if you are age 45 years or younger.

Individual Retirement Accounts (IRAs)

There are two types of individual retirement accounts: a traditional IRA and a Roth IRA. A traditional IRA permits you to contribute up to $2,000 annually. If you have no other employer-sponsored pension plan your traditional IRA contribution is fully deductible and begins earning tax-free income. However, if you are an active participant in an employer plan, the rules become a little more complicated, and the IRS begins to disallow the deduction at very low-income levels ($32,000 to $42,000 in year 2000 for single filers). Roth IRAs, which became available in 1998, offer more advantages than traditional IRAs, particularly if you have a longer time horizon until retirement. The contributions are not deductible, but the earnings on your contributions are tax-free and you can withdraw funds without paying any taxes (including earnings) if you meet the time and age requirements. Individuals can contribute up to $2,000 ($4,000 for couples) subject to a phase out between an adjusted gross income of $95,000 and $110,000 for individuals, and $150,000 and $160,000 for joint filers. One of the more attractive benefits of this retirement plan is that you can contribute the maximum amount to your SEP or Keogh and still contribute an additional $2,000 to a Roth IRA.

Keogh Plans

Keogh plans are designed for self-employed individuals, (including partners in a partnership and S-corp shareholders). Self-employed individuals can contribute to a profit-sharing plan annually, based on a percentage of the self-employment income (up to 20 percent) and subject to a $30,000 ceiling. If you are a self-employed investor planning for retirement, I advise utilizing the services of an accountant or certified financial planner to set up a Keogh plan.

SIMPLE Plans

SIMPLE plans are available to employers who have 100 or fewer employees (or a self-employed individual) not maintaining another employer sponsored retirement plan. The plan can take the form of an IRA established for each participant and the earnings will be tax exempt like any other IRA. The plan can also take the form of a 401(k) arrangement. Elective deferrals up to $6,000 per year can be made by each employee, with the employer matching from 1 to 3 percent of the employees wages, much like the 401(k) matching. The benefits of the tax-deferred earnings have been explained above.

Simplified Employee Pension (SEP) Plans

These basic retirement plans permit you to contribute up to 13.0435 percent of self-employment income. The maximum contribution is $24,000 (as of 1999). These contributions can be deducted from your tax returns. SEPs are more flexible and easier to establish than Keogh plans. You can literally start one in one day, through a commercial bank, brokerage company, or mutual fund company.

Variable Annuities

A variable annuity is the financial opposite of a life insurance policy. An annuity pays you a cash flow when you are alive. Insurance pays your dependents after you die. Basically, a tax-deferred variable annuity is an agreement between you and an insurance company. You invest a certain amount with the company, which, in return, agrees to pay you at a later time, usually after retirement (after age 59 ½). The benefit of an annuity is that it provides tax-free earnings until retirement. However, you will pay taxes when you withdraw the funds (as either a lump sum or monthly payments). There is no ceiling on what you can contribute to an annuity.

Be aware that annuities are associated with unusually high annual fees, commissions, and withdrawal penalties. In addition, the contributions to annuities are not tax-deductible.

Rebalancing Your Retirement Portfolio

It is crucial for investors to understand the importance of rebalancing their retirement portfolios. Rebalancing means keeping the composition of a portfolio up-to-date over a period of time. For example, at age 30, the composition of your retirement portfolio may consist of 100 percent equities, to take advantage of the historical observation that equity returns outperform bond returns for periods of 20 years or longer. However, as you approach age 50, you may wish to reallocate a substantial (e.g., 25 percent) portion of your portfolio to bond investments because your new retirement investment horizon has changed from 35 years (age 65–30) to 15 years (age 65–50).

Another reason for rebalancing is the natural drift in composition of any portfolio over time. Suppose your $100,000 retirement portfolio is comprised of 75 percent equities (i.e., $75,000) and 25 percent bonds (i.e., $25,000). If you earn a 30 percent return on your equity portion and a 5 percent return on your bond portion over a one-year period, the value of the portfolio will rise to $123,750: $97,500 in stocks and $26,250 in bonds. However, the composition of your portfolio has changed from a 75/25 to a 79/21 stock/bond split. If your retirement objective is to maintain a 75/25 split, the portfolio must be rebalanced. One way to accomplish this is to sell stocks and buy bonds until the portfolio composition is back to a 75/25 split. This strategy makes sense if the entire portfolio is in a 401(k) plan or any other retirement plan that has no tax consequences for buying and selling investments. A more practical strategy, particularly if there are tax consequences for buying and selling securities, is to reallocate future stock purchases or redirect the existing equity investments' distributions (dividends and capital gains) into bond investments until your portfolio reaches the desired 75/25 split.

Building Your Retirement portfolio

When you are investing for retirement, don't try to outguess the markets. Be consistent in your investment strategies, and invest for the long term. There is no place for a steady dose of market-timing trading in a retirement portfolio. Your portfolio will achieve healthy growth if you maintain the investment mix that's right for you.

Although it may be difficult at times, you should ignore the economic environment to some degree. Your retirement funds are in for the long term, regardless of whether you are in bad times or good times. There will be opportunities to make simple market-timing plays. For example, when a bull stock market is clearly turning into a bear market, it may be wise to shift some of your retirement stock investments to bonds and/or cash (i.e., money markets), particularly in a retirement plan that has no tax consequences for selling and buying securities. But, in general, your stock investments (particularly where there are tax consequences) are there for the long term. Endure the rocky ride through the bad times and wait for the good times to reappear.

Retirement investments should target mutual funds: stock funds, bond funds, or balanced funds. Because they are usually comprised of a varied menu of stocks, bonds, or both, mutual funds provide investors with the benefits of diversification. There are times, however, when it is acceptable to invest in individual stocks. If you have a tax-free/tax-deferred retirement plan, it makes sense to invest in dividend-paying stocks because you will not be taxed immediately on those dividends at a regular income tax rate. Conversely, nondividend growth stocks are probably better off in your nonretirement investment portfolio because the only major tax consequence they carry is a lower (relative to the income tax rate) capital gains tax rate when the stock is sold. Selecting dividend-paying stocks over growth stocks for a retirement portfolio is also consistent with the advice that investors should choose to take on less risk as they approach retirement.

At times, you may want to consider investing directly in bonds, particularly as you get closer to your retirement date. To limit your exposure to the interest rate risk inherent in bonds, consider laddering your bond investments. To create a laddered portfolio, purchase a set of similar bonds, ranging from short- to long-term maturities. For example, if your objective is to own bonds with a 5-year maturity, you could ladder your bond purchases in equal amounts of 1-year, 3-year, 5-year, 7-year, and 9-year Treasury securities. The average maturity in this portfolio would be 5 years. The benefit of laddering is that you are essentially insulated from interest rate changes. If interest rates rise in one year, you will have the proceeds from the maturing 1-year bond to reinvest at the current higher rates. On the other hand, if interest rates fall in a year's time, a significant portion of your laddered bond portfolio will be locked into relatively high rates.

There is no set rule for the optimal composition of a retirement portfolio. Portfolio composition depends on two factors: (1) the length of time to retirement and (2) the investor's risk profile. The further out to retirement (i.e., 20 years or longer), the greater the emphasis on the growth potential of stock investments. Similarly, the closer to retirement, the greater the emphasis on a stable and consistent cash flow of bond investments. If you are aggressive and willing to take on some risk, your investment portfolio may lean heavily toward stocks. (With a 20-year or longer investment horizon, you may be 100 percent invested in equities.) Conversely, if you are risk-averse, you may lean toward the safety of bond investments over the volatility of equity returns.

Retirement Investment Rules

Successful strategies for retirement investing are usually independent of whether the economy is experiencing bad times or good times. Investment strategies are more dependent on retirement horizons—the number of years until retirement. For this reason, the first three groups of investment rules given below are linked to time horizons: 20 years or longer; 5 to 19 years; and less than 5 years. Individuals with retirement horizons of 20 or more years have an opportunity to experience the full power of compounding. *Invest early and often* is the number-one rule for retirement investing. People with distant retirement dates also face a one-dimensional investment choice: *Invest in stocks and only stocks.* People who expect to retire within the 5- to 19-year range need to begin thinking about bonds and other fixed-income securities, in an effort to reduce the volatility of their returns and principal. People who are within 5 years of retirement should not lean too heavily on "safe" bond investments versus stocks. Equity investments' superior returns need to be assigned an integral part in any retirement portfolio, regardless of the time to retirement.

Retirement Horizon: Twenty Years or Longer

INVESTMENT RULE 1

Put up to 100 percent of your new investment dollars in stocks if you have a 20-year or longer retirement horizon.

Rationale. According to the past 70 years' of investment data, when the investment horizon is at least 20 years in length, stock investments are superior to bond investments. Compared with fixed-income investments, stock portfolios (i.e., large- and small-company stocks) generated the highest returns in 55 out of a possible 55 20-year investment holding periods from 1925 to 1999.

INVESTMENT RULE 2

A retirement portfolio with a 20-year or longer investment horizon should be a well-diversified equity portfolio, preferably in stock mutual funds.

Rationale. To take advantage of the historical observation that stocks always outperform bonds for investment horizons of 20-years or longer, make sure that your retirement portfolio is well diversified and represents a significant portion of the stock market. Investing directly in well-diversified stock mutual funds (which could also include international stocks), or in a stock index fund, is a convenient and easy way of accomplishing this goal.

INVESTMENT RULE 3

Avoid selling off quality blue-chip stocks in your retirement portfolio just because the economy is in a recession and/or the stock market has turned bearish.

Rationale. A downturn in the economy is not an excuse to sell current stock holdings that are earmarked for retirement, particularly if the underlying companies have a history of being solid performers. Equity holdings regularly provide superior returns to bonds when held for long periods (at least 5 years or more), and they always provide superior returns for 20-year or longer holding periods.

INVESTMENT RULE 4

Prioritize your retirement investments. Before investing retirement funds in taxable investments, use up your annual contributions to a 401(k) and other tax-advantaged retirement plans.

Rationale. The government is subsidizing your retirement investments in 401(k) and other retirement plans. Take advantage of these opportunities. Stay fully invested in these plans to achieve the highest returns possible and the maximum tax advantages.

INVESTMENT RULE 5

If you believe the stock market has turned bearish, avoid potential losses by selling selected stocks out of your 401(k) plan or other retirement plans. There are no tax consequences on the sale of stocks in these plans.

Rationale. There are situations in which you may "market-time" your retirement portfolio, particularly your 401(k) plan. Purchases and sales are nontaxable events in these tax-advantaged retirement plans. If you feel strongly that a negative turn in the stock market is imminent, selling a portion of your portfolio may help you avoid loss of principal.

INVESTMENT RULE 6

If your retirement horizon is longer than 20 years, place a greater emphasis on investing in growth stocks versus dividend-paying stocks. Growth stocks offer higher expected returns, and their price volatility is minimized by the lengthy holding period.

Rationale. Historically, because they generate higher returns than dividend-paying stocks, growth stocks are more attractive for long-term investment horizons, which minimize price volatility.

INVESTMENT RULE 7

For retirement horizons of 20 years or longer, in general, favor small-cap companies over large-cap companies, as a way of raising the long-term return of your portfolio.

Rationale. Over the past 70 years, small-cap companies have provided superior returns, compared to large-cap companies. For example, small-cap companies earned a 12.4 percent average return versus 11.2 percent for large-cap companies during this time period.

Retirement Horizon: Five to Nineteen Years

INVESTMENT RULE 8

As your retirement horizon dips below 20 years, place a greater emphasis on the stable and consistent cash flows of bond investments. Permit a certain percentage (determined by your risk-taking desires) of bonds to become part of your equity-dominated retirement portfolio.

Rationale. As your investment horizon dips below 20 years and eventually approaches zero (retirement age), stocks become increasingly risky compared to fixed-income investments. The closer you get to retirement, the more you should emphasize the stable and consistent cash flows of bond investments. There is no set formula for a bond/equity composition in these intermediate investment years, but, historically, it pays to place a greater emphasis on equity investments. If you are aggressive and willing to take on some risk, your retirement portfolio may lean heavily toward stocks (with a 5- to 19-year retirement horizon, you may be close to 100 percent invested in equities). This strategy will probably raise the overall return to your retirement portfolio. Remember, equity holdings regularly provide superior returns to bonds when held for long periods (at least 5 years or more), and they always provide superior returns for 20-year or longer holding periods. Conversely, if you are risk-averse, you may prefer the safety of bond investments over the volatility of equity returns. By making bonds a meaningful portion of your investments, you can reduce the price variations of your retirement portfolio.

INVESTMENT RULE 9

To achieve greater intermediate returns, continue emphasizing growth stocks over dividend stocks when you have an intermediate retirement horizon (5 to 19 years).

Rationale. Historically, growth stocks generate higher returns than dividend-paying stocks, making them more attractive for long- and intermediate-term investment horizons. Growth stocks (e.g., small caps), although more erratic than dividend-paying stocks, generate greater returns within the 5- to 19-year horizon.

Retirement Horizon: Less Than Five Years

INVESTMENT RULE 10

When your retirement horizon is less than 5 years, it may be acceptable to invest in dividend-paying stocks, particularly in a tax-free/tax-deferred retirement plan.

Rationale.   There are times when it is acceptable to invest in individual stocks. If you are in a tax-free/tax-deferred retirement plan, it makes sense to invest in dividend-paying stocks because those dividends would not be taxed immediately at a regular income tax rate. Selecting dividend-paying stocks over growth stocks for a retirement portfolio is also consistent with the advice to take on less risk as retirement approaches.

INVESTMENT RULE 11

If you are placing a greater emphasis on bonds, you may want to ladder your bond investments so that their maturities range from a short to a long term.

Rationale.   In an effort to reduce your exposure to the interest rate risk inherent in bonds, consider laddering your bond investments. To create a laddered portfolio, purchase a set of similar bonds with maturities ranging from a short to a long term. For example, if your objective is to own bonds with an average 5-year maturity, you can ladder your bond purchases by buying, in equal amounts, 1-year, 3-year, 5-year, 7-year, and 9-year Treasury securities. The average maturity in this portfolio would be 5 years. The benefit of laddering is that you are essentially insulated from interest rate changes. If interest rates rise by the time the 1-year bond matures, you can reinvest the proceeds at the new higher rates. If interest rates fall in a year's time, a significant portion of your laddered bond portfolio is now locked into relatively high rates.

Other Retirement Rules

INVESTMENT RULE 12

A basic rule of thumb in planning for retirement is that you'll need about 70 to 80 percent of your preretirement gross income to maintain your standard of living when you stop working.

Rationale.   This is a popular rule of thumb for most retirement plans. To illustrate, suppose you have been earning $100,000 per year for the past 10 years, and you are planning on retiring next year. The rule says that the amount you have in retirement savings should be able to generate an annual income stream equivalent of about 70 to 80 percent of your current income.

INVESTMENT RULE 13

For retirement investing, economic downturns and recovery periods should almost always be viewed as opportunities for buying stock in blue-chip companies.

Rationale. Historically, stock prices, as measured by the S&P 500 Index, are usually flat or falling throughout an economic downturn. This presents a rare opportunity for long-term investors to bottom-fish. Blue-chip stocks are the largest and strongest companies in the United States. They give investors the comfort of knowing that they will survive recessions and will flourish during the recovery and expansion periods. For retirement investing purposes, it makes sense to put new investment dollars into blue chips during a recession and/or recovery. In the long term, these companies' stock prices will eventually rise above the recession purchase price. Take advantage of good companies when they are down.

INVESTMENT RULE 14

As a general rule, investors need to rebalance their portfolios every two years.

Rationale. It is crucial for investors to monitor the composition of their portfolio at least every two years, to ensure that they are adhering to their own portfolio composition investment strategies. Rebalancing means keeping the composition of the portfolio up-to-date over a period of time. For example, if your retirement objective is to maintain a 75/25 split, you should rebalance your portfolio every two years. One way to accomplish this is to sell stocks and buy bonds until the portfolio composition is back to a 75/25 split. This strategy makes sense if the entire portfolio is in a 401(k) plan or any other retirement plan that has no tax consequences for buying and selling investments. A more practical strategy, particularly if buying or selling securities inflicts tax consequences, is to reallocate future stock purchases or redirect the existing equity investments' distributions (dividends and capital gains) into bond investments until the portfolio regains the desired 75/25 split.

INVESTMENT RULE 15

Given the current tax rules, take advantage of a Roth IRA account, but with a cautious eye toward future tax rule changes.

Rationale. Roth IRAs, which became available in 1998, offer more advantages than regular IRAs. A regular IRA (deductible) permits you to make a contribution of up to $2,000 annually, but the deduction is phased out for individuals with adjusted gross incomes between $150,000 and $160,000. With Roth IRAs, contributions are nondeductible, but the earnings on your contributions are tax-free, and you can withdraw your funds (including earnings) without paying taxes. Individuals can contribute up to $2,000 ($4,000 for couples), subject to a phase-out of an adjusted gross income between $95,000 and $110,000 for individuals, and $150,000 and $160,000 for joint filers. One of the more attractive benefits of this retirement plan is that you can contribute the maximum amount to your SEP or Keogh and still contribute an additional $2,000 to a Roth IRA. Retirement investors need to take advantage of this generous tax provision, but be mindful that Congress has been known to change the rules in the middle of the game. For this reason, do not convert all of your current IRA accounts to Roth IRAs.

INVESTMENT RULE 16

A meaningful portion of your retirement portfolio needs to include large-cap (especially blue-chip) companies, particularly when the investment horizon approaches your retirement date.

Rationale. Large-cap (including blue-chip) companies are the most highly capitalized and financially strong companies in the economy.

Retirement investors can trust that these stocks will provide stable returns compared with small-cap companies. As your retirement horizon diminishes to less than 10 years, large-cap companies may offer higher returns than bonds (your other alternative for reducing investment risk).

INVESTMENT RULE 17

Invest in zero-coupon bonds only when (1) you are purchasing them for a tax-deferred retirement account, (2) you are seeking to invest a relatively small amount of funds, and (3) you are willing to forgo regular interest payments.

Rationale. Zero-coupon bonds are attractive to investors who want to invest only a small amount of money now and receive a large return many years out. Depending on the interest rate, a 30-year zero-coupon bond with a face value of $1,000 may cost you only $50 on the date of issuance. These bonds have become popular investment vehicles for children's college education accounts and/or retirement accounts (e.g., IRAs and Keoghs). In these accounts, the negative impact of paying taxes without receiving interest is minimized because a child is usually exempt from paying taxes (or pays a low tax rate), or the account involved is a tax-deferred investment.

INVESTMENT RULE 18

Invest in specific equities and real estate categories that are the primary beneficiaries of the long-term spending patterns of the baby boomer population group.

Rationale. The aging baby boomers are now in their peak earning and buying years. The boomers are projected to spend large amount of funds in such industry sectors as financial services, health care, and real estate (retirement homes, second homes, trade-up homes, and vacation homes). Invest in some of these boomer-related assets, to take advantage of the positive impact that boomer spending patterns will have on retirement horizons.

PART THREE

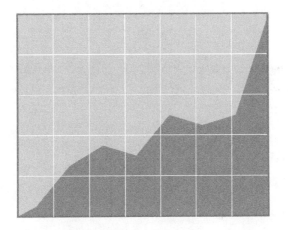

THE NEW
INFORMATION
ECONOMY

12

INVESTING IN THE NEW
INFORMATION AGE

I f there is one concept that readers should take with them from this
book, it is that the technological revolution is real and will transform
the investment world forever. The revolution has already produced:

- The Internet-driven information age.
- The real beginning of a transformation of communications and
  commerce from the physical world to the virtual (electronic) world.

Today's technological changes are not short-term phenomena in new
innovations. They are truly a revolution in advanced technology, and they
bring serious long-term implications for investments as well as for the
economy itself. The basic laws and values of the old economy may no
longer apply in today's new information economy. There is a new set of
laws and values emerging in the new economy that are heavily influencing consumer and business activities, promising to impact the value of investments for years to come.

Investors need to acknowledge what creates value and activity in the
new economy. In the old economy, *tangible assets* such as steel and oil pos-
sessed great value, even though they were clumsy and costly to transport.
There was also a premium placed on *location*, which helped determine
the success of a business or the value of a person's home. *Scarcity* is what
gave a particular asset value (demand exceeding supply, e.g., gold).

Conversely, in the new economy, *information,* an intangible asset, possesses the greatest value. Information can be easily and inexpensively transported throughout the economy. Information is also not scarce, and the more information a business provides to its customers, the more valuable that information source is to the markets. Furthermore, location is a dying concept in the new economy. In the virtual (electronic) world, business can locate anywhere and be anywhere with a click of a mouse. The concept of *time* has changed dramatically as well. In the new economy, consumers can shop for and businesses can offer products and services on the Internet 24 hours a day, 7 days a week. And finally, the new economy has *empowered* the consumer. The Internet has brought the world an abundance of information, products, and services for every consumer viewing a PC screen. Consumers are getting smarter and businesses are customizing (targeting) their products to satisfy individual needs. Attention and personalization to the consumer has become a valuable commodity in the new economy.

The transformation of communications and commerce from the physical world to the virtual world has created unprecedented investment opportunities. In this new Internet-driven information age, nonprofessional investors also have access to investment information that was previously available only to professional investors. Opportunities to invest like professionals are open to those who learn how to gather and use the information responsibly. The changing technological landscape is likely to provide a more favorable backdrop for equity and bond investments during the next decade.

This chapter provides investors with a practical step-by-step approach to investing in the new information economy. The steps involved are:

Steps	Investment Recommendations
1	Review your current investment portfolio.
2	Scan economic/investment environments.
3	Monitor changes in economic indicators.
4	Monitor company/industry performance. (Use fundamental and technical analysis.)
5	Review daily/weekly economic and investment commentaries (and/or broker tips or recommendations).
6	Develop investment rules for current, annual, and retirement horizons.
7	Obtain real-time stock/bond quotes.

8   Execute trades via online brokerage accounts (in the virtual world), discount, or retail brokerage (in the physical world).

STEP 1   Review Your Current Investment Portfolio

In any successful investment process, the first step is to key in your current investment portfolio on an Internet investment site and monitor its performance on a regular basis (ideally, once per business day). Literally hundreds of investment sites permit you to enter your portfolio and will then provide you with updated performance information on the portfolio. To illustrate, an investment portfolio comprised of 100 (shares) each of America Online, Cisco Systems, Lucent Technologies, Merck, and Sun Microsystems was created and entered on the America Online Personal Finance page, under portfolio display. Performance monitored via the AOL "My Portfolio" area, was depicted as shown in the box on page 267.

The performance of this portfolio is easily reviewed. For example, the current NAV (net asset value, or stock price) of AOL is $155⅝, down 4⅜ from the day before. The original purchase price was $125.938; current gain is $2,968.70. The market value of the holdings of AOL totals $15,562.50. To date, the value of the portfolio totals $51,954.25, providing a 19.25 percent return.

For each company in your portfolio, you can also monitor other performance measures: the price/earnings ratio, the earnings per share, the beta coefficient, and the market capitalization. By double-clicking each

			My Portfolio			
Symbol	Shares	NAV	Last Change	Purch Price	Gain/ Loss	Value
AOL	100	155⅝	−4⅜	125.938	+2,968.7	15,562.50
CSCO	100	84¾	+¼	115.438	−3,068.80	8,475.00
LU	100	77	−½	58.438	+1,856.20	7,700
MRK	100	77¼	+1¼	71¼	+600	7,725
SUNW	100	124¹⁵⁄₁₆	−1¹¹⁄₁₆	64⅝	+6,031.25	12,493.75

Portfolio Current Value: $51,954.25
                           +8,387.35
                           +19.25%

investment, you can receive more specific information. For example, if you clicked on CSCO, you would receive the following information for CISCO Systems, Inc.:

Exchange:	Nasdaq NM
Last Price:	84¾ at 16:01 EST
Change:	Up ¼ (+ 0.30%)
High:	86³⁄₁₆ at 10:58 EST
Low:	84½
Open:	85
Previous Close:	84½ on 11/16
Volume:	19,065,600
30-Day Avg. Vol:	21,673,000
Shrs Outstanding:	3,271,334,750
Market Cap:	277,217,334,750
52-Week High:	84.43
52-Week Low:	32.12
Beta:	1.36
Yield:	Nil
P/E Ratio:	141.25
EPS:	0.60
Currency Units:	US Dollar

On most investments, you can also receive investment research, such as mutual fund reports, stock reports, earnings estimates, financial statements, ratio comparisons, and company overviews. For each investment (particularly stock companies), most sites will provide you with the current news reports on a specific company, its competitors, and other industry-related companies. In summary, most investment sites provide the opportunity to monitor your own investment portfolio's performance with little effort and time spent. After reviewing your current portfolio performance, you will be able to make informed, intelligent decisions about your future investment activity.

STEP 2   Scan Economic/Investment Environments

Which economic stage (i.e., recession, recovery, or expansion) and investment environment (bull or bear market) are you currently in? The Investor

---

Investor Checklist: Economic/Investment Indicators

Economic Indicators

Real GDP (quarterly rate)	Current Mo.	_____	Previous Mo.	_____	1-Year Avg.	_____
Inflation (CPI monthly rate)	Current Mo.	_____	Previous Mo.	_____	1-Year Avg.	_____
30-Year Treasury Yield	Current Mo.	_____	Previous Mo.	_____	1-Year Avg.	_____

Investment Indicators

S&P 500 Index	Current Mo.	_____	Previous Mo.	_____	1-Year Avg.	_____
Federal Funds Rate	Current Mo.	_____	Previous Mo.	_____	1-Year Avg.	_____
Market Psychology	Bullish	_____	Bearish	_____		
Federal Reserve	Accommodative	_____	Restrictive	_____		
Federal Budget	Surplus	_____	Deficit	_____		

Investment Preferences

Stocks (S&P 500)	In Favor	_____	Out of Favor	_____
Bonds (30-Year Treasury)	In Favor	_____	Out of Favor	_____

Checklist provides information on the important economic and investment indicators that help determine the parameters of the economic/investment environment. By monitoring just a few monthly economic reports and a handful of market/investment indicators—the growth rates of GDP, inflation, and interest rates—and comparing these primary indicators to their previous-month and one-year averages, you will know (1) whether the economy is in a recession, a recovery, or an expansion, and (2) whether these environments are characterized by high inflation/high interest rates or low inflation/low interest rates. For gauging the investment environment, you need to track such measures as the S&P 500 Index, the federal funds rate, market psychology, Federal Reserve policy, and the federal budget. All of this economic and investment information is readily available on most Internet investment sites (e.g., bloomberg.com).

Before the Internet was available, completing the Investor Checklist was time-consuming and cumbersome for most nonprofessional investors. In today's information age, updating is virtually automatic; most investment sites already present this information (and much more) in an organized manner. If you are comfortable with a specific site, there is no need to complete the Investor Checklist. Instead, bookmark the relevant pages on your investment site so that you can receive this information on a regular basis.

The information you collect has value only if you know how to use it. Where possible, look at charts and the actual data for each variable.

Monitoring GDP growth rates will identify the phase of the business cycle you are currently in—downturn, recovery, or expansion. As we learned earlier, if the growth rate of GDP falls in two successive quarters, the economy is in a downturn period. If GDP growth turns positive after registering a negative quarterly growth rate, the economy is in a recovery period. And if GDP growth is positive and its levels exceed its prerecession highs, the economy is most likely humming along in an expansion mode.

It is equally important to view economic growth in the context of the direction and level of inflation and interest rates. If the economy experiences a downturn, history would suggest that both inflation and interest rate pressures would eventually dampen. Conversely, if the economy experiences an expansion and operates near capacity, we would expect some upward pressure on costs, raising both inflation and interest-rate pressures. History also suggests (see Chapter 5) that a low-inflation/low-interest-rate environment provides a very favorable backdrop for investing in the stock market. Conversely, a high-inflation/high-interest-rate environment is unfavorable for investing in stocks.

It is important to monitor market psychology (Are investors bullish or bearish?), Federal Reserve behavior, and the amount of the federal budget deficit/surplus. Tracking market psychology is relatively easy. By reading the investment commentary at an Internet investment site or in the business section of a major newspaper, you should know whether investors are bullish or bearish on stocks and bonds. To confirm your take on investors, monitor the trend in the S&P 500 Index and the 30-year Treasury bonds.

Investors need to know whether the Fed is being accommodative or restrictive in the markets. The Fed's accommodative monetary policy permits interest rates (e.g., the federal funds rate) to fall; its restrictive monetary policy applies upward pressure on interest rates (e.g., the federal funds rate). The size of the federal budget also has some influence on the direction of interest rates. A large deficit exerts upward pressure on interest rates, a large surplus exerts downward pressure, and a balanced budget should not tilt interest rates in either direction. Another category might be appropriate for your investing checklist: unusual events that influence investment values. For example, if Intel announces a better-than-expected earnings report, investors can be expected to react by purchasing shares and bolstering the stock prices of other computer-related businesses, because Intel is viewed as a reliable indicator of the prospects for the entire computer industry. Keeping your eye on some of these unusual noneconomic events may provide opportunities for successful investing that you would otherwise miss.

STEP 3   Monitor Changes in Economic Indicators

Monitoring changes in economic indicators can be time-consuming, but it may prove most financially rewarding. Retrieving the monthly releases of the economic reports is relatively easy. (The appropriate investment/economic sites are listed in Chapter 13.) I recommend limiting your study of monthly economic developments to ten or fewer reports. For starters, you should monitor the influential economic reports presented in Chapter 4:

Employment Report
Retail sales
Consumer Confidence Index
Capacity utilization
National Association of Purchasing Managers' Index
Housing starts
Merchandise trade balance
Durable goods orders

Look at the monthly changes in each indicator. Identify the investment implications resulting from these changes, and then apply an appropriate investment strategy. For example, suppose the economic environment has been characterized by a robust expansion pressing against capacity (the capacity utilization rate has been dangerously high), and inflation, as measured by the Consumer Price Index (CPI), has been averaging a 2.5 percent rate for the past 12 months. You retrieve this month's CPI report and observe that it registered a 0.6 monthly rate, or an annualized rate of 7.2 percent. This report should represent a yellow flag; there may be upward inflationary pressures in the market. Investors might react negatively to this report, believing that the values of both stocks and bonds may retreat in response. Your investment strategy (or rule) may be (1) to postpone any bond or stock purchase for that day or week, or (2) to avoid inflation/interest-rate-sensitive stocks such as financial services companies, and to purchase inflation-hedge stocks such as oil and energy-related companies.

Consider setting up an Economic Indicator Spreadsheet that lists, for each indicator: monthly change, annual rate, previous 12-month annual rate, flag (yellow or green), and recommended investment strategy. A yellow flag means that the monthly change in the indicator has generated a meaningful change in your investment strategy. Your spreadsheet might look like this:

Economic Indicator Spreadsheet (Sample)

Indicator	Monthly Change	Annual Rate	Previous 12-Month Annual Rate	Flag	Investment Strategy
CPI	0.6%	7.2%	2.5%	yellow	Postpone bond/stock purchases, or invest in inflation-hedge stocks such as oil and energy-related companies.

STEP 4   Monitor Company/Industry Performance

As presented in Chapter 6, there are two primary methods for evaluating stocks: fundamental analysis and technical analysis. Fundamental analysis involves evaluating the financial performance of a company by monitoring some of its key financial indicators. Technical analysis involves studying the historical and recent patterns of stock prices and trading volumes of a particular company, as a way of anticipating its future stock price movements. Information for both methods is readily accessible on the Internet. Literally hundreds of Web sites offer detailed information and analyses of company and industry performance. Similarly, many investment sites include a section on technical analysis in which the technical indicators are reviewed and charted. (Chapter 13 identifies the major Internet investment sites that offer fundamental and technical analyses for investors.) Because fundamental analysis is the primary focus of this book, I recommend that you focus your attention on the eight performance measures presented earlier (see Chapter 6 for discussion):

1. Earnings per share (EPS)
2. Dividends
3. Debt/Equity
4. Price-to-Earnings ratio
5. Price-to-Book ratio
6. Return on equity
7. Market value
8. Beta coefficient

They are most helpful in evaluating the current and future performance of company stock values, and they are easily accessible, on most Internet investment sites, for every company traded on a major exchange. Most sites also provide some performance evaluations by expert market analysts.

STEP 5 Review Daily/Weekly Economic and Investment Commentaries

Reviewing economic and investment commentaries on a regular basis is an important activity for any investor. The task of gathering data and developing market and company views for thousands of potential investments is close to impossible for the individual investor. Expert commentary from professional stock analysts is a necessary aid in developing successful investment strategies. Investors should review, at least weekly, a selected number of market analysts' reports on the economy, industry sectors, and specific companies. All of this information is accessible at the same investment sites that provide investment data and analysis.

STEP 6 Develop Investment Rules for Current, Annual, and Retirement Horizons

At a minimum, investors should develop their investment strategies based on the investment rules listed in this book. Identify the rules that are comfortable and relevant for your situation, and put them to use. Give particular consideration to the top ten rules for each investment tool presented in this book: stocks, bonds, real estate, options/futures, international investing, and retirement investing.

STEP 7 Obtain Real-Time Stock/Bond Quotes

Stock quotes and/or bond quotes, delivered 15 to 30 minutes after being posted on the exchanges, are readily available on the Internet. Real-time quotes are available at freerealtime.com and quotes.com. Some Web sites, such as thestreet.com, charge fees for real-time stock/bond quotes. Most investment sites offer quotes delayed 15 to 20 minutes (e.g., fidelity.com, bloomberg.com, and quote.yahoo.com).

STEP 8 Execute Trades via Online, Discount, or Retail Brokerage

The most convenient method for investing on the Internet is to utilize a site that offers one-stop investment shopping. Fortunately, most investment sites that offer data, analyses, and stock quotes provide their own online brokerage services (e.g., fidelity.com) or offer links to the major online brokerage services, such as DLJDirect and Waterhouse Securities. Identify an investment site that allows you to monitor comfortably the information you need. Then set up an online trading account with the investment site itself (if it offers online brokerage services) or with an online broker that is linked to the investment site you have chosen.

Concluding Remarks

Wise investors will adopt the above eight-step Internet-based investment plan. To accomplish this, the following approach is recommended:

- Select your primary Internet investment site (e.g., bloomberg.com) and enter the site into your bookmark list.

- Enter your current investment portfolio into the site and monitor its performance weekly (at a minimum). Select a designated time to monitor your portfolio performance (e.g., 10:00 A.M. on Saturday).

- Identify the pages in the investment site that scan the economic and investment environments and offer the information necessary to monitor the changes in the influential indicators. The site must to be able to (1) monitor performance measures from specific company/industry reports (by using fundamental and technical analysis) and (2) review daily/weekly economic and investment commentary.

- Utilize the investment rules presented in this book for current, annual, and retirement investment horizons.

- Obtain stock/bond quotes and execute trades via online brokerage accounts (in the virtual world) or via stockbrokers/discount brokers (in the physical world).

Although there are no guarantees and certainly no set formulas for successful investing, by following closely the above approach to investing, and by using the investment rules presented in this book, you will place yourself firmly on the road to growing rich.

13

INVESTMENT SOURCES ON THE INTERNET

In today's new information economy, investors have direct access to a full array of financial and investment information via the Internet. Each month, the number of people investing online and/or obtaining investment information on the Internet is increasing dramatically. The growth in the number of companies offering investment sites or online brokerage services has equally been impressive. Even if you're not yet investing online, chances are you are visiting some of the investment sites offered on the Internet. And if you are confused by the long and varied lists of investment sites, or intimidated by the online investment process, you are not alone. Before you click the buy, sell, or trade prompts on your computer screen, you need to become comfortable with the world of Internet investing. That means learning how to locate the information needed for formulating your investment strategies and becoming familiar with the online investment shops offered on the Net.

Locating investment information on the Net is simple—information is virtually everywhere and is readily accessible. The federal government, state and local governments, and other organizations release reports on important indicators of economic activity almost every day. Investment and financial information is offered by a wide variety of sources: brokerage houses, mutual fund companies, financial news networks (e.g., CNN, Bloomberg), and business magazines and newspapers, to name just a few. On the Internet, the most influential economic reports, stock quotes, bond yields, and exchange rates are all readily available, and literally thousands of organizations provide relevant and timely market and financial data.

This chapter offers a cursory glance at the seemingly endless, and always growing, list of information sources and online investment sites on the Internet. The information contained herein is not intended to be a complete directory. Sources and uses of investment information on the Internet are growing by leaps and bounds. The chapter makes no attempt to capture the universe of sites or to rank the investment sites listed. It simply identifies a limited number of Internet sites that offer useful information and/or services to investors seeking to gather information or to invest online. The sites listed were identified as of February 2000. Additional sites worth visiting will inevitably continue to appear. Any omissions of quality investment sites established before the cutoff date are unintentional.

The remaining pages of this chapter are divided into two major sections. "Information Investors Should Know About" identifies all the types of economic and investment information that are available in today's marketplace. "Online Investing Sources" identifies investment sites that provide effective monitoring of the economic and investment environments and/or online investment services.

Information Investors Should Know About

All types of economic and investment information are available in today's marketplace. Here, they are placed in the following categories:

- Economic and Financial Data (for stocks, bonds, futures/options, and international data).
- Company/Industry-Specific Information.
- Mutual Funds.

For each category, the data that are readily accessible and useful to investors are identified, as are the major organizations (and their Web sites) that offer these data to the public.

Economic and Financial Data

Given below is an abridged list of the key economic and financial data that are available on the Internet and are useful for monitoring movements in the economy and in specific investment markets. Most of the data are reported by various U.S. government agencies and other key survey organizations. You can go to each agency's Web site and pick off the data, or you can go to the "macro" Web sites that offer most of the data in one place (e.g., Federal Reserve Bank of St. Louis (http://www.stls.frb.org/fred/data).

Government Agencies

1. U.S. Department of Treasury (www.fms.treas.gov)

   Federal Government Debt

   Federal Surplus or Deficit

   Federal Debt Held by Foreign Investors

   Federal Debt Held by Private Investors

   Federal Receipts

   Federal Outlays

2. U.S. Department of Labor, Bureau of Labor Statistics (http://stats.bls.gov:80)

   Employment Cost Index

   Productivity and Cost

   Consumer Price Index

   Producer Price Index

   Employment Situation: Household Survey and Establishment Survey

3. U.S. Department of Commerce, Census Bureau (http://www.census.gov)

   Manufacturing and Trade, Inventory and Sales

   Manufacturers' New Orders

   Retail Sales

   Housing Starts

4. U.S. Department of Commerce, Bureau of Economic Analysis (http://www.bea.doc.gov)

Auto and Light Truck Sales

Gross Domestic Product and Related Measures

Personal Income and Its Disposition

Government Receipts and Current Expenditures

Price Indexes and Deflators

5. Federal Reserve Board (http://www.federalreserve.gov)

Industrial Production

Flow of Funds: Outstanding

Burden of Debt Service Payments

a. *Exchange Rates (to the U.S. Dollar)*

Australian Dollar

Austrian Shilling

Belgian Franc

Brazilian Real

Canadian Dollar

Chinese Yuan

Danish Krone

Euro

Finnish Markka

French Franc

German Mark

Greek Drachma

Hong Kong Dollar

Indian Rupee

Irish Pound

Italian Lire

Japanese Yen

Malaysian Ringgit

Mexican Peso

Netherlands (Dutch) Guilder

New Zealand Dollar

Norwegian Krone

Portuguese Escudo

Singapore Dollar

South African Rand

South Korean Won

Spanish Peseta

Sri Lankan Rupee

Swedish Krona

Swiss Franc

New Taiwan Dollar

Thai Baht

United Kingdom (British) Pound

Venezuelan Bolivar

Trade-Weighted Exchange Index: Broad

Trade-Weighted Exchange Index: Major Currency

Trade-Weighted Exchange Index: Other Important Trading Partners

b. *Leaders in Exports and Imports*

Canada	Japan
France	Mexico
Germany	United Kingdom

c. *Selected Interest Rates*

Federal Funds Rate

3-Month AA Financial Commercial Paper

1-Month CD Rate

3-Month CD Rate

6-Month CD Rate

3-Month Treasury Bill Rate

6-Month Treasury Bill Rate

1-Year Treasury Bill Rate

1-Year Treasury Constant Maturity Rate

2-Year Treasury Constant Maturity Rate

3-Year Treasury Constant Maturity Rate

5-Year Treasury Constant Maturity Rate

7-Year Treasury Constant Maturity Rate

10-Year Treasury Constant Maturity Rate

20-Year Treasury Constant Maturity Rate

30-Year Treasury Constant Maturity Rate

30-Year Conventional Mortgage Rate

Other Organizations

6. Conference Board, Business Cycle Indicators (http://www
    .tcb-indicators.org)

    Composite Index of Leading Indicators

    Composite Index of Lagging Indicators

    Composite Index of Coincident Indicators

7. National Association of Purchasing Managers (http://www/napm.org)

    National Association of Purchasing Managers: Composite Index

8. Survey Research Center, University of Michigan (http://www
.isr.umich.edu/src)

University of Michigan: Consumer Sentiment

Company/Industry-Specific Information

Literally hundreds of Web sites offer detailed information about the stock
market and individual companies. Hook into a site and you can get current stock quotes, research financial performance, tune in to live broad-
casts of company earnings reports, and buy and sell stock. The list of
companies that now offer online information is long and varied but includes all the major Wall Street investment banks and brokers, most of
the discount brokerage houses, a new group of e-trade companies, most of
the major mutual funds, the major insurance providers, companies that
manage 401(k) retirement plans, and the financial media services. These
sources monitor and provide the stock information investors need. Go to
any search engine, type in *stocks* or *personal finance,* and your screen will
be filled with hundreds of sites similar to those described above.

Individual Stock Information

Recent stock price	Price/Book ratio
52-week high/low	Price/Cash flow
Average daily volume	Earnings per share
Beta coefficient	Sales per share
Market capitalization	Book value per share
Shares outstanding	Return on equity
Dividend yield (%)	Return on assets
Annual dividend	Return on investment
Dividend payout ratio	Gross margin
Current ratio	Operating margin
Long-term debt/equity	Profit margin
Total debt/equity	Growth rates for sales and earnings
Price/Earnings ratio	
Price/Sales ratio	Income statement

Balance sheet

Cash flow statement

Performance comparisons with industry averages

Stock Market Information

Dow Jones Industrial Average

S&P 500 Index

Wilshire 2000 Index

S&P 100

S&P 1500

S&P/Barra Growth Index

S&P/Barra Value Index

S&P Indexes

Bank Composite

Basic Materials

Capital Goods

Chemical Composite

Communication Services

Consumer Cyclicals

Consumer Staples

Energy Sector

Financial

Health Care Sector

Industrials

Insurance Composite

Oil Composite

Pharmaceutical Composite

Retail Stores Composite

Technology Sector

Transportation

Utilities

Mutual Funds

More than 9,000 mutual funds are offered in the United States today. To help investors select among them, there are services that rate mutual funds and provide performance information. Two popular mutual fund Web sites—www.morningstar.com and www.sageonline.com—provide the top 25 or the top 50 ratings for overall mutual funds and for the different fund categories. America Online's Personal Finance site has a mutual fund area that offers investors fund information and comparisons, to help them make better investment decisions. Also, Brill's mutual funds interactive, brills.com, provides useful information for investors who are considering mutual fund purchases.

Investors need to know (1) the types of mutual funds that are offered in today's marketplace, and (2) whether information on the funds is accessible on the Internet. The following fund categories are readily accessible on the Internet. Morningstar and Sage Online offer rankings of the funds within most if not all the categories.

Large-Cap Growth Funds	Pacific/Asia Ex-Japan Stock Funds
Mid-Cap Growth Funds	Japan Stock Funds
Small-Cap Growth Funds	Emerging Markets Funds
Large-Cap Blend Funds	Latin America Funds
Mid-Cap Blend Funds	Intermediate Government Funds
Small-Cap Blend Funds	Short-Term Bond Funds
Large-Cap Value Funds	Ultrashort Bond Funds
Mid-Cap Value Funds	High-Yield Bond Funds
Small-Cap Value Funds	Multisector Bond Funds
Precious Metal Funds	International Bond Funds
Natural Resources Funds	Muni National Long Bond Funds
Technology Funds	Muni National Intermediate Bond Funds
Utilities Funds	
Health Funds	Muni Single State Long Bond Funds
Financial Funds	
Real Estate Funds	Muni Single State Intermediate Bond Funds
Communication Funds	
Convertible Funds	Muni Bond Funds
Foreign Stock Funds	Balanced Funds
World Stock Funds	Retirement Funds
Pacific/Asia Funds	

Here is a brief list of some of the more popular mutual funds in the United States today. All of these funds are available through the Internet or are evaluated (ranked) by an Internet investment site.

Aetna	Alliance Capital
AIM	American

American Century	Nuveen
BT Funds	Oakmark
Calvert	Oppenheimer
Dreyfus	PaineWebber
Fidelity	Phoenix
Flag	PIMCO Funds
Franklin	Prudential
INVESCO	Putnam
J.P. Morgan	SAFECO
Janus	Salomon Smith Barney
John Hancock	Scudder
Kemper	Seligman
Legg Mason	Shroeder
Mainstay	State Street Research
Merrill Lynch	T. Rowe Price
MFS	Van Kempen
Nationwide	Vanguard
Neuberger Berman	Zweig
Nicholas	

Online Investing Sources

Because of the great amount of information on the Internet, novice Internet investors spend an inordinate amount of energy and time "surfing the Net" unproductively. To assist investors with Internet access, we identified some of the more popular categories of investment sites. They range from online discount brokers that offer high-speed trading executions and basic investment research information to more sophisticated investment sites that can provide a wider range of investment products and research information and tools. In addition, investors can visit www.investorama .com, which offers links to almost 10,000 other investment-related Internet sites, ranging from online brokers to equity research specialists, real estate investment sites, and futures/options sites.

Online Discount Brokers

Out there on the Internet, a new breed of company is taking the financial industry by storm: the online discount broker. Over 100 genuine online brokers are now on the Internet. According to a survey conducted by *Time Digital Magazine* (www.timedigital.com), in May 1999, the top ten online discount brokers (based on execution, size, and service) were:

1. DLJDirect   www.dljdirect.com
2. Quick & Reilly   www.quickwaynet.com
3. Web Street Securities   www.webstreetsecurities.com
4. Discover Brokerage   www.discoverbrokerage.com
5. Charles Schwab   www.charlesschwab.com
6. Waterhouse Securities   www.waterhouse.com
7. A.B.Watley   www.abwatley.com
8. Suretrade   www.suretrade.com
9. E*Trade   www.etrade.com
10. Datek   www.datek.com

Web-based discount brokers help investors evaluate and manage their portfolios, as well as buy and sell securities at a discounted price. Commissions can be as low as $9.99 per trade. (A full-service broker can get about $120 per trade.) These discount brokers are now placing orders as promptly as their Wall Street counterparts. Fidelity and Charles Schwab are perhaps the largest. Most online discount brokers offer investors relatively low commissions, easy-to-use trade screens, research tools, performance statistics, and a varied menu of product offerings and securities. Stock, bond, and option/futures activity can be monitored daily from these sites.

Investors need to select these sites according to their investment needs. For investors who plan to be very active (e.g., day traders), consistent and fast execution of trades is a high priority because a delay in execution can result in an investor's missing a market timing opportunity. Day traders appear to be leaning toward sites such as E*Trade and Web Street Securities. Occasional traders, for whom research and investment tools are more important than quick execution, appear to be leaning toward sites such as Fidelity and Charles Schwab.

Taking subjectivity out of the mix, the most popular online brokers, as measured by market share at year-end 1998, are:

Company	Market Share
Charles Schwab	27.4%
Waterhouse Securities	12.4
E*Trade	11.8
Datek	10.0
Fidelity	9.4
Ameritrade	7.6
DLJDirect	3.7
Others	17.7

Source: Crédit Suisse First Boston Corporation.

Investment Sites Offering Market Quotes

In addition to the online brokers, a host of sites offer market quotes (mostly for bonds, stocks, options, and futures) in either real time or 15- to 20-minute response times. Here is a brief list of selected sites:

Company	Site
Massachusetts Mutual	www.massmutual.com
Bloomberg Financial Services	www.bloomberg.com
Yahoo	www.quote.yahoo.com
Quicken	www.quicken.com
America Online	Personal Finance section
Yahoo	Finance section
Intuit	www.quicken.com
PCQuote	pcquote.com
Microsoft	www.investor.msn.com
LycosQuote.comInvesting	www.investing.lycos.com
Dow Jones	dowjones.com
Just Quotes	justquotes.com

Real-time stock quotes and real-time discussions about companies are also available on the Internet. Real-time stock quotes are available at www.freerealtime.com and www.quotes.com.

Investment Sites Offering Advice and Information

Company	Site
Motley Fool	www.fool.com
Value Line	www.valueline.com
Value Call	www.vcall.com
Cents Financial Journal	www.lp-lc.coom/cents
Zack's Investment Research	zacks.com

The Motley Fool and Value Call Web sites provide opportunities for investors to discuss specific companies and to listen as analysts question the companies about performance. Among the Web sites that charge fees for their information, Value Line evaluates the performance of over 1,700 companies and offers buy recommendations. Cents Financial Journal offers market commentary from leading economists and strategists at Moody's, Morgan Stanley, and other companies. Zack's Investment Research is a reliable source for earnings-per-share estimates, including company reports and stock market commentary.

Direct Online Company Investing

The Internet also gives investors the ability to invest directly in a particular company without using a broker or Internet trading service. The following companies and their Web sites offer this service to the public:

Company	Site
Direct Purchase Plan Clearinghouse	www.enrolldirect.com
Direct Investor	www.netstockdirect.com
DRIP Investors	www.dripinvestor.com
The Moneypaper	www.moneypaper.com
Netstock Direct	www.netstock.com

Institutional Sites

Company	Site
NASDAQ	www.nasdaq.com
Bond Market Association	www.investinginbonds.com
American Association of Individual Investors	www.aaii.com
National Association of Investors Corp.	www.better-investing.org
Thomson Investors Network	www.thomsoninvest.net
New York Stock Exchange	www.nyse.com

Other Investment Sites

Company	Site
Street.Cop	www.stockdetective.com
IPO Maven	www.ipomaven.com
Bigcharts	www.bigcharts.com
IndexTrade.com	www.indextrade.com

Street.Cop monitors investment sites that may have had trouble with the federal government and may be subject to Securities and Exchange Commission (SEC) actions. IPO Maven provides the necessary data for initial public offerings. Bigcharts offers technical analysis and charts for equity investing. IndexTrade.com, a site that provides specialized services in index trading, helps investors take advantage of broad market moves in stocks, commodities, currencies, and bonds.

Company	Site
TheStreet.com	www.thestreet.com
Business Week	www.businessweek.com
CBS	www.cbsmarketwatch.com
CNN	www.cnnfinancial.com
Standard & Poor's	www.personalwealth.com
Wall Street City	www.wallstreetcity.com
Morningstar.net	www.morningstar.net

Investment Sites Specializing in Bonds

Among the many online investment sites that offer a wide variety of investment products, the following sites are recommended by *Business*

Week (May 24, 1999) as sites for purchasing bonds and obtaining useful bond investment information:

Company	Site
BondAgent	www.bondagent.com
Discover	www.discoverbrokerage.com
E*Trade	www.etrade.com
U.S. Treasury	www.publicdebt.treas.gov
Bonds Online	www.bondsonline.com

Investment Sites Specializing in Real Estate

Company	Site
National Association of Real Estate Investment Trusts	www.nareit.com
REITNet	www.reitnet.com
RealtyStocks & Funds	www.realtystocks.com
Mortgage Bankers Association	www.mbaa.org
National Association of Realtors	www.nar.com
National Association of Homebuilders	www.nahb.com
Homestore	www.homestore.com
Intuit	www.quickenloans.com
Microsoft	www.homeadvisor.com

INDEX